RCSmith

The Art of

Hand Analysis

The Art of
Hand Analysis
Mir Bashir

FREDERICK MULLER LTD

First published in Great Britain 1973
by Frederick Muller Limited,
London, NW2 6LE

To
KHAVER and YAVER
who insist that it
should be dedicated
to THEIR MOTHER

design/computer composition/print in England
by Eyre & Spottiswoode Ltd at Grosvenor Press
Bound by Pitman Press, Bath

ISBN: 0 584 10017 5

CONTENTS

page

INTRODUCTION   1

TECHNIQUE AND TERMINOLOGY   5

THE BACK OF THE HAND — Profusely hairy hand —
Hairy hand — Thick hair — Thin hair, male hand   11

THE TEXTURE OF THE SKIN — Fine texture — Firm
texture — Leathery texture   13

THE FINGERS — SMOOTH AND KNOTTED —
Knotted fingers — Knotted top joints — Knotted second
joints — Knotted top and second joints — Even third
joints — Uneven third joints   15

THE TYPES OF FINGER TIPS — Conic finger tips —
Square finger tips — Spatulate finger tips — Mixed finger
tips   18

THE SIGNIFICANCE OF NAILS — Long nails —
Oblong nails — Short nails — Feminine short nails —
Broad nails — Narrow nails — The nails' moons — Moons
absent — Large moons — Half moons   22

THE PHALANGES OF THE FINGERS — Third
phalanges longest — Middle phalanges longest — First
phalanges longest   26

OUTWARD AND INWARD FINGERS — Inward-bent
fingers — Outward-bent fingers   29

INCLINATION OF FINGERS — Towards each other —
Straight (unbent) fingers — Spaces in the fingers —
Index and middle fingers: inter-space — Second and
third fingers: inter-space — Second and third fingers:
close — Second and third fingers: equal in length —
Third and fourth fingers: inter-space — Third and fourth
fingers: close — Fourth finger inclined inwards   31

THE INDEX FINGER — The finger of power — Top phalange longest — Top phalange shortest — Top phalange thin — Top phalange stout — Second phalange longest — Second phalange shortest — Second phalange thin — Second phalange stout — Third phalange longest — Third phalange shortest — Third phalange thin — Third phalange stout — Index tip conic — Index tip pointed — Index tip square — Index tip spatulate — Length of the index — Index shorter than third — Index as long as the middle 35

THE MIDDLE FINGER — The finger of destiny — First phalange longest — First phalange shortest — First phalange stout — First phalange thin — Second phalange longest — Second phalange shortest — Second phalange stout — Second phalange thin — Third phalange longest — Third phalange shortest — Third phalange stout — Third phalange thin — Fingertip conic — Fingertip pointed — Fingertip square — Fingertip spatulate — Middle finger much longer than the third — Middle and third fingers equal — Middle finger shorter than the third

40

THE THIRD FINGER — The finger of art — First phalange longest — First phalange shortest — First phalange stout — First phalange thin — Second phalange longest — Second phalange shortest — Second phalange stout — Second phalange thin — Third phalange longest — Third phalange shortest — Third phalange stout — Third phalange thin — Fingertip conic — Fingertip pointed — Fingertip square — Fingertip spatulate 46

THE LITTLE FINGER — The finger of eloquence — First phalange longest — First phalange shortest — First phalange stout — First phalange thin — Second phalange longest — Second phalange shortest — Second phalange stout — Second phalange thin — Third phalange longest — Third phalange shortest — Third phalange stout — Third phalange thin — A rare phenomenon — Fingertip pointed — Fingertip conic — Fingertip square — Fingertip spatulate 50

SIGNATURE OF THE THUMB — Normal angle of the thumb — Narrow angle — Wide angle — Right angle — Inflexible thumb — Flexible thumb — Short thumb — Medium thumb — Exceptionally long thumb — Top phalange — Long second phalange — Short second phalange — Top and second phalanges equal — Top phalange conic — Top phalange pointed — Top phalange square — Top phalange bulbous — Out-turned thumb — Inturned thumb   56

COMPARATIVE LENGTHS OF FINGER AND PALM — Fingers longer than palm — Fingers shorter than palm   63

WIDTH OF THE PALM — Narrow palm — Wide palm — Lean palm — Consistency of palm, flabby or firm — Hard palm — Silky palm   65

PURE MOUNT TYPES — Mount of Jupiter: fleshy elevation; apex, skin ridge design; physical features; psychological features; health and ailments — Mount of Saturn: physical features; psychological features; disposition of the mount; health and ailments — Mount of the Sun: physical features; psychological features; health and ailments — Mount of Mercury: physical features; psychological features; health and ailments — Mount of Mars: upper and lower Mounts of Mars; physical features; psychological features; health and ailments — Mount of the Moon: physical features; psychological features; health and ailments — Mount of Venus: physical features; psychological features; health and ailments   68

THE MOUNTS OF THE HAND — General characteristics — Mount of Jupiter: good mount, excessive mount, low mount — Mount of Saturn: good mount, excessive mount, low mount — Mount of the Sun: good mount, excessive mount, low mount — Mount of Mercury: good mount, excessive mount, low mount — Mount of Mars Negative: good mount, excessive mount, low mount — Mount of the Moon:

good mount, excessive mount, low mount — Mount of Venus: good mount, excessive mount, low mount — Mount of Mars Positive: good mount, excessive mount, low mount   89

DISPLACED MOUNTS OF THE HAND — Jupiter towards thumb — Jupiter towards Saturn — Jupiter towards the head line — Saturn towards Jupiter — Saturn towards the Sun — Saturn towards the heart line — Sun towards Saturn — Sun towards Mercury — Mercury towards the Sun — Mercury towards the percussion — Mercury towards the heart line — Mars Negative towards Mercury — Mars Negative towards the palm proper — Mars Negative towards the Moon — Moon towards Mars Negative — Moon towards the percussion — Moon towards the wrist — Moon towards Venus — Moon towards the middle of the palm — Venus towards the thumb — Venus towards the life line — Venus towards the Moon — Venus towards the wrist — Mars Positive towards Venus — Mars Positive towards the Thumb — Mars Positive towards the middle of the palm   97

LIFE LINE — Origin and end — Long life line — Index to the book of life — Delineation of origin — Line of demarcation — Dating system — Origin: marks at start — Life and Head Lines joined — Life and Head Lines separate — Life and Head wide apart at start — Very wide apart — Origin at Jupiter — Sweeping Life Line — Straight Life Line — Terminating inwards — Terminating towards the Moon — Terminating in large fork — Offshoots — Travel lines — Ending in a tassel — Minor marks: break, square — Accident or injury — Worries, ill health — Internal defect — Varying shades of thickness — Thin — Extra thick — Circle on line   102

THE LINE OF HEAD — Origin — Head Line linked to Life Line — Independent start — Origin Jupiter — Origin inside Life Line — Straight — Short — Long — Of medium length — Sloping — Drooping too low — Deep

and clear — Defective — Shallow — Upward branches —
Very short — Very long — Flawless and long — Gently
sloping — Edge to edge — Double — Termination —
Arched — Wavy and twisted — Fragmented — Branches
— Branches to Heart Line — Breaks and Gaps — Broken
pieces overlapping — Island middle — Islanded
throughout — Crosses, stars — Head Line/Heart Line
interspace 116

THE LINE OF HEART — Origin and termination —
Idealism in love — Origin between index and middle
fingers — Origin below middle finger — Origin below
third finger — From the edge to the percussion — Long
and short Heart Lines — Colour — Flawless, crossing
entire palm — Twisted — Wavy extremities — Sister
Heart Line — Sign of great misfortune — Low at the
start — Touching Head Line below Saturn — Forked
start — Downward branches — Branch cutting Fate Line
— Upward branches — Three offshoots at start —
Offshoot towards Mercury — Broken Heart Line —
Defects — Island — Circle — Square — Cross — Merging
into Fate Line — Giving rise to Sun Line 126

THE LINE OF FATE — Origin and end — Origin first
bracelet — Origin close to wrist — Origin Life Line —
Origin Mount of Venus — Origin Plain of Mars — Origin
Mount of Moon — Origin Mounts of Venus and Moon —
Origin Head Line — Revealing termination — Natural
point of termination — Termination on Head Line —
Termination on Heart Line — Termination Mount of
Saturn — Recurring obstacles — Termination third
phalange of middle finger — Termination towards
Jupiter — Termination Mount of Sun — Course of Fate
Line — Wiry and thin — Wavy and irregular —
Dominating other lines — Origin an island — Loss of a
parent — Formidable obstacle — Major change of
situation — Major disaster — Military success — Mark of
protection — A serious change — Unfortunate
occurrences — Major step forward — Intellectual success
— Success in science or industry — Marriage of great

advantage — Union or marriage — Heart-breaking romance — Strong emotional ferment — Submissive partner — Islanded influence line — Painful affair of the heart — Time on Fate Line   134

THE SUN LINE — Origin — Good — Glorious life — Origin inside Life Line — Origin on Life Line — Origin Mount of the Moon — Origin middle of palm — Origin Fate Line — Origin between Head and Heart Lines — Origin Head Line — Origin Heart Line — Success in different fields — Short — Stopping at Head Line — Stopping at Heart Line — Thin Sun Line — Thick — Fading — Mark of a scandal — Mark of jealousy — Wavy — Fame and brilliance — Speculative interests — Pecuniary success — Major financial loss — Money from the family — Loss through a close relative — Lawsuit with a relative — Mutually beneficial partnership — Disastrous partnership — Loss and unhappiness through marriage — Success through a guilty love affair   146

THE LINE OF HEALTH — Origin and end — Absent — A long life — Origin Mount of Venus — Twisting — Thin and wiry — Mark of longevity — Origin Life Line — Cross with Head Line — Cross in area of Mount of Moon — Triangle with Head and Fate Lines — Islanded — Broken — Mark of sterility — Yellow — Success in science or industry   155

THE LINE OF MARRIAGE — More than one emotional link — Short marriage, long marriage — The unmarrying type — Partner lives shorter — Mark of divorce — Forked start — Terminating in a fork — Brilliant union — Union with a wealthy person — Loss of worldly position — Mark of separation — Opposition to marriage — Marks of children — Guilty intrigue — Great sexual urge   159

THE LINE OF INTUITION — Uncommon mark — Origin and end — Gift of intuition and prophesy — Disciplined mediumship — Interest in divinatory techniques — Gift of eloquence — Literary genius —

Control of intuition — Strong hypnotic power — Disturbing presentiments — Terminating on upper Mount of Mars — Gift of prophesy — Wavy — Originating from an island — Mark of a sleep walker — Formed like a rosary — Broken — Family opposition to occult interest   163

THE GREAT TRIANGLE — Formation — Spacious and large — Ill-shaped — Narrow — The upper angle — Materially insecure — Life and Head Lines separate — Too wide angle — Second or inner angle — Very sharp angle — Extremely nervous disposition — Third angle — Mark of active living — Deceit and faithlessness   168

THE QUADRANGLE — Table of the hand — Regular quadrangle — Psychological imbalance — Too wide quadrangle — Honest and straightforward — Careless about public opinion — Careful about public image — Narrow and self-centred — Calm and steady — Restless and irritable — Aptitude for the occult — Excitability and haste — Brilliant career — Success in science — Research and scientific study — Lack of self-control — Eye trouble   172

THE GIRDLE OF VENUS — Origin, course and termination — Symbol of aesthetic sense — Generally fragmentary — Danger of loss — Talent for literary work — Multiple Girdle of Venus — Life of vice — Terminating beneath Mount of Mercury — A bad character — Cutting Line of Marriage — Fragmentary Girdle of Venus — Islanded — Star — Flirtatious and fickle — Loss due to a member of opposite sex   176

THE RASCETTE — Wrist lines — Potential longevity — First wrist line — Chained first wrist line — Sign of dissipation — Bow-shaped wrist line — Magic bracelet — Marks of journeys — Successful journey — Fortunate sea voyage — Hazardous journey — Sinister mark — Distinction abroad — Wealth through a journey — Vain and deceitful — Angle on the Rascette — Inheritance — Triangle in Rascette — Travel lines   181

THE UNUSUAL MARKINGS — Small Triangle — Uncanny gift of divination — Mystic Cross — Church dignatories — Superstitious practices — Ring of Solomon — Ring of Saturn — Medical Stigmata   185

THE MINOR MARKS — Dot — Island — Circle — Triangle — Square — Cross — Star   188

MINOR MARKS ON INDEX FINGER — First phalange: vertical line; cross; star; clear triangle; square; circle; islanded formation; grille — Second phalange: vertical line; horizontal line; wavy lines; slanting fork; cross; cross at the joint; star; triangle; square; circle; grille; line from Jupiter to second phalange — Third phalange: vertical line; multiplicity of wavy lines; cross lines; forked line; cross; star; square; circle; grille   198

MARKS ON THE SECOND FINGER — The middle finger — First phalange: vertical line; several vertical lines; wavy lines; cross; star; triangle; square; circle; grille — Second phalange: vertical line; cross lines; thick cross line; cross; star; square; triangle; circle; grille — Third phalange: vertical line; oblique line; multiplicity of lines; cross lines; slanting fork; cross; star; triangle; square; circle; grille   202

MARKS ON THE THIRD FINGER — First phalange: vertical line; multiplicity of lines; cross lines; cross; star; square; triangle; circle; grille — Second phalange: vertical line; slanting fork; cross lines; cross; star; triangle; square; circle; grille — Third phalange: vertical line; cross line; cross; starr; triangle; square; circle; grille   211

MARKS ON THE LITTLE FINGER — First phalange: vertical line; cross lines; cross; star; triangle; square; circle; grille — Second phalange: vertical line; cross lines; cross; star; triangle; square; small circle; grilled formation — Third phalange: vertical line; wavy lines; cross lines; clear cross; star; triangle; square; circle; grille   218

MARKS ON THE THUMB — First phalange: vertical line; multiplicity of lines; cross line; cross; star; triangle; square; circle; grille — Second phalange: vertical line; multiplicity of vertical lines; cross lines; cross; star; triangle; square; circle; grille   224

MARKS ON THE MOUNTS — Mount of Jupiter: ascending line; cross; star; triangle; square; grille — Mount of Saturn: ascending line; cross; star; triangle; square; grille — Mount of Sun: ascending line; cross; star; triangle; square; grille — Mount of Mercury: ascending line; cross; star; triangle; square; grille — Upper Mount of Mars: ascending line; cross; star; triangle; square; grille — Mount of the Moon: ascending line; cross; star; triangle; square; grille — Mount of Venus: ascending line; cross; star; triangle; square; grille — Lower Mount of Mars: ascending line; cross; star; triangle; square; grille   228

SCRAPBOOK — Aldous Huxley — Robert Helpmann — Herbert Lom — Walter Pidgeon — Vicki Baum — Jawaharlal Nehru   239

INDEX   253

PREFACE

The human hand is a map of life. It reveals the potential of an individual, indicates events which have happened or will happen in his life and provides an accurate assessment of both his psychological and physiological make-up. Such information, however, can come only as a result of a careful and comprehensive study of the hand.

Hand analysis is a science; it is also an art. It is a systematic body of knowledge with fundamental laws which must be clearly understood; its real value lies in the proper application of these laws, in the ability of the palmist to balance what are perhaps contradictory markings before coming to a final judgement on the character and destiny of the individual.

Chirology is the name we give today to the technique of hand interpretation. It comprises two distinct systems of analysis: cheirognomy, which is the study of the shape of the hand, finger formations, skin texture etc.; and cheiromancy, or the study of the lines and markings engraved on the palmar surface of the hand. It would be wrong, however, to assume that these two parts are independent of each other. In fact, the information acquired through one method can be assessed only with reference to that acquired through the other; there can be no true analysis unless one takes into account this interdependence.

Chirology originated in the East, and it is there that the art still has its real home. The Chaldeans, the Persians, the Chinese and the Indians seem to have an ancient chirological tradition, and in the South of India the art is kept alive and practised daily in every town and village. Quite a few books on the subject, written in the almost archaic Tamil language which is still the lingua franca of that region, are read and understood even today. One of the oldest such manuscripts is attributed to Valmika Maharishi, a legendary figure mentioned in the religious literature of four or five thousand years ago. This book, known as *The Teachings of Valmika Maharishi on Male Palmistry*, is assumed to have been a revelation to him from a divine source and is regarded as a definitive work on the art of handreading. It is written in exquisite poetry and comprises 567

1

stanzas; each eight-line stanza covers one marking or formation.

There is a high degree of close association between astrology and chirology in Eastern thought, a fact well demonstrated in *Nadi* literature. *Nadis* are books dealing with the lives and destinies of individuals; each book is written on palm leaves (ingrained with a fine chisel) and is handed down from father to son or guru to trusted *chela* (student). In the case of those dealing with handreading (*hasthrikha*), the reader of the *nadi* scans the palm with a magnifying glass to find what is an individual signature. This is a specific mark formed by the skin ridge lines, which are unalterable. Having found it, the reader refers to the index of the book and proceeds with the reading. This first gives the time, date, month and year of birth. Then it states the planetary position of the zodiac, thus giving an extremely accurate horoscope of the individual.

I have in my possession quite a few readings in Tamil, Sanskrit, Telegu and Singalese. All of them describe my profession and the main events of my life, and one or two of them have revealed to me some hidden secrets of the technique of chirology, including how to find the date of birth from the hand.

Although the West is becoming increasingly inquisitive about the predictive chirological technique, the study was regarded as a fringe activity for many centuries and is only now gaining the respect which it deserves.

The oldest treatise on the subject is supposed to have been written by the Greek philosopher Aristotle, and there is evidence that palmistry was practised during Roman times. The study was given great impetus during the closing decade of the last century, primarily through the work of two French practitioners, Capt. D'Arpentigny and Desbarrolles. The former concentrated on the cheirognomic aspects of the art, the latter on the cheiromantic ones.

Chirology then achieved further respectability with the work of Dr. Carl Jung. Though physicians in the East have always considered the physiological aspects of the hand in their diagnostic work, Jung can be regarded as the first Western pioneer in this respect. An outstanding clinical psychologist, he was not only a great scholar but a man of infinite wisdom. To help clinical research, he kept an open mind and investigated the potential significance of chirological indications. He certainly would not have continued to use the findings of Julius Spier, the hand analyst, for a quarter of a century unless he had discovered data valuable for his work. Jung himself observed that "the totality conception of modern biology, which is based on the evidence of a host of observations and research, does not exclude the possibility that hands whose shape and functioning are so intimately connected with the psyche, might provide revealing and therefore interpretable expressions of psychical peculiarity, that is, of the human character".

Despite its wider acceptance today, the condemnation to which handreading has been subjected in the Western Hemisphere in previous centuries (divination of any kind was always included in legislation against witchcraft and sorcery) lingers on, together with scepticism which is a product of our technological age. The general impression is that chirology is a parlour game of fortune telling, a seaside entertainment which has no value other than that of catering to the needs of silly women who are looking for an emotional outlet or to those seeking a refuge from anxiety, fear and insecurity. Because much of palmistry concerns itself with prediction, the usual assumption is that only weak people go to the so-called hand-reader, in order to find solace, or "comfort foretelling".

In practice, of course, this is not the case. Chirological studies have a variety of uses, ranging from indications of an individual's vocational potential to assessments of the true state of a person's physical and emotional health. Nor can it be said that palmistry is the province of the weak. After living in the West for over a quarter of a century it seems clear to me that, despite the apparent scepticism of the modern man, he is every bit as inquisitive about his future as the more mystical Oriental. This is amply proved by the thousands of my clients from all over the globe, among whom are prime ministers, ambassadors, politicians, university dons, writers, painters, musicians, businessmen, doctors, psychiatrists, barristers, engineers, architects, actors, scientists — in fact, all manner of men and women, from world figures to homemakers.

TECHNIQUES AND TERMINOLOGY

For ease of study, this book has been divided into two sections: the first treats the cheirognomic aspects of the hand and the second the cheiromantic markings. There is a particular technique which it is best to follow when attempting hand analysis and, similar to any other system of knowledge, chirology has a specific terminology which must be learned.

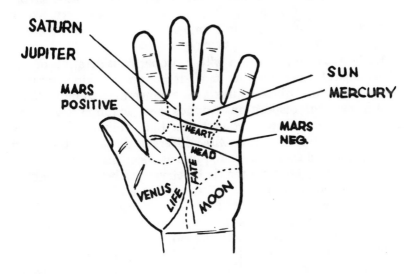

figure I

The best way to begin a systematic approach to hand analysis is to collect a number of handprints of close friends and relatives. To do this you will require a photographic roller, approximately five to six inches long, an ordinary glass plate, a tube of ink and some paper for the prints. Quite a good quality print can be achieved by rolling the roller in the ink on the plate until it is evenly covered, inking the subject's hand and then ensuring that he or she places the inked palm neatly and firmly on the paper. The date of birth of the individual, as well as the date on which the print is taken, should be noted for reference.

Before taking the handprint, it is essential to make a careful

5

study of the various cheirognomic aspects of the hand, such as the back, the formation of the finger tips, the type of hand itself, the texture of the skin and the prominence of the mounts. Although some of these can be ascertained from the prints themselves, a thorough examination ensures that no characteristic of the hand will be overlooked.

The analysis should be completely objective and based only on the information which the hand itself presents. Delineation is a most difficult and important part of hand analysis and without accuracy in this connection one could be wide of the mark; instead of being helpful one could create very wrong impressions which might, in turn, cause confusion in the life of the person whose prints are being observed.

Each study should begin with a proper consideration of the physiological aspects of the hand. It is from this cheirognomic analysis that one obtains information concerning an individual's health pattern, dispositional trends and acquired traits and tendencies. There are certain terms that should be carefully studied, their association with different parts of the hand understood and their indications clearly recognised. These are in the main connected with the fleshy elevations below the fingers, thumb and along the edges of the palm; each of these fleshy pads is known as a mount. Each mount has a name, and the finger above each elevation shares both the name and the characteristics connected with the mount.

The *Mount of Jupiter* lies at the base of the index, or first, finger. It is associated with social and religious consciousness, pride and ambition. When well-formed and centrally located, it indicates a high sense of integrity, deep religious feelings and a potential for distinction; its owner tends to be magnanimous and is capable of good leadership.

Below the second finger lies the *Mount of Saturn*, an elevation associated with balance and reflection. A strong and centrally located Mount of Saturn shows constructiveness and a deep sense of the metaphysical in its owner.

The *Mount of Sun*, or *Apollo*, is connected with fame, brilliance and artistic aptitudes. It lies below the third finger and when well-formed it indicates a good sense of humour.

The fleshy pad below the little finger is given the name of the scribe of the heavens and the god of speed, *Mercury*. Its

6

associations are with science, commerce and industry.

Situated below the Mount of Mercury is another elevation on the percussion, or edge, of the palm. Its boundaries are determined by the two main horizontal lines that cross the palm; the Heart Line near the fingers and the Head Line towards the middle of the hand. This is the *negative Mount of Mars* (the palm is divided vertically in half, the thumb side being positive and the percussion side being negative) and it is connected with the power of resistance, courage, stamina and patience.

Below this and close to the wrist line there is yet another fleshy pad. This is the *Mount of the Moon* which extends upwards into the palm to meet the negative Mount of Mars and is associated with romanticism, imagination, mysticism and travel.

Across the palm from the Mount of the Moon, just under the thumb on the positive side of the hand, is the *Mount of Venus*. A well-developed mount represents affection, love of harmony, sensitivity and a liking for music.

Above this, and beneath the Mount of Jupiter, lies the *positive Mount of Mars*, which is associated with aggressiveness and combativeness.

Another feature of the palm which must be included in the cheirognomic study are the skin ridge lines. These are found all over the palmar surface, and on the fingers and thumb. Members of the medical profession have recently given careful consideration to these lines, and have termed the study of them dermoglyphics. These skin ridge lines must be even more closely considered where they form a triangular shape, known as an apex, on each of the mounts of the hand. These apices are of paramount importance and give exceptionally useful clues regarding the physique of an individual, his health and lifestyle.

After one has given close attention to the cheirognomic factors, a study of the lines and other palmar markings is necessary. Cheiromantic indications fall into two categories: the major lines and the minor marks. The major lines can be assumed to be channels which show the ebb and flow of mind-body trends, whereas the minor marks may be accepted as peak points of these trends when, through the interaction of individual make-up and the outer environment, there is produced what can be called events or occurrences.

There are six major lines in the palm: Life, Head, Heart, Fate, Sun and Hepetica or Health.

The *Line of Life* begins between the index finger and the thumb on the edge of the positive side of the palm and makes a curved formation around the Mount of Venus, ending close to the wrist under the mount. From this line one can read the span of an individual's life, his constitution, the state of his health and any psychological factors which might be associated with his physical well-being. It is generally accepted as the most important marking in the human hand.

The *Head Line* originates from the same area as the Life Line, but crosses the palm horizontally in the direction of the percussion. It reveals all that is associated with the brain and head, and with the processes of the mind. A proper understanding of this line is essential for any psychological assessment of individual character, and it is a reliable indicator of mental attitude.

The *Heart Line* expresses emotional attitudes and concerns all matters of love, affection and sensitivity. It is also intricately connected with health, and can be used to diagnose any weaknesses of the heart or nerves. It normally begins below the index finger and crosses the palm horizontally to end just below the Mount of Mercury.

The *Fate Line* is the dividing mark between the positive and negative halves of the palm. It begins near the wrist, and rises vertically to end below the middle finger. This line is generally thought to be associated with the material aspect of the individual pattern of life, and denotes sense of direction, degree of security and vocational aptitudes.

The *Sun Line* runs parallel to the Fate Line, beginning near the wrist and ending below the base of the third finger. It is not a very common mark and usually is present only between the base of the finger and the Heart Line. When a good Sun Line can be seen, it indicates brilliance, fame, and material and social success that gives high personal satisfaction.

The *Line of Health* begins near the wrist and rises vertically to end below the little finger. Its presence shows some dormant delicacy of health; in fact, its absence is welcome.

Using the Life and Fate Lines in conjunction, it is possible to

8

construct an adequate dating system. There are quite a few methods of doing this, but perhaps the most reliable is the system of ten. Consider the origin of the Life Line to be zero, and then divide the line into ten equal spaces. Mark the Fate Line with the same standard measurement, calling the middle of the first wrist line zero. Each space on the lines indicates a span of ten years; if further accuracy is desired, each interval can be sub-divided into ten equal parts. By referring to events which have already taken place the accuracy of the measure can be checked, and if any discrepancy is discovered the dating system can be adjusted accordingly. The difficulty with any method of dating is that each individual hand has its own particular measurement, to which standardised measurements can not always be adapted. (See XXIX.)

The minor marks on the hand lie in no specific area; they can be found in the body of a main line or on any other part of the hand. The position in which a mark lies is of great importance, for it is only by considering the mark itself and its location in conjunction that its meaning becomes clear. Some minor marks are the dot, island, cross, star, square, circle, triangle and grille.

In addition to minor marks, some hands contain what are known as unusual markings. These include the Ring of Solomon, the girdle of Venus, the Ring of Saturn, the Medical Stigmata, the Line of Intuition, the Mystic Cross, the Via Lasciva, the Line of Mars, the Lines of Marriage and the Three Bracelets: though the last two are common to all hands. Again it is important that the marking be considered only in the context of its position on the hand, as will be seen in the chapters concerning these formations.

It is generally assumed that one is born with the left hand and makes the right one. (This would obviously not apply to those who are born left-handed and continue to use the left hand predominantly throughout their natural life span.) This is quite an erroneous assumption for we are born with both the hands; however, the right hand is the active and operative instrument of mankind and for this reason one is inclined to allocate to it the constructive, formative characteristic of making things and aiding progress and development.

A careful study of both the hands and the markings thereon will clarify the point: there is a certain disparity with regard to

9

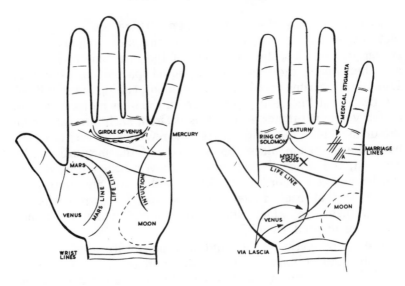

figure II

the shape and markings of both the hands. For an accurate hand analysis, all the similarities as well as the dissimilarities of the left and right hands have to be taken into consideration; and then and only then should one arrive at conclusions. In a specific sense, the left hand may tend to reveal certain unconscious and inherited tendencies, whereas the right may indicate the more applied aspects of the same.

In the Eastern system it is the left hand of the female and the right hand of the male which is studied with the most thoroughness, but the other hand is never neglected. The ultimate analysis always has to be based on the comparative study of configurations of both the hands, and it is with the back of the hands that one should begin.

THE BACK OF THE HAND

The correct procedure with regard to examination of a hand is, initially, to have a thorough look at its back. The hairy or bare surface of the back of the hand is of special importance. All male hands are normally hairy. Feminine hands usually have hair, but it tends to be fine and not quite noticeable at first sight; this of course is quite in keeping with femininity.

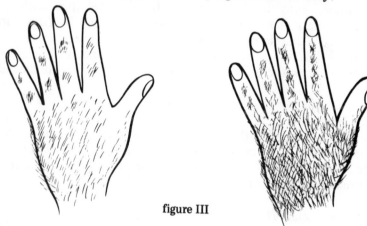

figure III

Profusely Hairy Hand

When the back of the hand is profusely covered with firm, coloured hair and the skin is invisible, it indicates excess of animal instincts, vitality and a propensity towards accentuated love of the physical, particularly as regards sexual relationships and eating.

The owner tends to be rough and quite often is incapable of appreciating all that consititutes the refined milieu of personal intimacies. He is also devoid of taste with regard to delicacies of the table. He loves quantity and is too apt to be undisciplined. Possessive and crudely affectionate, he tends to be aggressive, explosive and physically punitive if thwarted in the satiation of his pronounced physical appetites.

He enjoys a robust constitution and is naturally suited to hard, rough kinds of work. Actively inclined, he is capable of a great deal of physical exertion.

11

He is, however, unable to stand any form of mental strain and in times of crisis usually acts like a scared animal. In matters of health, he tends to suffer from the ill effects of indulgence in his physical appetites.

Hairy Hand

When the back of the hand is hairy, but the skin is visible, it reveals durable vigour, virility and manly qualities. There is a measure of essential discipline with regard to physical appetites. Its owner tends to appreciate delicacies, relating both to intimate relationships and to the table. He can be firm and responsible. Capable of hard work, he would use his powers of the mind predominantly, though if necessary he can call upon his physical resources for the accomplishment of his duties and tasks.

Thick Hair

When such hairs are thick, there is a leaning towards animal instincts; when the hairs are firm and fine, the owner would be more intellectually inclined and appreciative of discipline, culture and refinement.

Thin Hair — Male Hand

When the hairs are very thin and sparse on the back of the hand it is, in the case of a man, an ill omen. Such a person has very little manly vigour, or virility. He is apt to be weak. Unable to be masculine, he tends to be unreliable, submissive to pressure, and lets others wear the trousers. Neither dignified nor determined, he suffers from feelings of inferiority, lacks self-reliance and is too inclined to shirk responsibility. Besides want of physical strength, he is lacking in persistence and intellectual stamina. He can be cunning and evasive, and is most probably inclined to be deceptive. His is hardly an enviable lot. He usually suffers from ill effects of nervous and psychological weaknesses.

THE TEXTURE OF THE SKIN

The texture of the skin on the back of the hand also reveals useful information. It may be fine and silky, firm, or leathery.

Fine Texture
When the skin is fine and silky, it indicates an accentuated aesthetic taste, as well as a tendency towards love of the passive and refined pursuits. Apt to be lazy, such a person nevertheless is endowed with an alert and observant mind, and usually can show artistic and cultural interest. He likes luxury and comfort, and generally tends to use his fine intellectual acumen suggestively, to his own personal advantage.

He is given to excesses and, unless some discipline is maintained, may fall victim to luxurious living, expensive drinks and, of course, decorative adornment.

In a female hand, fine skin texture certainly indicates astuteness, clever manoeuvring, deftness (although always with a touch of evasion), and suggestive acumen. Such women can be expensive, and are inclined to be pleasure-loving.

In matters of health they are prone to the evils of boredom, and slight neglect by the opposite sex can incline them towards things which may prove none too healthy — the bottle, perhaps, or drugs. They do however love high living and would usually be extremely sensitive, and of excellent taste. They can shine in vocations which provide expression for refined taste and scope for presentation of decor.

Firm Texture
A firm texture, neither too fine nor too coarse, indicates a healthy cohesion of the physical and the intellectual. Its owner shows an ability for activity, energy, and intellectual potential. He is also able to realize those fine points of human relationship which form the basis of fruitful living. Active both physically and mentally, he is a capable individual and inclined to be efficient and firm.

Leathery Texture
When the skin is leathery, it shows a robust constitution and a

love of the open air. Its owner has a complete disregard of the inclemencies of weather and as a rule enjoys sound and fit health. He is more inclined toward pursuits associated with the countryside and is not in favour of urban living.

Inclined to be exceptionally healthy, he is liable at times to take undue risks with his well-being. His power of recuperation is good and minor chills and ills hardly worry him, but he can be prone to serious disorders due to over-eating and can have mishaps resulting from his interest in hazardous pursuits.

THE FINGERS — SMOOTH AND KNOTTED

The fingers have a specific significance, both individually and collectively. When all of them tend to be smooth, without any indication of knotty formations around the joints, they speak of quick process of the mind and a measure of intuitional correctness. Their owners usually go by their first impressions which, when emotions are not involved, do tend to be correct. However, they are apt to be given to impulsive reactions and quite often do things without much forethought. Though spontaneous and quick on the uptake, they do seem to lack seriousness of thought.

Knotted Fingers
When fingers happen to be knotted, smooth flow of ideas is checked. Their owner tends to be thoughtful, is slow in arriving at conclusions and usually takes time before implementing any idea into actual practice. He cannot be rushed into anything. He must have time to formulate his thoughts and consider the alternatives open to him.

Knots are signs of restriction. They also reveal love of order and method. The three phalanges of the fingers, from the top downwards, represent the ideal, the mental and physical realms.

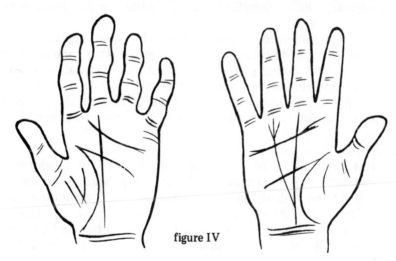

figure IV

15

Knotted Top Joints
When fingers have knotty formations around the top joints only, it indicates an extremely analytical and fastidious intellect. Their owner is unable to undertake anything without going into all the essential details. He tends to ruminate over every aspect of a problem most exactingly and in a thoroughly orderly and logical manner. However, being too introspectively inclined, he is often not able to see a situation in its totality. He is endowed with an excellent capability for critical evaluation of ideological work, and can shine as a critic, analyst or logician. Such an individual can be most aptly occupied in pursuits which involve preparation of indices, catalogues or dictionaries.

He can be terribly slow, painstaking, over-cautious and most meticulous. In everyday life he can prove to be very tiring, dull, boring and too difficult to please. He is prone to mental anxiety and nervous tension and is quite often given to nervous disorder.

Knotted Second Joints
When the fingers are knotted around the second joints only, their owner tends to look for order and method in the things around him. He is, in the main, concerned with tangible objects and his analytical trend is usually applied in arranging things in an orderly manner. He likes to work and live in accordance with a routine, which normally reveals discipline and a sound quality of usefulness.

Though somewhat exacting, when things are organized in a set and disciplined manner he likes to get on with implementing his ideas and clearing up the work load. A cautious, slow and critical individual, he does not allow abstract thinking to influence his workday life, he prefers to stay on the physical plane, and thus is able to keep his feet firmly on the ground.

Knotted Top and Second Joints
When both joints of the fingers are knotted, it produces a character which is extremely difficult to cope with. Their owner tends to be calculative, systematic, logical, analytical and extremely thoughtful. He wants order in the realm of ideas as well as on a material plane, and is unable to be satisfied with anything. He lives in a world of his own making and should be

16

allowed to pursue his own inclinations. He could be unrivalled in intellectual and academic work demanding precision, logic and analysis. He is ideally suited for research and can truly prove to be a great thinker and analyst.

Inclined to be sceptical, he is neither a good eater nor an outdoor man. He likes to do things indoors, undisturbed, and unfortunately usually ruins his health by being too shut up. When he can work in conditions suited to his innate aptitudes, he can flourish and even maintain a fair fitness of health.

Even Third Joints
The knuckles form the third row of joints. When these form an even line they indicate a great yen for personal hygiene and neatness. Their owner is meticulous about cleanliness and shows neat dress sense. He usually endeavours to maintain a wholesome, though somewhat fastidious, approach to matters of health, physical fitness, food and clothes.

Uneven Third Joints
When one of the knuckle joints, particularly around the root of the little or the index fingers, drops low there is a marked unevenness. This betrays lack of tidiness and occasionally the owner tends to be none too careful with regard to habits of hygiene, health or cleanliness. Inclined to be irregular and careless, he unconsciously tends to be undisciplined, unpunctual and untidy by disposition. He is also irregular in regard to times of meals, personal neatness, and general demeanour. Obviously he is not able to live a healthy or a fit life.

figure V

17

THE TYPES OF FINGER TIPS

Finger tips, chirognomically, are of paramount importance: they reveal innate dispositional trends as well as health. Finger tips as a rule assume three main shapes. These constitute the conic, the square and the spatulate. Usually the hand as a whole falls in line with the basic finger tip pattern and is known by the same name. However, nature tends to individualize each person, and in practice one comes across a mixture of types. The forefinger may be conic, the middle square and third spatulate. There can be other combinations too.

Conic Finger Tips
When all the fingers from the roots onwards gently taper to a cone-shaped ending, the hand is known as conic. When it tends to be very narrow at the terminus, it is called the pointed or the psychic. This is an accentuation of the conic type.

When all the finger tips are conic, it indicates sensitivity, aesthetic potential and quick processes of the mind. The owner, besides being artistically inclined, is endowed with a good intuitive faculty. He is comfort-loving, careless and lazy. He is neither punctual nor able to conform to any rigid code of

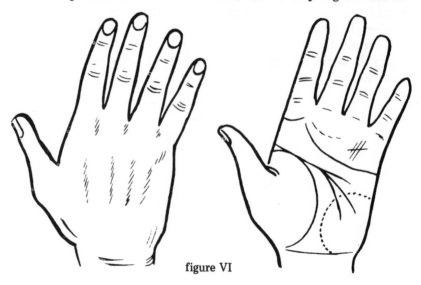

figure VI

18

discipline. Capable of quick flashes of intuition, he can be an excellent judge of people, and his first impressions are generally correct. Unable to concentrate on detail he tends to be temperamental and moody. When the spirit moves him, however, he can accomplish a lot at a go.

In matters of health he is hardly sturdy, and in fact too often given to nervous and digestive discomfort. His constitution is not strong, nor has he much physical stamina.

Square Finger Tips

When all the fingers proceed evenly from the root upwards and terminate in the form of a rectangle, these are known as square finger tips. At the nail phalange, such a finger looks like a well-defined rectangle.

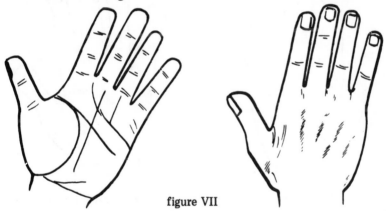

figure VII

The owner is realistic by disposition. He likes to keep his feet firmly on the ground, endeavours to be punctual, is careful about his demeanour and follows a strict routine. He likes to do things in a methodical manner and enjoys a good day's work. Neither a shirker nor lazy, he is a worker by nature. He is logical, essentially conventional and prefers the established way to anything new or out of the ordinary. He does not try to go out of his milieu, and would like to live and work in familiar surroundings. He is the type one would like to call the salt of the earth. Though hardly original or artistic, he is capable, efficient and hard working. He is endowed with a sound constitution, and tends to be alert about his well-being. He times his work and pleasure and is always appreciative of punctuality, regularity and disciplined living. He likes his food at the right time, and also prefers to sleep and rest at the appointed hour. He may be a bit of a stickler for routine, but the wheels of life would not go round without the likes of him.

Spatulate Finger Tips

When the finger tips assume the form of a spatula, the knife chemists use for mixing powders, they are known as spatulate. Such fingers tend to be smooth from the roots up to the first phalange, but then begin to spread out and end in a semi-circular form.

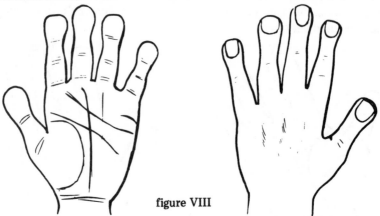

figure VIII

Such finger tips are hallmarks of energy, enterprise, invention, and the spectacular. Their owner loves open spaces, usually travels extensively, and tends to build up new settlements, colonies or enterprises.

He is also endowed with considerable engineering talent, and when this is properly developed can prove exceedingly good in any field of industrial engineering.

He is, however, a restive being, unable to settle down; he likes mobility, movement and change. He loves to plan big things and is completely unconventional. A revolutionary by disposition, he is none the less constructive and sound. He likes the tangible, the original and out of the ordinary.

Constitutionally, the spatulate type is robust, strong of bones and sturdily built. He usually enjoys good health. He is fond of outdoor sports, and cannot be hemmed in all the time. He is capable of a great deal of physical exertion, and when an occasion demands can show exceptional stamina and work long hours. He cannot sit still and always needs something to occupy him. When not engaged he is liable to be nervous, and can be ill-tempered and aggressive. He is likely to suffer from nervous tension and strain and in some cases could be accident prone, but being endowed with enormous powers of recuperation, he is always able to get over any physical trouble or strain readily.

Mixed Finger Tips
When finger tips in a particular hand are of mixed type, it denotes versatility and, of course, aptitude for more than one type of pursuit. Due to diversity of interests, the owner is able to make essential changes with regard to his work and way of living, and usually shows a great deal of adaptability. Predominance of one type, however, does tend to determine the basic dispositional trend, and this has to be taken into consideration with regard to choice of work and life style. As a rule he settles down to a life which follows a specific interest, though he does tend to develop a hobby or two according to the less dominant finger tip formations.

THE SIGNIFICANCE OF NAILS

"When we consider," said Balzac, "that the line where the flesh ends and the nail begins encloses the inexplicable and invisible mystery of the continuous transformation of our fluid content into horn, we must admit that nothing is impossible in the marvellous modifications of human matter."

Nails, chirognomically considered, have a special value. It has to be clearly understood, however, that the portion that loses touch with the flesh due to growth is not of importance.

Nails essentially show health but, unless confirmed by other palmar markings regarding the presence of an ailment, they only indicate dispositional trends in connection with matters of health.

When studying nail formations their colour, shape, texture and a variety of other aspects have to be taken into careful consideration. However, the shape is of greatest significance, and nails generally fall into four categories, *viz*, long, short, broad and narrow. Of course the usual colour variations include white, blue, yellow and shades of red.

Long Nails
Long nails belong to individuals who live in a world of imagination. Emotional, and sympathetically inclined, their owner tends to be frank and somewhat lacking in critical faculties. He also often lacks vigour, and has a predisposition towards delicate health. Though none too strong, he can occupy himself usefully, at a somewhat leisurely pace.

Long nails mainly tend to indicate a disposition towards ailments that affect the upper part of the body. When narrow and long, the delicacy of health is accentuated and most probably some ailment is present in the system.

Oblong Nails
When long nails assume an oblong shape, though indicative of a predisposition towards weak health, they are sure signs of a sweet temper. Their owner dislikes contention, dispute or any form of aggressiveness. He is in fact gentle by nature and belongs to the peace-making wing of human society.

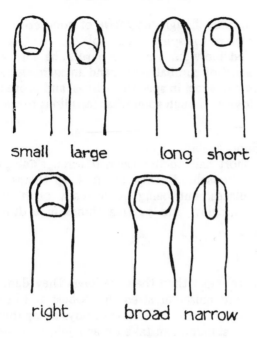

small   large   long   short

right   broad   narrow

figure IX

Short Nails

When nails are short and round they betray a critical attitude. Their owner tends to be sceptical, and takes delight in argument, contention and contradiction. He is too apt to be suspicious and though endowed with a quick wit and confidence, he is liable to be sharp-tongued, and enjoys mocking those he opposes.

Proud by nature, he does not give in easily, and when defeated in an argument can be badly hurt. He is impatient and irritable, and prone to ailments appertaining to nerves. Rather hot-tempered, he can be given to heart weakness.

Short-nailed individuals can prove excellent critics, and shine in the legal profession as well. However, when nails appear to be

23

short as if bitten, though suggestive of good critical faculty, it indicates a lack of the spirit of control.

Short-nailed individuals can, as a rule, be hard workers and do show a spirit of combativeness and an aggressive approach to things. They can excel in specific callings, and prove reliable and sound employees, though somewhat fastidious bosses.

Feminine Short Nails
In women, short nails incline them to arrange and put things in order in the household. They try to keep things tidy and in their right places, but being never really satisfied they lean towards re-arranging, and putting things in a different order every time.

Broad Nails
Broad nails are wider than they are long. They denote a sound constitution and muscular strength. Robust and healthy, their owner likes to be active and fit. He enjoys doing things, and by virtue of sheer stamina can take on any job, however difficult, and do it well.

He is inclined to dominate and be quarrelsome. There is a streak of stubbornness in his make-up and he usually feels superior to others. Naturally an optimist, he gets ahead in life by sheer dint of hard labour.

Narrow Nails
Narrow nails are none too good to own, for they indicate a predisposition towards delicate health. Their owner tends to suffer readily from nerve fatigue, and does not seem to have much vitality or vigour. He is usually nervous and apprehensive. Most probably due to general debility and weak will, he is not able to take on any strenuous job. He needs to preserve his energy potential just to get through the day.

The Nails' Moons
At the bottom of the nails, where they are embedded in the skin, there are normally moon-shaped white portions visible. These are known as moons, and tell quite a tale.

Moons Absent
When the moons are absent or only appear like dim crescents they are ill omens, for they betray a strong tendency towards low blood pressure, and poor or irregular circulation. When this is the case the owner should not ignore his well-being.

Large Moons
When the moons are large, on the other hand, it indicates over-action of the heart. There is a tendency towards nervous hypersensitivity and an excitable temper.

Half Moons
When there are clear half moons they are the right ones to have. They indicate a balanced blood pressure, good circulation, and a fairly cool and stable temper.

THE PHALANGES OF THE FINGERS

The phalanges of the fingers are of specific value both individually and collectively. In point of fact, they provide reliable clues with regard to vocational aptitudes, as well as some salient aspects of character make-up.

Each finger has three segments. The lowest, close to the palm, is considered the third, the middle the second and the top the first.

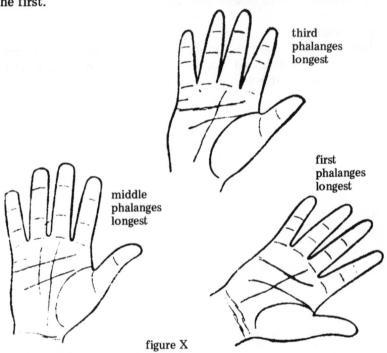

third
phalanges
longest

first
phalanges
longest

middle
phalanges
longest

figure X

Third Phalanges — The Longest

When the lowest phalange of each finger is the longest as compared to the other two, it is a point worth noting. These segments are associated with animal instincts and physical propensities. When dominant, the owner is predisposed to live in a world conditioned by physical needs. He is neither intellectually inclined nor endowed with high spiritual values.

Usually robust and well-built, nature provides him with a physique capable of rough and hard work. He can be seen in all walks of life which require physical vigour and a good constitution. He is not too bright, and cannot adequately take up any responsible position; farm labour or any unskilled type of work usually suits his disposition. In the factory, office or field he can hold a job which does not require a high degree of intelligence, but is associated with activities having a bearing on physical stamina, capacity for exertion, and a healthy constitution. He can be conditioned to a set routine, and obeys his superiors. He is also seen in some of the semi-skilled jobs — lorry driver, packer, dustman, etc. He is hard working, but does need guidance and direction. In a set, routine job, he can fairly discharge his duties.

He loves physical comforts, and usually goes for quantity in food. He enjoys athletics and an outdoor life, and generally develops hobbies which provide scope for the expression of physical energies.

Inclined to show a herd instinct, he mixes well with his kind, and according to his own standard of living and intelligence tends to prove a good citizen, host or friend. He likes family life and enjoys home comforts. He is not very good on his own!

Although often rough in his ways and abrupt, he can also be humorous and kind. So long as his physical appetites are gratified he is happy, lives amicably, and proves a good neighbour.

Middle Phalanges — The Longest
When all the middle phalanges are the longest the owner, though disposed to enjoy normal physical comforts and appetites, is however inclined to take to pursuits which require a higher level of intelligence, training and education. An intellectual approach to things tends to predetermine his choice of work and associations.

Usually professional individuals, businessmen, scientists, doctors, journalists, in fact the whole range of people who work predominantly with their heads rather than with their hands, have fingers whose second phalanges are the longest.

One of the interesting features of such a person is that he is capable, efficient, and inclined to learn progressively; he adds steadily to his accumulated knowledge and experience in his specific field of work.

His values, too, are sound and constructive. He usually adheres to accepted codes of behaviour, socially as well as professionally. He is perceptive, observant and believes in building up prestige, social status and worldly assets. He can be a hard worker, though he does not devote all his time to mere work. He can be a good home-lover, a family man and a useful and conscientious citizen.

First Phalanges — The Longest

When the top phalanges of all the fingers are the longest their owner is less inclined towards physical things. It is an indication of idealism, and an innate urge towards devotion to spiritual and moral causes. Such an individual is sensitive, metaphysically inclined, and seems to reach out for a school of thought, philosophy, ethic or religion to which he can devote his whole being.

None too practical, he is, however, highly intelligent and perceptive. He tends not to notice his own lack of practicality, and his ideals so absorb him that he often comes to be a kind of living symbol of metaphysical and divine interest. Such an individual is pre-eminently suited for missionary work, or such academic interests which may have bearings on moral philosophy or reform work.

He too often neglects physical comforts, and as a result grows isolated; even if he lives in an active world of his own choice he does so as a hermit. Nonetheless, he can have a profound impact on those with whom he does come into contact.

His appetites are subdued, and he can be quite indifferent to the delicacies of the table, or to personal intimacies of an emotional nature. He would ever endeavour to pursue austerity, and tends to be ascetic with regard to physical needs.

Not too strong physically, he is liable to show a paucity of vigour and stamina and often suffers from malnutrition. Highly sensitive by disposition, he is given to nervous troubles. With care, however, he can live adequately and maintain a fair fitness of health.

OUTWARD AND INWARD FINGERS

Inward-Bent Fingers

When all the fingers bend palmward, especially at the tips, the hand loses its beauty and shape. It reminds one of the claw of a beast rather than the human hand. It is a symbol of avarice and greed. People with these fingers are prone to be covetous, selfish and extremely mean. Cowardly and suspicious when thwarted in their selfish efforts, they can prove to be utterly ruthless. Such a palmward bend should be natural and not caused by any ailment. When natural, fingers are inflexible and do not yield to pressure. Such individuals are devoid of finer feelings or lofty ideals. In the main animal appetites rule them, and self-gratification seems to be the height of their ambition. (XI).

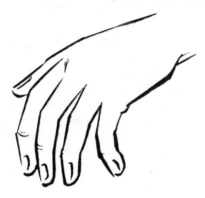

figure XI

Out-Bent Fingers

One of the most amusing memories of my early youth is associated with an old friend of the family. Grandpa Gossip, as he was commonly, though discreetly, known, had a gift for eavesdropping. He had a remarkable talent for collecting society gossip. His curiosity to assimilate juicy bits of social scandal, love, intrigues and anecdotes about personal appearances and behaviour was truly insatiable. And as soon as a piece of news reached his ears his tongue would spin the most fascinating

29

yarns which would pass from ear to ear in the twinkling of an eye. His hands used to fascinate me, especially the marked outward bend of the tips of his fingers. They seemed to be turning towards the back of his hand. Such an outward bend of the fingers betrays an inability to hold anything. He was quite incapable of keeping any secret; he could not hold his tongue. It is a symbol of great curiosity, a tendency to gossiping and eavesdropping. True to the type he was generous to a fault and never had a penny to his name. (XII).

figure XII

Specimens of this type are fairly well known and no social group is without them. These people soon acquire a name for their particular "gift", and as a rule prove to be very entertaining. You will never have a dull moment if you are with a friend with such fingers. But you must neither take him too seriously nor be too hard on him. These people can be such fun and often bring a lively interest into the dull routine of daily life. Of course they would not spare you if you could be the next target of their spicy remarks when they visit someone else. As a rule they are interesting characters, lively, human, and jovial company. One of the most endearing aspects of their character is that although they often get into awkward situations and are liable to suffer, they never seem to bear a grudge or hatred for long. Mind you, when an occasion arises, they are sporting enough to gossip at their own expense too!

INCLINATION OF FINGERS

Towards Each Other
The inclination of fingers towards each other is of special interest. When all the fingers curve at their tips toward the middle finger, you are sure to notice a streak of secretiveness in the make-up.(XIII, 1.) People with this type of finger are apt to be cautious and apprehensive. They show want of courage and are disinclined to trust others. They seem to be on their guard all the time.

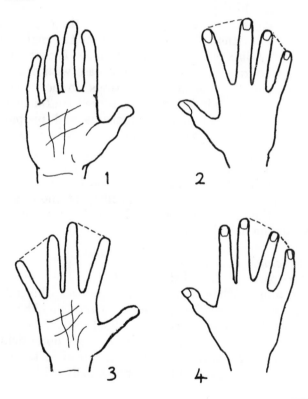

figure XIII

31

If you have someone among your circle of friends whom you have known for some length of time with these fingers you will observe that he or she is inclined to be reserved. Such people hardly ever open up. They give the impression that they are striving for self-preservation, in the process of which they do not take risks. In fact they appear to be trying to feel their way all the while and are prone to show lack of self-confidence. Generally they are slow and hesitant in their decisions. They are extremely careful in what they do, and are neither much fun nor good sports.

Straight (Unbent) Fingers
When the fingers are straight (XIII, 2), there is a natural aptitude to be efficient. These fingers point to capabilities that can be usefully directed in the right channels. People with these fingers show courage and seem to be at ease with others. They are neither suspicious nor unduly cautious. In fact they are fair and have an open mind. They show self-confidence and a remarkable capacity to handle situations and people. They favour a straightforward way of life.

Spaces in the Fingers
When straight fingers are in a state of relaxation they seem to fall well apart from each other, especially at the tips. Curved fingers, on the contrary, are inclined to overlap the top phalanges of the neighbouring fingers.

Index and Middle Fingers: Inter-Space
This inter-space or the distance between the fingers is an important point. When it is greatest between the index and middle fingers it reveals independence of thought. The capacity to form independent views is innate. Such people tend to have their own way in life. In fact, they show potentialities of leadership (XIII, 2). When this space is curtailed the capacity for freedom of thought shrinks proportionally with its narrowness (XIII, 4).

Second and Third Fingers: Inter-Space
The second and third fingers generally seem to be very close together. They appear to be difficult to separate (XIII, 3).

In some hands, however, these fingers also fall well apart, but this is quite rare. When they do, it shows marked independence of circumstances (XIII, 4). Such people show an inborn capacity to act and think in such a fashion that they do not allow circumstances to force them into submission. They are inclined to be unconventional and are likely to have a touch of the reformer in their make-up.

Second and Third Fingers: Close

When the fingers are close together freedom of action is lacking. Such a restriction is brought about by the force of circumstances over which these individuals apparently have no control, and their life seems to be chalked out by some unavoidable restrictive condition which leaves no choice open for them. The pattern of their routine is set and they seem to be forced into a groove.

Second and Third Fingers: Equal in Length

A curious thing in some cases is noticed to bring in an element of relief: the third finger is predominant and almost equal in length to the second (XIII, 2). This length of the third finger denotes the ability to take risks. Such individuals show a spirit of adventure and enterprise, and endeavour to take chances to achieve mastery over their circumstances. Generally they seem to succeed in their attempt and feel happier with the results of their gamble. Lack of space between these two fingers is limiting and often creates a frame of mind which lacks optimism and hope.

Third and Fourth Fingers: Inter-Space

When the third and the little fingers are well apart there is freedom of action. Such persons show a great capacity to do things on their own and do not allow outside conditions to hamper their activities. There is a touch of unconventionality in their make-up which often urges them to take part in unusual and out of the ordinary interests. They seem to be quite at home in such pursuits and as a rule achieve good results. Active courage seems to be their great asset. (XIII, 3).

Third and Fourth Fingers: Close
When the interspace between the third and fourth fingers is narrow, it shows contrary results (XIII, 4). In some instances the space is rendered narrow by the marked inclination of the little finger toward the third, particularly due to an inward twist at its top phalange; this is not at all good.

Fourth Finger Inclined Inwards
A slight bend of this finger toward the third denotes elements of tact and diplomancy in the character, but when it is twisted and shows a definitely marked distortion in its formation it betrays a tendency to cheating and falsehood. Such individuals are evasive and tend to be extremely sly and slick. They are tactful in speech and careful in approach, with a shrewd sense of handling situations and people to their own advantage, which is by no means healthy. They are apt to be clever, and skilfully manoeuvre to outwit others. Strangely enough they often get caught and lose more in the long run than they have usually gained at the beginning of a contact.

THE INDEX FINGER

The Finger of Power
Fingers individually, besides giving positive indications regarding potential aptitudes for a variety of talents and capabilities, also denote some important and cardinal characteristics. The index finger, usually known as the pointing finger, shows ability to command, religious inclinations, pride and ambition.

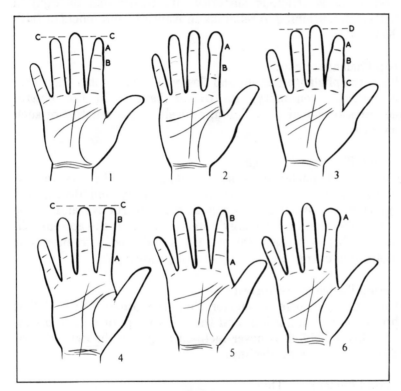

figure XIV

Top Phalange — The longest
When the first phalange is the longest (XIV, 2A), it indicates a deeply religious nature and intuitional quickness. Its owner is capable of accurate first impressions, as well as a deep sense of the religious.

35

Top Phalange — The Shortest
When it happens to be shorter than the other phalanges (XIV, 3A), it shows material instincts, and a strong streak of scepticism. Its owner is pretty well devoid of deep feelings for religion, is unable to show a faith in human nature, and seems to be going after the goods of this earth.

Top Phalange — Thin
If this phalange is spare and thin, it shows a strong predisposition towards religious austerity. Its owner can be rigid in matters appertaining to religious conventions and tenets of faith (XIV, 1A).

Top Phalange — Stout
When the phalange is stout and fleshy (XIV, 2A), it betrays love of religious sensuality. Its owner believes in the blissful pleasures ordained by religion, as well as the sanctity of such practices.

Second Phalange — Longest
The second phalange, when it happens to be the longest (XIV, 2B), is a veritable symbol of sturdy and determined ambition. Its owner shows a positive, constructive and persistent application of his energy potential towards the accomplishment of his ambitious dreams. He is endowed with enormous intellectual energy and usually uses it positively.

Second Phalange — Shortest
When the phalange is shorter than the others (XIV, 1B), it shows want of ambition, and there is very poor energy potential. This individual is never inclined to put in the right kind of effort to improve his destiny.

Second Phalange — Thin
When a long second phalange is spare (XIV, 2B), it reveals a great and abiding desire for glory. Its owner is capable of ambitious domination, and would ever be on the go to achieve material advantages which can bring him prominence, fame, and worldly fortunes. He just cannot take a back seat.

Second Phalange — Stout
When the phalange is stout and fleshy (XIV, 3B), it shows love of comfort and personal pleasure. Its owner, though ambitious, does not seem to seek glory or great power. He strives for such advantages which can enable him to enjoy personal comforts and, of course, the pleasures that may be near to his heart.

Third Phalange — Longest
The third phalange, when longest (XIV, 4A), indicates a tremendous urge to rule. Its owner is very proud by nature, and as such would reach out for a place of distinction. His love in life is to dominate others and to dictate.

Third Phalange — Shortest
When the third phalange happens to be shorter than the others (XIV, 5A), its owner is quite satisfied with his humble station in life. He does not endeavour to rise high or to a powerful position, nor is he really concerned with lofty ideals. In fact, he enjoys a certain degree of self-effacement, and would usually like to be left alone to pursue his own interests.

Third Phalange — Thin
When the long third phalange is spare and thin (XIV, 4A), it shows a definite tendency towards an ascetic way of life. Its owner does not hesitate to indicate his contempt for the so-called pleasures of life, and would be more interested in sober pursuits and self-denial.

Third Phalange — Stout
If it is stout and fleshy (XIV, 3C), this phalange betrays egotism, love of comfort, and a tremendous amount of greed. There is in fact a preponderance of sensual leanings, and such a person would stop at nothing to satisfy his cravings.

Index Tip — Conic
The index finger assumes a variety of shapes at its tip. When it happens to be conic (XIV, 1A), that is, tapering gently without being too pointed, then it indicates love of ecstasy and an intuitional rapidity. The impressions of its owner generally seem to be correct. However, he does not adhere to any method or

order. He is religiously inclined, though in an unconventional manner.

Index Tip — Pointed
When the finger is rather pointed (XIV, 5B), then the tendency towards lack of discipline in ambition or religious matters is accentuated. However, there is an inclination towards contemplation, and its owner shows a keen sense of the mystical.

Index Tip — Square
If the tip is squarish in shape (XIV, 4B), it is another matter. It stands for search for reality, and its owner is usually engaged in the pursuit of truth. He is conventionally inclined in all matters pertaining to religious decor or ceremony, and demands complete submission to the accepted procedures associated with spiritual or ethical codes. Likely to be a disciplinarian, he can also be a teacher of sound calibre.

Index Tip — Spatulate
When the index finger assumes a spatulate form at the tip (XIV, 6A), though rare, it is significant. It shows an urge to command, an active mysticism, and a certain bigotry in spiritual or religious matters.

Length of the Index
When compared with other fingers, the index should be longer than the thumb and the little finger. If it is as long as the third finger (XIV, 1CC), it reveals a great love of fame, and its owner shows tremendous potential for success in whatever field of life he chooses.

Index Shorter than Third
When the index finger is shorter than the third (XIV, 3D), it shows an ambition which can be quite violent. This person cannot stand any opposition to his aspirations, and may tend to display an inflammable disposition. He is too apt to react strongly to any restrictive conditions, and often suffers from an inferiority complex.

Index as Long as the Middle
It is rare that the index finger is as long as the middle finger (XIV, 4CC). When this is the case, it shows an excessive urge for domination. Its owner tends to be a despot, and unfortunately has a knack of getting authority in his hand. He does not seem to care how he reaches his objective, and having once achieved power he is capable of using it very sternly. He seems to rule over his fellow beings almost blindly, and would not hesitate to eliminate, or render harmless, those who might dare to oppose him. He is never loved, and usually feared. He is also very fond of his pleasures and persistently indulges in them.

THE MIDDLE FINGER

The Finger of Destiny
The middle finger, in all normal cases, is the longest as compared with the others, and dominates in all essential aspects. It indicates deep interest in the occult and its owner tends to investigate the unknown areas of human life and destiny (XV, 1A).

It also denotes love of solitude, introspection, concentration and a fondness for gardening and nature. There is also a taste for all that pertains to human culture, especially with regard to refinements that may have an ancient heritage.

First Phalange — The Longest
Its phalanges are expressive of salient aptitudes and characteristics. The first phalange, when it happens to be the longest, denotes a quality of prudence and an ability for the persistent application of energy potential (XV, 1A).

When it happens to be unduly long (XV, 2A), it betrays a strong tendency towards melancholy and sadness. Its owner is apt to be given to fantasies of the mind which are of negative character. He is also inclined to be superstitious and is hardly able to sparkle with a zest for living.

First Phalange — Shortest
When the first phalange is short as compared with the others (XV, 3A), it reveals a predisposition towards resignation. Its owner is neither aggressive in his aspirations nor possessed of a great desire for the goods of the earth. There is a kind of gentle contentment about him and he is able to accept what is given to him by his destiny. However, it in no case means that he does not strive to improve his lot, but he keeps a calm and steady disposition and is not unduly disturbed by the vicissitudes of fortune.

First Phalange — Stout
When it is stout and fleshy (XV, 4A), irrespective of its size, it is hardly a welcome formation. It shows want of refinement and

40

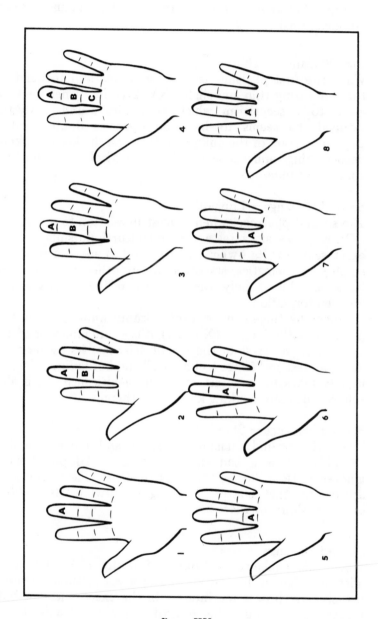

figure XV

41

culture. Its owner tends to be coarse, and his manners are apt to be objectionable.

First Phalange — Thin

When the first phalange is spare, without fleshiness and therefore appearing thin and slight (XV, 2A), its owner tends to be given to a scepticism which tears him asunder. Mystically inclined, he seems to be wide open to doubts and even disturbing fears of the unknown. However, he keeps looking for deeper things and his sense of the mystical helps him to have glimpses of inner reality.

Second Phalange — Longest

The second phalange, when longest in relation to the other two (XV, 6A), reveals a taste for agricultural pursuits, as well as exact sciences. Its owner can be good in areas of work which employ mathematics, statistics, or any other exact techniques. However, this is only the case when the fingers assume a knotted formation.

When the fingers are smooth without knots and the second phalange is the longest (XV, 6A), it is a sure indicator of a deep and abiding interest in the occult sciences. Its owner shows a keen interest in "fringe techniques" and borderline subjects. He usually takes to some art of occult significance and is able to achieve adequate working knowledge therein.

Second Phalange — Shortest

When the second phalange is short and looks insignificant (XV, 2B), it is a bad sign. Its owner is disposed towards ignorance. He makes no constructive effort to learn any science, art or, for that matter, anything worthwhile about life. He seems, in short, to waste his time.

Second Phalange — Stout

When this phalange is stout and fleshy (XV, 4B), it is an adequate sign of a good aptitude for agricultural pursuits. Its owner may show some interest in the exact sciences, but his innate trend would be towards agriculture and its allied interests.

Second Phalange — Thin
When it happens to be slight, spare and hollow in appearance (XV, 3B), it is a sure indication of love of exactitude and scientific interest.

Third Phalange — Longest
If the third phalange of the middle finger is the longest of all (XV, 4C), it denotes avaricious inclinations. Its owner tends to be greedy and covetous, and may not be able to remain within any ethical domain in the acquisition of his objectives. He is usually unable to hide this native trait of character.

Third Phalange — Shortest
When this phalange is short (XV, 5A), it shows a strong predisposition for economy. Its owner is frugal and tends to be watchful of waste. He plans intelligently and puts a lot of consideration into his approach to the economics of living.

Third Phalange — Stout
When it happens to be fleshy and stout (XV, 8A), it indicates sociability and its owner shows a gregarious instinct. However, his sense of sociability is tempered by a measure of seriousness and he maintains a dignified approach in his contact with people.

Third Phalange — Thin
When the third phalange is slight and hollow, and therefore spare (XV, 7A), its owner does not seem to mix well with those with whom he comes into contact. He is not able to keep pace with life or the progress of events and circumstances. He is too apt to feel dissatisfied and unhappy with himself and does not enjoy the fruits of his endeavours.

Middle Finger Tip — Conic
When the middle finger assumes a conic shape at its tip it is an interesting point to note. This finger is symbolic of seriousness, melancholy and superstition in general, but when it terminates in a cone shape, it tends to negate some of these characteristics, so that its owner is not as apt to be sad or melancholic.

Middle Finger Tip — Pointed

When the finger is pointed and exceptionally narrow towards the end, it loses its serious character altogether. This formation indicates a form of intuitional quickness which its owner is able to apply in solving problems of a difficult nature, especially those associated with philosophy, metaphysics and ethics. He is capable of optimism, and is generally free of restrictive and melancholic influences.

Middle Finger Tip — Square

The middle finger ending in a rectangular shape, generally known as the square finger, shows strict adherence to moral principles, religious conviction and an inability to be broad-minded with regard to any doctrine or principle of a moral nature. Its owner is innately serious, and apt to be rather too solemn and reflective in his approach to life.

Middle Finger Tip — Spatulate

A spatulate formation of this finger is not too good, for it also shows a very strong predisposition towards melancholy and pessimism; its owner is capable of suicidal thoughts and is always inclined to be deeply interested in matters such as getting rid of the mortal coil, and trying to be free of the restrictive influences of the human body. He is not likely to live a normal life and seems to isolate himself from others. He is serious by nature and has a great deal of depth in his being; when artistically inclined, the sombre and the melancholy will predominate in his creative works.

Middle Finger Much Longer than the Third

The length of the middle finger as compared with the others is of great importance and when normal it should be the most dominant and the longest of all the fingers. However, when it is much longer than the third finger the owner is likely to cause himself a great deal of harm through morbidity and melancholy, especially in his pursuit of art and literature. As the third finger is also associated with money, it is unlikely that he would be able to make any great financial success.

Middle and Third Fingers Equal
When the middle finger is equal in length to the third, this, too, is not a good sign. Its owner would be disinclined to allow serious thought to mould his character or his interests. He is apt to have very strong gambling instincts and would be compulsively drawn towards speculative enterprises. Obviously, he is liable to live a kind of life in which the element of risk is rather strong, causing uncertainty, insecurity and even losses.

Middle Finger Shorter than the Third
If the middle finger is shorter than the third finger, it denotes a desperate character who takes to risky enterprises which can and do bring him to ruin. He appears, in fact, to be almost insane in the manner in which he behaves and usually ends up as nothing short of a severely unbalanced person.

THE THIRD FINGER

The Finger of Art
The third finger, in all normal instances, is shorter than the
middle, longer than the little, and about the same length as the
first. It is associated with art, talent and merit. When properly
shaped and normal (XVI, 1), its owner instinctively seeks glory
and shows a deep feeling for the ideal, the great and the
beautiful. He is pre-eminently endowed with a sense of the
aesthetic and looks for recognition and fame.

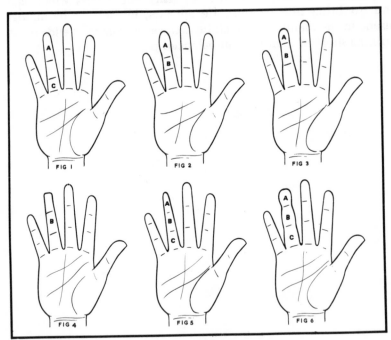

figure XVI

First Phalange — Longest
The phalanges are expressive of his innate longings; for example,
when the first phalange is the longest (XVI, 1A), its owner
tends to enjoy all that is noble and beautiful in the realm of
thought. He has a keen intelligence and a love of all that is lofty
in art.

46

When in excess, it betrays eccentricity and intellectual asceticism, and such an individual is apt to pose rather than show a true love of art.

First Phalange — Shortest

When the first phalange is short as compared with the others (XVI, 3A), it stunts the artistic sense, and its owner neither is lofty in his artistic feelings, nor goes after the ideal. He is inclined to show simplicity in his behaviour, use of language and dress sense, and is devoid of the pose and vanity of the intellectual artist.

First Phalange — Stout

If the phalange happens to be stout and fleshy (XVI, 6A), irrespective of its size, it is a definite indication of feeling for beauty in form as well as aesthetic sensualism. Its owner, although conscious of the beauty of thought, is none too inclined to seek beauty in the realm of the ideal or purely artistic. He is positively disposed towards the enjoyment of formalized beauty in preference to the ideological concept of all that is lovely and artistic.

First Phalange — Thin

When the first phalange is spare, thin, and depressed in shape (XVI, 5A), it is symbolic of a feeling for beauty in ideas and aestheticism. There is a fine spirituality about this person; anything that pertains to beauty in form is, in his eyes, of a lower standard than his idealistic nature would like it to be.

Second Phalange — Longest

Originality and talent in artistic endeavours are indicated when the second phalange is the longest (XVI, 4B); its owner seeks the useful and the reasonable in art. He prefers common sense blended with talent to idealism and is a stern adherent to this approach in matters concerning art and beauty. When this phalange is excessively long, however, its owner tends towards eccentricity and can be too logical in artistic matters.

Second Phalange — Shortest

When the second phalange is obviously short in relation to the others (XVI, 2B), it betrays an individual who is unable to succeed. He possesses little inspiration; this stifles any natural potential and only adds to his failure.

Second Phalange — Stout
A fleshy and stout second phalange (XVI, 6B) reveals the realist in art. Its owner is endowed with that expressional talent which enables him to give practical form to his ideas. Due to this faculty he is usually able to make impressive headway and to contribute something worthwhile in his own right.

Second Phalange — Thin
When this phalange is spare and depressed (XVI, 5B), it denies form. Its owner is neither lavish nor expressive; he prefers to stick to bare essentials and his manner of expression is brief and succinct. His artistic inclinations are towards the austere and he has little liking for richness of form, colour or expressional decor.

Third Phalange — Longest
When the third phalange of the third finger is the longest (XVI, 6C), it shows love of form and materialism. Its owner has no feeling for beauty in art. Rather, he wants to shine in a material world, and seeks riches, decorations and honours.

Third Phalange — Shortest
If this phalange is short (XVI, 1C), it betrays lack of skill in art. It is also indicative of a paucity of potential for success and unfortunately its owner does not usually make any great headway, either in life or in art.

Third Phalange — Stout
A fleshy and stout third phalange (XVI, 6C) indicates an instinctive urge for comfort. Its owner usually gives the impression of a love and appreciation of art by surrounding himself with valuable pieces of artistic significance. However, this is pretence only for he is devoid of any true appreciation. He suffers from the sin of those who amass wealth quickly.

Third Phalange — Thin
When this phalange is spare and depressed (XVI, 5C), its owner neither cares for comfort nor has regard for wealth. In fact, he is completely indifferent to such things as riches, honour and fame. He lives in a world of his own, and can do without most things.

Third Finger Tip — Conic
The formation of the tip of the third finger is of great significance, and reveals some very exceptional characteristics. When it is cone-shaped (XVI, 1A), it reveals an aptitude for commerce and a spirit of artistic thought.

Third Finger Tip — Pointed
When the tip formation is pointed (XVI, 5A), it indicates idealism in art and an aptitude for poetry. Its owner is endowed with inspiration in matters appertaining to art and taste. He is also intuitive, mystical and has intense feeling for the beautiful. A born dreamer, his visions of the beautiful are too idealistic to be realized.

Third Finger Tip — Square
A squarish formation at the tip (XVI, 4), shows love of riches, and quest for truth in art. Its owner is so positive that inspiration seems to be lacking in him. He can never be a true artist of high calibre.

Third Finger Tip — Spatulate
When the tip is spatulate (XVI, 6A), it is a mark of histrionic talent. Its owner tends to apply artistic power and energy to matters of movement. It does spotlight true potential of great distinction. Its owner can be a great painter, dramatist, dancer or writer. Spatulate formation predominantly reveals a talent for animation, movement and originality.

c

THE LITTLE FINGER

The Finger of Eloquence
The little finger deserves careful consideration, as it shows the expressional potential of its owner. It deals with such characteristics as eloquence, taste for study, science and intuition. Its individual phalanges give definite clues to the preponderance or otherwise of these various traits.

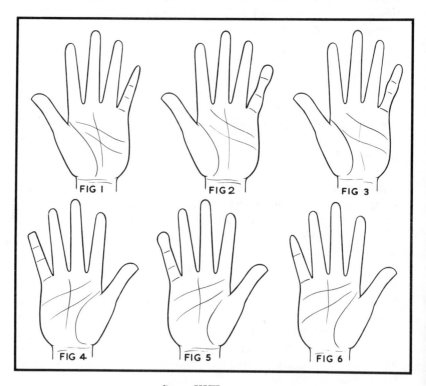

figure XVII

First Phalange — Longest
When the first phalange is the longest of the three (XVII, 3), it denotes a love of science for the sake of science. Its owner is endowed with an innate taste for study and research, and is

50

capable of expressing his views and ideas with eloquence. He investigates words and literary styles, and is always keen to find ways in which he can better convey his views to others.

First Phalange — Shortest
When this phalange is short (XVII, 2), it betrays a lack of intellectual alertness; its owner tends to be mentally lazy, and is hardly willing to undertake any form of serious study. None too appreciative of the delicacies of words, he remains somewhat dull.

First Phalange — Stout
It is important to note whether this phalange is fleshy and stout, or spare and depressed. When it happens to be fleshy (XVII, 2), irrespective of its size, it shows a lack of astuteness. Its owner could be stupid, uncultured, and rather backward spiritually. He certainly lacks urbanity.

First Phalange — Thin
When it is spare and thin (XVII, 1), it is a reliable symbol of innate tact and a fine taste for words. Its owner is usually an engaging conversationalist.

Second Phalange — Longest
When the second phalange is the longest of the three (XVII, 2), its owner seeks a rational approach to things. He is instinctively inclined towards commerce and industry, and usually takes to the useful and practical in life. Unless he finds a reasonable basis for a proposition he will not accept it. Neither the purely imaginative nor the artistic are his domain of interest. A realistic, business-like attitude determines his pursuits and life interests.

Second Phalange — Shortest
A short second phalange, however (XVII, 3), shows a lack of both enterprise and acumen in business, and its owner tends to adhere to things he knows without any measure of rational approach. He is, in fact, liable to be wanting in any sense of initiative, and would not speculate with anything. He displays a loyalty to things he is used to but this loyalty is often due to an

innate fear for anything out of the ordinary. In his eyes this would amount to a speculative enterprise.

Second Phalange — Stout
When the phalange is fleshy and gives the impression of stoutness (XVII, 3), it denotes a good aptitude for business. Its owner knows the ropes, and enjoys both making money and success. He usually gets what he wants, most probably without any consideration for scruples or conscience. Materialistically inclined, he may not worry unduly about the means he has to resort to in order to reach his ends.

Second Phalange — Thin
A spare and thin second phalange (XVII, 2), speaks of an individual who is more inclined to be a merchant banker or a financier; he feels more at home in theory than in practical application of his financial interest. But he is none the less astute in financial matters, and would show exceptional acumen in the manoeuvering of his commercial and investment interests.

Third Phalange — Longest
If the third phalange is longest (XVII, 4), it is indicative of skilfulness. However, its owner is cunning, and uses his faculties of mind for gain through the use of hypocrisy and falsehood. He is endowed with good persuasive powers, and is able to eloquently manoeuvre situations in a somewhat low, dishonest — though skilful — manner, to his advantage. Such a phalange is, in fact, a sign of a charlatan. In whatever field of life he happens to be, he is unable to resist the temptation of pulling a fast one. Usually he succeeds for a short time, though in the long run he is found out, and properly rewarded for his deceitful practices and hypocritical pursuits.

Third Phalange — Shortest
The short third phalange (XVII, 5), on the other hand, is a clear symbol of simplicity, and sometimes gullibility. This individual is often not very intelligent but he is neither a trickster nor deceitful. He is a simple, ordinary person, who can be easily taken in.

Third Phalange — Stout

The fleshy third phalange (XVII, 2) is a clear sign of immodesty and accentuated material tastes. Its owner loves the pleasures of living and does not hesitate to seek them, without regard for morality or accepted codes of behaviour. He is often tempted to take liberties with others' property or privileges, and when caught so doing he can be pretty barefaced about it.

Third Phalange — Thin

When this phalange is spare (XVII, 3), its owner is naturally inclined to be a matter-of-fact person. In his way of looking at things there is nothing beyond the fact that two and two makes four. Devoid of imagination and enterprise, he lives by rule of thumb. He lacks a spirit of endeavour, a zest for living, and knows nothing other than a mechanical approach to life.

A Rare Phenomenon

Though only very rarely, I have come across little fingers with only two distinct phalanges (XVII, 6). In such a case the three other fingers have the regular three phalanges, and the little finger and the thumb have two each. This is an extremely rare and very revealing phenomenon. When the top phalange is the longest of the two, it indicates that intellectual and scientific aspects determine the owner's way of life. This is a symbol of a highly gifted individual who should be able to make exceptional contributions to his specific field of work, whether it happens to be science, industry or art. In addition he is devoid of any form of cunning.

When the second phalange is the longer of the two, the opposite is the case. Its owner is dominated by his materialistic and practical instincts. He would be dextrous in the use of his skill and potential, and would reach out for material advantages. He is capable of tremendous commercial acumen, and his material instincts dominate his artistic or intellectual potential. He would achieve his ends, in a very realistic and practical manner, having used all his skills to do so. He would possess neither idealistic considerations nor any very high degree of moral calibre.

Little Finger Tip — Pointed

The little finger tip, due to its variety of formations, gives positive clues to its owner's disposition and aptitudes. Assuming a pointed formation (XVII, 1), it speaks of a natural gift for the understanding of the occult sciences. Its owner is able to recognize out-of-the-ordinary phenomena, and usually possesses intuitive talents.

He is also gifted with eloquence, can be an excellent talker, and displays a special form of skill and cunning which he is able to use in the execution of his plans and objectives. However, he has a kind of dream-like approach to things.

Little Finger Tip — Conic

When the tip tapers to a cone shape (XVII, 3), there is a greater sense of an artistic, though realistic, approach to things. Its owner is naturally endowed with qualities of the spirit which, when cultivated, can lead to his success and progress, and he achieves this much more constructively than in the case of the individual with a pointed tip.

Little Finger Tip — Square

The rectangular or square formation of the little finger tip (XVII, 4) is indicative of reasoning and logic, and its owner tends to be practical in his approach to life. He seeks explanations and data, rather than the impressional form of intuition, as his guideline. He can be found in any of the fields which require acquired skill — as a physician, teacher, businessman, in fact in any work which would be practical, logical, and essentially useful to life. This person shows an aptitude for research, analysis, discovery, and all that is associated with science or business.

Little Finger Tip — Spatulate

When the tip assumes a spatulate formation (XVII, 5), it denotes an innate aptitude for movement or animation. Its owner would be interested in the science of movement, and would show a good deal of moving eloquence, performance, acting, etc. If mechanically inclined, he would be interested in the mechanics of machinery, as well as gymnastics. The entire character is predominantly movement conscious, and whatever field of life or work he would be interested in, he would go for all that may have something to do with movement, animation and physical mobility.

SIGNATURE OF THE THUMB

In the history of law, we come across the expression "witness my thumb and seal". It is used in connection with legal documents. In the West the use of the thumb is a thing of the past. In the East, however, the practice still exists.

When a person is literate, signature alone is valid; a "seal" is used in privileged instances. But in the case of illiterate people, the imprint of the left thumb is affixed to legal documents.

We are all familiar with the universal use of finger prints to aid detection of criminals. Ridge-patterns in the finger tips are unalterable and completely individualistic. In the Indo-Pak subcontinent where the art of Hastrik — the study of the lines of the hand — has flourished from the dawn of human history, these ridge-patterns are accepted as basic and dependable symbols of human conduct and destiny.

It is an established fact that no two thumb imprints have been discovered that bear identical line formations. The thumb constitutes the symbol of man's individuality. It is his unfailing seal, his unique and reliable signature that no one can change or duplicate.

Man's most outstanding and distinctive physical feature, as compared to other animals, is his hand. The nearest approach to a human hand in the entire animal world is to be found in the chimpanzee. The thumb in particular, in its formation and length, is peculiar to man. Unlike the other fingers, the thumb has only two segments — the top and the second phalange — which represent will and reason respectively. The formation and length of these denote the type and strength of these attributes.

Angle of the Thumb

Normal Angle
The angle of the thumb with the palm is to be carefully studied. In all normal cases it forms an angle of around 45°. When thus placed, it shows a good capacity for adherence to all normal standards of life, fair power of the will and a common-sense outlook.

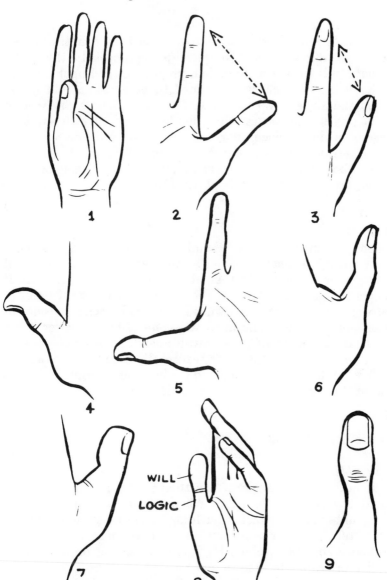

WILL
LOGIC

figure XVIII

Narrow Angle

When the thumb forms a narrower angle, it denotes limited power of the will and a more selfish approach to things. Its owner tends to be small-minded, prejudiced, and unable to see wider issues of life. He is inclined to be covetous and mean. When the angle is very narrow, he is apt to be a prisoner of sheer physical appetites. He is neither endowed with any high degree of intelligence, nor able to show grit, or volitional characteristics. He can be stubborn and self-bound. There is not much about him that can make him likeable or capable of rising to importance in any sphere of life. (XVIII, 3.)

Wide Angle — Right Angle

When the angle of the thumb is wider, it denotes more individuality of character and a stronger personality. When it forms a right angle with the palm, it is a rare phenomenon. It shows tremendous power of the will and an incessant urge for reformative activities. Its owner is capable of being a leader of men and tends to shine in some sphere of life; whether it is a political, social or religious involvement, he stands out as a reformer, leader and fighter for causes. He usually makes a mark in life and leaves a name behind for his unusual contribution to the welfare or advancement of mankind. (XVIII, 5.)

Flexibility of Thumb

Inflexible Thumb

It is not only the angle of the thumb which is important, its flexibility is also significant. When the thumb happens to be firm, unbending, in fact unyielding, it shows great rigidity of character. Its owner seems unable to compromise, and is usually stubborn and stiff-necked. He is not an easy person with whom to live or work. He is stern and rather firm in his attitudes and views. He would like to be a law unto himself. He can be very determined, and shows a great deal of potential for hard work, discipline and application of energy potential for anything he takes up. Normally people are either afraid of him or critical of his stubbornness and the difficulties which it presents.

58

Flexible Thumb

When the thumb is flexible, it is a symbol of adaptability and intelligence. Its owner is capable of manoeuvring around any situation and can demonstrate tact and diplomacy. His ability to adjust to people, situations, and all sorts of conditions enables him to be a sound public relations man, a good negotiator, and a fine salesman. His most effective rôle is to smooth out involved matters and usually he tends to be a kind of peacemaker, though he may be quite firm and determined in so doing.

When the thumb is so flexible that it wilts under pressure it shows a good ability for adaptation to situations and people, but its owner is not very independent and too often yields to pressure. He is not quite able to stick to anything firmly.

The Length of the Thumb

Short Thumb

The length of the thumb is also of great importance. When it is short, and looks stunted, it betrays a lack of will. Its owner is neither too intelligent nor too tenacious. Yet he can be obstinate, and without rhyme or reason may put his foot down firmly on a particular issue. He is narrow-minded in his outlook and can often be abrupt. (XVIII, 1.)

Medium Thumb

When the thumb is of medium size in relation to the palm and fingers, its owner is intelligent and endowed with a sound power of the will. Neither excessively firm nor easily swayed, he prefers a middle course. He likes to be adaptable, and uses common sense to guide his actions. When necessary he can be tenacious and firm, but he always endeavours to weigh the pros and cons before really showing his resolution. (XVIII, 4.)

Exceptionally Long Thumb

An exceptionally long thumb is a mark of greatness. Its owner has a great deal of intelligence and a strong will; he can also show tremendous potential for influencing situations and the public. He is inclined to be an opinion maker; his gifts of greater intelligence and superior volition enable him to be a leader of men. He is never a failure and has a forceful individuality and a large amount of courage. His ability to deal with any situation, however odd, difficult, or critical, can be tremendous. He always seems to rise to any occasion. He is seen in industry, politics, literature, the arts, in fact in all fields of human endeavour — and always as a captain, a leader and originator of big things. (XVIII, 5.)

The Phalanges of the Thumb

The Top Phalange
The two segments of the thumb are of importance individually. The first is associated with will and the second with logic. When the first phalange dominates the thumb and appears to be broad, long and strong, the power of the will can be terrific. Its owner is capable of tremendous energy and hard work but he is not always willing to listen to his own reason. He believes in determined action and at times is liable to become domineering and somewhat illogical. However, he does prove to be a very hard worker as well as a hard task master. (XVIII, 8.)

Long Second Phalange
When the second phalange is long and dominating, it reveals a great deal of logical faculty; however, such a person tends to argue too much, goes into details more than necessary, and is unable to make up his mind. He is endowed with brilliance of mind and intellect, but due to lack of decisive action is too apt to lose chances of making headway in life. Usually he talks too much, though of course brilliantly. Always putting forward new ideas, he is liable to get resentful when others make free use of them; but in no case does he seem to learn to keep his tongue, or his views and ideas, to himself. Even if he were to do so, he would not be able to summon enough self-discipline and will power to put them into practice.

He can be usefully employed as a man of ideas and should prove a perceptive and intelligent analyst. Usually he is able to see things rationally and can look at both sides of an issue with a great deal of perception and interest. If he associates himself with a man of action who is honest, both of them can really work wonders.

Short Second Phalange

A short second phalange indicates a lack of rationality in an individual. Its owner is liable to be illogical, stubborn, and sometimes downright stupid. He can, however, work well at routine jobs under direction.

Top and Second Phalanges — Equal

Will and reason co-exist in a proportionate degree when the phalanges are equal in length. It is a rare combination but, when found, harmonious co-operation between will and logic results. Such persons are suited to positions of authority and responsibility. They show great initiative and know how to wield power. They tend to achieve high offices in various walks of life.

Top of the Thumb

Top Phalange Conic

When the top phalange is cone-shaped, it is a sign of an impulsive nature. When it is short as well the individual is too apt to react quickly and without forethought. He is inclined to be emotional, and is none too determined or logical. Very often he gets hurt by involvements with other people.

Top Phalange Pointed

A thin and narrow top phalange as shown in XVIII, 3 also betrays a weak will. Such people lack decision and the power of resistance. When placed in circumstances where firm will alone can carry the day, they fail to rise to the occasion.

By nature, they are underlings and need to be guided. Leadership is not for them. When left to their own initiative, they fall prey to indecision and hesitation. They can be good routine workers and, when well-directed, can be useful subordinates. They will, however, abuse privilege the moment they notice any relaxation of vigilance.

Top Phalange Square

Sometimes the thumb is squarish at the top and sides, as in XVIII, 6. The top phalange is thus rendered rectangular or square. This denotes a strong will and a person capable of realistic and decisive action. Such people are constant and

61

persistent by nature. They have great endurance and make
reliable friends. Though firm in their ways, they are open to
reason and are neither obstinate nor ruthless.

Top Phalange Bulbous
In very rare cases, the first phalange is top heavy, as in XVIII, 7.
It is bulbous in appearance; and the second phalange is thick.
Such a thumb lacks refinement of form and is ugly to look at. It
indicates that both will and reason are subordinate to brute
force in the individual, who can be obstinate and extremely
difficult to handle.

Such a thumb is frequently associated with a murderer, but
this is hardly fair; it is not a definite index to homicidal
tendencies. However, such people are ruled by passion and are
highly inflammable. If wrongly attacked they are prone to be
overwhelmed by blind fury.

Out-turned Thumb
The inclination or bend of the thumb is also worthy of note.
When it bends away from the palm, thereby extending the
stretch between its tip and that of the forefinger (XVIII, 2), it
shows a nature free from inhibitions and narrowness of mind.
Such people are usually generous.

Inturned Thumb
When the bend is palmwards, thereby narrowing the above
mentioned stretch (XVIII, 3), it is indicative of a restrictive
attitude. Such people are slaves of their own selfishness. They
are inclined to be acquisitive and mean.

COMPARATIVE LENGTH OF FINGERS AND PALM

The length of the fingers as compared to the palm is an important factor. There is more than one method to ascertain relative length, but the most accurate and practical way is to measure the palm from the first wrist line up to the crease beneath the middle finger and then measure the middle finger from the crease to its tip. Lengths of 4½ inches (palm) and 3 inches (finger), indicate a normal proportion. Obviously, with a 4½-inch palm, a finger length of less than 3 inches is relatively short, a finger length of 3½ inches or over relatively long.

When fingers and palm conform to proportionate measurements the owner is endowed with good common sense and is neither given to impulse nor too inclined to reflect unduly over minutiae.

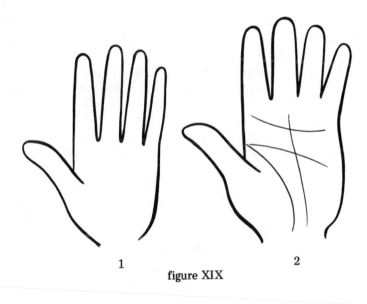

1   2

figure XIX

Fingers Longer than Palm
Fingers which are long in relation to the palm symbolize a persisting urge for analysis and a love of detail. This person tends to be over-critical, fastidious, and always gets involved in

things in such a manner that he is not able to see any situation as a whole. His approach, however, is unemotional. His slow and methodical mental processes make him well-suited to research work, though he is inclined to look for such data which may satisfy his analytical investigation. He is usually drawn towards intellectual pursuits.

His slow, analytical, and critical faculties would never allow him to be rushed into anything. He wants time for deliberation, reflection, and is usually overly cautious. (XIX, 1.)

Fingers Shorter than Palm

When fingers are shorter in relation to the palm, the owner shows a tendency towards quick processes of the mind. Impulsive by disposition, he endeavours to look at a given situation as a whole and cannot be bothered with details. He is intuitive and goes by first impressions, which in a strange kind of manner do turn out to be correct. He is also able to act quickly and too often undertakes things without forethought; when this happens he is apt to get himself involved in awkward situations. (XIX, 2.)

He is somewhat gullible and, being none too critical, liable to be taken in. Of course, other aspects of his hand may minimize this tendency but, in the main, he is impulsive, quick-tempered, and impatient with regard to details.

He is often successful in pursuits which require rapidity of action and accomplishment of tasks without serious consideration.

He looks at things *en masse*, and is simply unable to sit down and study details of data that may involve careful examination. However, he can deal with matters efficiently on a broad basis, and is endowed with executive talent. When rightly placed he can get things done and, though impatient of results, is able to accomplish a lot at a go.

WIDTH OF THE PALM

Besides the comparative length of the palm and the fingers, there are a variety of other features which reveal a great deal about their owner. Take, for instance, the width of the palm. When the palm conforms to the size and build of its owner, it shows a measure of healthy balance in his character.

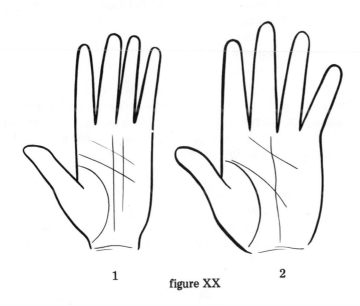

1   2

figure XX

Narrow Palm
A narrow palm is indicative of a self-centred individual, who not only tends to be mean and acquisitive, but is too apt to take a narrow view of life; he is liable to look at things from a purely subjective angle. This person does not demonstrate any social or gregarious instincts, and usually isolates himself. There is a kind of sadistic streak in his make-up and he can be cleverly ruthless and cold in order to achieve his ends. (XX, 1.)

Wide Palm
When the palm is wide, it is a sign of innate sympathy and a

65

great deal of common sense. Its owner is good at team work, knows how to get along with people amicably and is by nature both social and kind. Such an individual makes a good partner, spouse, or member of a group. A wide palm which also has well-developed mounts shows tremendous drive and energy potential, as well as an even larger degree of the sympathy and gregariousness indicated by the width. Its owner is usually associated with welfare work and public service. Due to his innate capacity for human service and his exceptional energy, he finds outlets in pursuits which bring him into contact with people and enable him to contribute to their well-being, happiness or entertainment. (XX, 2.)

Lean Palm
When the palm is lean and thin, without developed mounts, there is paucity of energy. Its owner is apt to tire quickly, and is not able to summon that kind of energy essential for the steady and useful application which produces results.

Palm — Consistency
The consistency of the palmar surface is a factor of great importance. To assess consistency, press the thumb of the right or left hand on to the palmar surface of the other. There will be a feeling of flabbiness, resilient firmness, or hardness.

Palm — Flabby or Firm
When the palm yields under pressure and feels flabby and lifeless, it betrays a lack of energy, love of laziness, and unwillingness to undertake anything active or fruitful. Yet this person is usually cunning and can manoeuvre situations in such a way as to make others do his work for him while he sits back and enjoys life. He is inclined to be untidy and is never punctual or efficient.

A firm, yet springy, palm indicates an active disposition. Its owner enjoys being active, has a great deal of energy, and is capable of accomplishing a lot. He is also inclined to be practical, constructive and positive in his approach to life. He is found in all walks of life which require hard work, firm application and a steadfast disposition.

Palm — Hard

When the palm is hard and wooden the owner is apt to be too taut and nervous. Always on edge and anxious by nature, he is unable to relax or stay calm. He is too sensitive, does things rather nervously, and can hardly find the right words or approach to people or situations. His behaviour is erratic and he cannot cope well with serious responsibility. He can do good work under intelligent direction and in an appreciative atmosphere, but is liable to collapse if badly handled or unduly criticized.

Palm — Silky

In addition to these three palmar consistencies, there are some palms which feel silky, though firm, to the touch. This is the hallmark of an individual who is intellectually inclined and is best suited to activities which have a bearing on cultural interests. He works with his head more than his hands. He is also endowed with a fine sensitivity, and can specialize in fields which require refinement and intellect. These individuals usually show exceptional potential, and are often brilliant.

PURE MOUNT TYPES

The Mount of Jupiter
Having carefully examined the various indications of the fingers, it is essential to carefully study the fleshy elevations at their roots, generally known as the mounts. There are four padded formations at the bases of the fingers, and three in other parts of the palm. The fleshy elevation beneath the index finger is called the Mount of Jupiter.

Fleshy Elevation
Each mount has two aspects, the padded formation and the apex. The fleshy elevation gives the Mount its physical formation. If it is large, well padded and of firm to hard texture, it is known as a prominent mount. If, when compared to other mounts of the palm, it stands out, it would be known as the leading mount. When the Mount of Jupiter is thus formed, centrally located, with rightly placed apex, it reveals the pure Jupitarian.

Apex — skin ridge design
An apex is formed by those skin ridge lines, similar to fingerprints, which cover the whole of the palmar surface. These form a triangular design in the skin region in the area of the mount. When such a design or apex is located below the index finger in a central position this makes the mount the most prominent. When the above enumerated attributes produce a centrally located mount of Jupiter, they will give the pure type of Jupitarian.

It may be borne in mind that such archetypes as Jupitarians, Saturnarians, etc., are a rarity. However, when found, they conform to a very definite type.

Physical Features
A pure Jupitarian is of medium height. He is well built and inclined to be fleshy, though neither flabby nor stout. He is a large man and gives the impression of a person of some weight and significance.

68

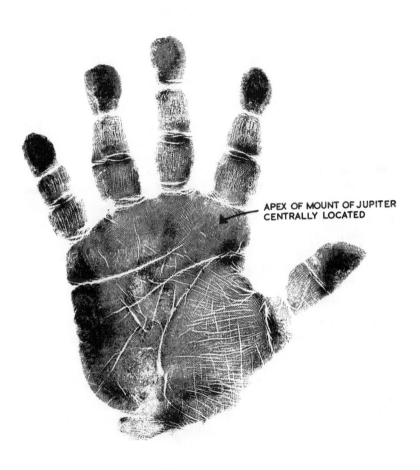

APEX OF MOUNT OF JUPITER
CENTRALLY LOCATED

figure XXI

His skin tends to be healthy, clear in complexion and smooth in texture. His eyes are expressive, eyebrows arched, and the nose is straight and fair in size. His mouth tends to be large with thick lips, the upper one giving the impression of being dominant. The teeth are long and usually the two frontal ones seem to stand out. The cheeks have a firm, soft appearance. The long chin tends to have a dimple. The ears are well-formed and close to the head, and add to his facial harmony and attractiveness. He has a well-built neck, round shoulders, and a sturdy back which is fairly fleshy but firm. He walks in a manner that gives the impression of strength, dignity and style. He has hair all over his body: however, he is inclined to lose the long and curly hair on the top of his head rather early. There is also a tendency to perspire.

His legs are inclined to be firm, of medium length, and strongly built. He owns rather large, strong lungs, to match his commanding voice, through which he is able to influence those who come in contact with him.

His physical appearance, in the main, indicates dignity, pride, strength and of course aristocratic bearing.

Psychological Features

He is endowed with an irresistible ambition and is proud and capable of leadership. In point of fact he is a born leader of men and, whatever the field he may happen to be in, he would reach out for authority and leadership. He loves power and, though he is very fond of high living and affluence, his first love is power rather than the goods of this earth. These he tends to accumulate in order to lend weight to his authority, to help him to hold his head high and to enable him to live in a dignified manner.

He tends to be rather vain and has a way of asserting himself rather too obviously. In spite of this trait he is a great humanitarian, warm-hearted, and can be rather kind and generous. He tends to fight for the underdog and would be quick to take up genuine causes and sponsor them. He is neither mean nor miserly, and in fact hates anything petty and underhanded.

Inclined to love pomp and splendour, he is also naturally religious and deeply moral. This inclines him to be conservative

70

and he would not dream of doing anything which would be beneath his dignity, or, for that matter, allow those around him to think of him as some one not up to the mark. He is a kind of born aristocrat and he would endeavour with all at his disposal to maintain that image.

He grows up early and usually endeavours to marry in the developing stages of his manhood. He also begins to make his success pretty early in life. Unfortunately he tends to expect too much from his partner, and in actual life this expectation may not always be realized.

He has a tendency to live well and is fond of seasoned rich food. He has a delicate taste and yet can be a big eater. He goes for the pleasures of the table in an epicurian manner.

Health and Ailments
As he suffers from the ills of rich living he is prone to be bilious and given to stomach disorders. Unless he is very careful he is apt to suffer from gout and impurity of the blood. This can lead to lung trouble too.

The Mount of Saturn
The Mount of Saturn is positioned beneath the middle finger. Its two aspects, fleshy elevation and the apex, both have to be carefully observed. When it is centrally apexed with well-developed and padded formation, it constitutes the leading mount. Its owner would be called the Saturnian type.

Physical Features
He tends to be taller than his fellow beings, gauntly built, yet thin and of pale colour. His skin is apt to be yellow, dry and usually appears wrinkled.

His hair is thick and black in colour, but he has a tendency to lose it early in life.

His face is thin and long, and the cheekbones tend to be high and stand out. His eyebrows grow thickly on his nose. The colour of his eyes is usually black. His nose is long, thin and is apt to be sharp and pointed. The mouth is large, though his lips tend to be thin; however, his lower jaw is strong and prominently formed. He has good teeth though they are usually inclined to decay at an early age. He has a large neck and an

71

outstanding chin. His distinctive feature is his prominent Adam's apple.

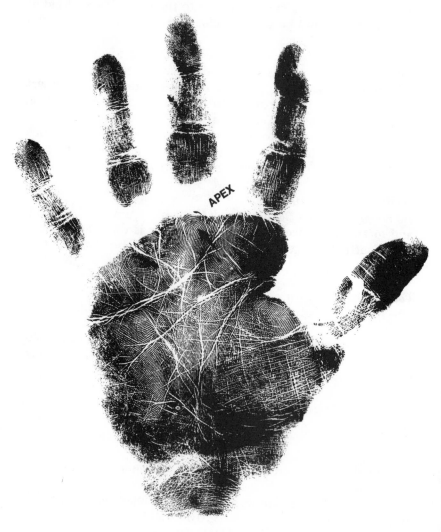

figure XXII

He has a tendency to stoop and also his arms hang pretty loose at his sides. His physical form, bearing and looks betray sadness.

Psychological Features

Naturally inclined to be gloomy, he lacks a buoyance of spirit: cynical and sceptical by disposition he can be called a killjoy. He is none too good company, and likes solitude and isolation.

He is a fatalist by nature and believes in Kismet. Morbid and sensitive, he does not believe in any religious creed or concept though he is a born lover of the occult.

His mien and attitude towards serious matters is philosophical and he goes for grave music and serious literature. He never takes to any calling that involves any measure of risk.

He has a deep love of agriculture and country life, and tends to be distrustful. He is, moreover, prudent, over-cautious, and rather inclined to be self-opinionated.

He is usually capable of research work, can be good at mathematics and any type of work which requires solitary, serious application of the intellect. He is little inclined to marry and usually avoids getting emotionally involved. He prefers to live and work independently and, as such, proves a very poor partner. And if he does choose to marry he can be exceedingly difficult to live with. He shuts himself away and is never open to communication.

The Disposition of the Mount

When the apex of the mount is high, close to the base of the middle finger, his worst characteristics come into operation. He is then liable to be given to suicidal ideas, is gloomy and can be excessively sad.

When the apex is displaced towards either the mount of Jupiter or of Sun, the excessive characteristics are greatly modified.

Health and Ailments

In matters of health he is bilious with a tendency to rheumatic complaints and nervous disorder. There is also a predisposition towards disorders of and accidents to the legs and the feet.

73

The Mount of the Sun

The fleshy elevation below the third finger, known as the finger of Apollo or the Sun, is called the Mount of the Sun. When this mount is the most prominent and has a centrally located apex, it produces the Apollonian type. It should be noticed that the padded formation as well as the apex should be placed in the central location, deviating neither to the left nor the right; also they should be neither too high nor too low.

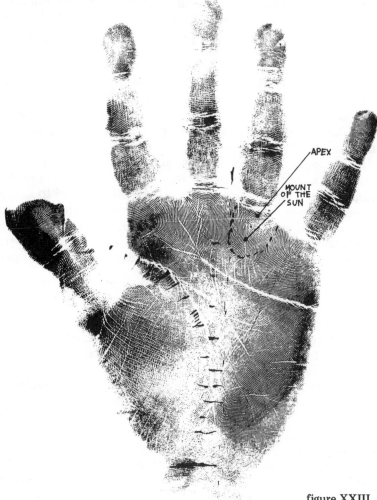

figure XXIII

74

Physical Features

A pure Sun type individual is handsome, shapely and graceful: he has an attractive physical appearance.

Above average height, neither too tall nor too short, he is supple and of athletic build. Gracefully muscular, his movements and general demeanour show a sense of proportion and physical balance.

His hair is thick, curly, abundant, silky and fine. When he grows a beard, that too is abundant and silky, and covers his chin, lips, and of course spreads high over his cheeks. His forehead is broad, though none too high, yet full. His eyes are almond-shaped, large and expressive, and there is a frank and honest look about them: they definitely seem to convey a certain personal sweetness. The eyelashes are long, the eyebrows are arched and crescent shaped. The cheeks are round and rosy, and the complexion is clear and of fine texture.

The nose is straight, as well as beautifully shaped with fine contours. His mouth is well formed, the lips being shapely, well proportioned, neither thick nor thin, and they are of course set in a delicately even manner. His teeth are well set and formed in a neat white row. The chin is round, without being large or small, and the ears are of medium size, set close to the head.

The neck tends to be long, though firmly built and giving the impression of grace and attractiveness. He owns a full chest, and this enables him to speak in a full though musical voice.

His lower limbs are well formed, neither stout nor lean, and generally his feet are of medium size and his gait elastic and graceful. His whole physical build is indicative of natural grace, handsome demeanour and firm strong appearance. He is healthy, active, and full of physical charm.

Psychological Features

He loves art, artistic things and beauty, though he is not a born artist. He is endowed with a potentially brilliant mind and an aptitude for success and fortune. He seeks fame and fortune and usually makes a substantial headway in life.

He is endowed with a kind of innate ability to sense things correctly and usually tends to be intuitive, sensitive and perceptive. He is not a plodder and would be most unwilling to work too hard, for he relies on his brilliant and agile mind and is usually able to make an impact because of it. Of course he is versatile, quick, and can show inventive ability, and he would most probably be good at making use of a small idea in a big way. He is able to attract attention, and usually gets credit for more than he is worth — but then he has a genius to shine in any field or any group of people. His essential trend is love of fortune, fame and wealth and, though he is unwilling to undertake hard labour to accomplish his objectives, he is endowed with a something extra which enables him to succeed in a quick and easy manner.

Adaptability and versatility are his very unique talents. He is capable of fitting in to any situation, and, since his intuitive and brilliant grasp of essentials quickly enables him to become the centre of attention, he is usually the focus of envy and jealousy. In fact he tends to make enemies, so much so that some of them really grow bitter. Yet he is warm-hearted, sunny by temperament and, though neither deep nor profound in his thoughts or nature, he is an extremely likeable individual. He has a creative instinct, though he is better as an imitator: he does, however, tend to brighten up anything he touches, and has a way of expressing himself clearly and without ambiguity. He has a kind of gift for making money, likes riches and enjoys living affluently, surrounded by objects of beauty and value.

One of his interesting traits of character is his short and short-lived temper: but not only does he get angry even when lightly provoked, he is also able to overcome this anger quite quickly. He is not the type who would harbour a grudge too long. He has an innate urge to be popular and too often he talks his way into getting on with people and making himself liked and admired. As I have said, he loves fame and esteem, and would not hesitate to do anything to get known. Not inclined to stoop to conquer he does tend to maintain a kind of dignified approach in his desire for distinction.

His worst fault is vanity, and he is unable to resist the temptation of self-exaggerating in order to get to the top. If thwarted and cut to his true size he really grows bitter and would not hesitate to lie or cheat. Though not endowed with any great artistic gifts, he is unwilling to accept that he is second to none. Should he not be fully successful in his pursuit of ambition, fame and artistic distinction, he seems to believe that he is victimized and being given less than his due. He appears to think that everyone is against him and envious of his great talent.

Health and Ailments
The pure Sun type, being naturally optimistic, is usually able to live a fit and balanced life. However, his weak spots are his eyes and heart. He is also liable to accidents by fire.

He is prone to complaints associated with eyesight, palpitation of the heart and sunstroke.

The Mount of Mercury
The padded formation located directly under the little finger is known as the Mount of Mercury. When it is correctly positioned in the area allotted to it, and contains a definite apex design pattern in its centre, and assumes fleshy prominence in respect to the other mounts of the hand, deviating neither toward the ring finger nor to the outer palm edge, then its owner is known as a Mercurian. Such a pure type, it must be stressed, is rare.

Physical Features
One of the distinguishing characteristics of a Mercurian is that he is of small stature. He is, however, well built and has a strong predisposition to retain a youthful appearance right up to his later years.

He owns a pleasant countenance, oval or elongated in formation, and his features in the main tend to be regular and well defined. The expression of his face changes rapidly, and reveals the play of his emotions and his quick mind. His skin is smooth and fine with a complexion of honey or olive colour.

His forehead is bulging and high. His hair tends to curl at the edges. His eyebrows are thin, joined and form neat curves. He owns deep-set eyes. He usually grows a beard, and tends to keep it well trimmed.

His nose is long and straight. His lips are fine shaped and evenly set, and he owns a long chin that is oval in formation. His neck is well built and his shoulders shapely and quite strong. His chest is broad and usually his limbs too have muscular strength. He certainly has graceful limbs, and tends to be agile and quick in his movements. His voice is neither too loud nor

77

too weak. His whole bearing and countenance speak of alertness, with his impressive and well-defined features, agility of movement. His face changes under emotion, right up to the point of blushing.

He is quite strong and well-built and is one of the most active of all the Mount types. He is not only physically agile, but his mind, too, is alert and active.

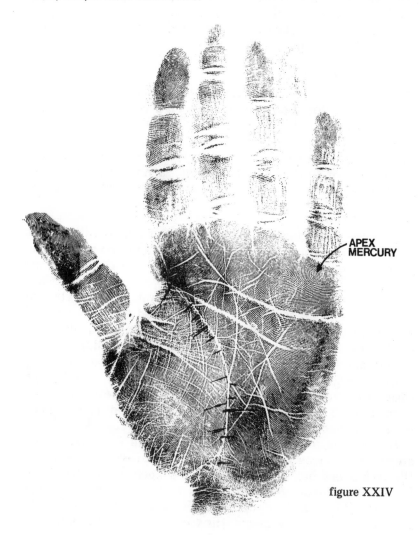

APEX
MERCURY

figure XXIV

78

Psychological Features

The salient characteristic of the Mercurian is that he is quick witted and enjoys rapidity of thought and action. He certainly endeavours to be graceful in all his actions. Not only mentally alert, he enjoys physical activity as well. Obviously he is able to acquire skill in all sorts of games, whether these happen to be indoor or outdoor. And he is at his very best when he has to take up a challenge.

One of his unusual talents is for oratory. He can speak convincingly and often enjoys debates, arguments and particularly those situations where he can make an effective use of his powers of repartee and eloquence. He is also endowed with a quick intuitive faculty and is able to deftly assess people and situations; and thus can make good use of his tact and finesse. As a good after-dinner speaker he is fully equipped with the graces that can win him friends and make him popular.

He has an inventive brain, and indefatigable energy potential. A deep student of human nature, he is also keenly interested in art and literature, though he can be a good mathematician and, given the choice, would take up a vocation which would involve use of this gift. Usually he is seen in business, to which he is admirably suited. He can in fact be an excellent businessman and always finds ways and means of making money. He is also found in the field of law, and can prove an excellent barrister. He is also a born actor.

In everyday life, he is affectionate, even tempered, intelligent and a reliable friend or acquaintance. He is a good parent and loves his partner and family. Very fond of travelling, he enjoys seeing the world. He is also inclined to be intuitive and can show some ability for divination.

When his evil propensities are stimulated he can be dangerous. He can cheat and get away with it. He schemes and plans vicious and daring enterprises, and can really be a menace. However, he is thoroughly superstitious, and when a failure he takes to the life of a tramp. When of the bad type he poses as an occultist and can deceive people with his gift of tongue and trickery of creating confidence in his unusual so-called mystical powers.

Health and Ailments

In matters concerning health, he is given to a nervous and bilious disposition. Obviously his weaknesses are associated with his digestive system and the liver. He is also liable to suffer from ailments connected with the hands and arms, and is also prone to accidents to these limbs, possibly to the extent of being accident-prone with regard to his hands and feet. A tendency to troubles associated with the mobile parts of the body and with movement often seems to have a bearing on his legs and feet.

The Mounts of Mars

The Upper and the Lower Mounts of Mars

There are two mounts of Mars, the upper one situated along the percussion of the hand, directly beneath the Mount of Mercury and located between the lines of the Heart and Head. The lower one is located directly below the Mount of Jupiter, extending from the palm edge, inside the Life Line, and forming a fleshy elevation, between a large crease shooting from the thumb and proceeding to touch the Life Line, the edge of the palm and the arched formation of the Life Line itself. The upper Mount of Mars is associated with resistance and the lower with the quality of aggression.

When either of these Mounts is predominant in the hand, the owner is said to be of Martian type. In some cases both are strongly developed and such a condition would point to a Martian archetype.

Physical Features

The Martian is of medium height. He is of strong build, however, without being heavy or fleshy, and gives the impression of great muscular strength. He has a small thick head and his face is round. The hair too is short, though curly and strongly textured. His large bright eyes have a commanding look about them. His mouth is large and firm though the lips tend to be thin, the lower one being thicker and more prominent. His eyebrows are thick and straight and usually grow very close over the eyes. He tends to frown and, when angry, the bushy eyebrows can look very menacing.

His nose is long, sharp in formation and of Roman shape. His neck is short, and his shoulders broad and well-developed. He owns a commanding voice and usually his whole demeanour is that of a strong, audacious and combative individual. Whether the qualities of aggression or resistance are predominant in his make-up, his appearance tends to convey the ability to defend himself and to indicate that he is not to be trifled with.

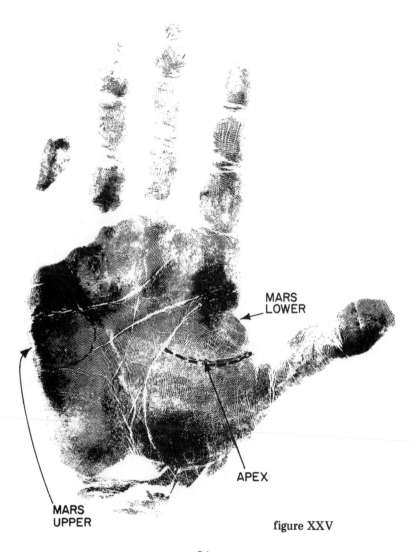

MARS LOWER

APEX

MARS UPPER

figure XXV

D

Psychological Features

The Martian, by nature, is a generous type and proves a loyal and a devoted friend. In point of fact, he loves spending for those he loves and generally does his best to make friends, going out of his way to do things for them. His aggressive spirit inclines him to fight on their behalf and, because of his magnanimity and devotion, he is admired and retains his friends.

He is endowed with a tremendous amount of energy and shows stamina, determination and ability to cope with all sorts of difficult and awkward situations, to get ahead and succeed. There is a spirit of enterprise about him. Due to his combativeness, he is naturally inclined to be a good soldier and quite often takes to the army.

He is not too mindful of delicacies in human relationships and usually is not refined in his approach to people. He tends, in fact, to be tactless and blunt, and without hesitation goes to the point in a straightforward manner. However, he does not really mean to harm anyone though he may at times unconsciously cause hurt to those he is dealing with. He accomplishes his aims with vigorous approach and with audacity and courage. He is also inclined to dictate and lay down the law.

In matters of love and affection he is amorous and passionate. He is usually attractive to the opposite sex and quite popular with them. When he sets his heart on an object of affection he goes straight for the person, and, by sheer forceful approach, wins the love he wants.

He is a good eater and enjoys plenty of good food. He is inclined to be fond of outdoor sports, games of hazard, circuses and anything that implies courage, challenge or giving battle. He is proud by nature, and seeks honours and decorations. He cannot take a back seat and ever endeavours to occupy the pride of place.

When his evil propensities predominate, he can take to crime and can be a dangerous member of society. He would become a thief or a killer and would undertake hazardous criminal activities. However, even in his worst form, he remains loyal to friends and is generous and courageous.

Health and Ailments
He has either too much or too rich blood. Usually prone to suffer from ailments associated with blood, he tends to have skin diseases, rush of blood to the head, and loss of blood through injuries. In the main he endeavours to maintain good health, and tends to be energetic, active and ever on the go. He likes pushing forward and usually makes headway.

The Mount of the Moon
The fleshy elevation covering an area close to the wrist along the percussion side of the palm, and roughly between the Fate and Head lines towards the outward palm edge, is known as the Mount of the Moon. When firmly textured and predominantly developed, with a clear apex, which either may be formed by tri radii or a concentric circle, the Moon or Lunar type is indicated.

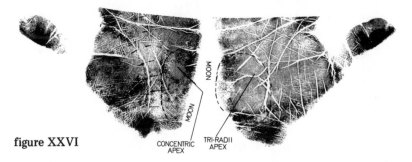

figure XXVI

Physical Features
The Lunar type is certainly tall in stature and is easily distinguished thereby. He tends to be fleshy, with a bulging stomach, heavy legs, and large feet. He is usually stout — soft and flabby, however, rather than muscular or firmly built.

He owns a round head, closely set and usually small. His forehead is low and his hair fine and of light colour. He has a broad and full face, the nose being small and round. The mouth, though small, is rather thick lipped, with large teeth which are unevenly set and irregular in formation. The eyes are quite large and round, often bulging, with large, thick eye-lids. His teeth have a tendency to decay early in life, and seem to have a grey hue about them. The same is the case in regard to his gums.

He has a long neck, which is usually inclined to be wrinkled, fleshy and quite noticeable. His chest too is fleshy, and his stomach large and protruding, usually standing out as the prominent feature of his physical make-up. His hands and feet are large and sometimes give the impression of being swollen. His otherwise dead white complexion is occasionally seen to have a pinkish colouring.

Psychological Features
The Lunar type is restless by nature, and tends to be fickle, untrustworthy and cold. He is certainly selfish and bone idle and never seems to be optimistic or joyful. He is melancholy, given to superstitions, and unwilling to really work. He is religious in a superficial way by nature, being liable to show a kind of respect for the mystic or supernatural aspects of religious beliefs.

He is endowed with a very rich imagination. He is a born traveller and tends to move about the Earth. He is unable to settle down, and is usually a very poor or unreliable lover or marriage partner. He is often given to daydreaming and tends to indulge in forebodings and misgivings of all sorts. Rather nervous and impressionable, he is liable to react to people and situations quickly and usually not in a constructive way. However, he is romantically inclined and shows love of poetry and artistic pursuits. He likes music and enjoys literature, usually of a romantic and imaginative nature. He is hardly a person who goes for facts, reality and data. He in fact is a creature of imagination.

In the case of male Lunar types there is a strong predisposition toward effeminate tastes and inclinations. Neither healthy and determined nor robust they tend to be changeable and vaccillating, and usually unreliable. In fact, they are rather weak.

In the case of female Lunar types, there is a tendency toward frivolity and insincerity. However, they have a kind of tenderness for those they think they love and care for. Rather selfishly inclined, they are, however, quite capable of imagining that they are truly devoted to their loved ones. Lunar subjects are strongly attracted by the sea, and their favourite professions do seem to be associated with the sea or water.

One of their worst defects is that they tend to over-do things. They may solemnly promise something, and talk about it a lot, but they never seem to keep to their word. They are like water — moving, changing and never still. They can be rather fond of strong drinks and alcohol. Some of their lower characteristics constitute cowardice, foolish talk, selfishness, insolence and of course infidelity and unreliability. They are soft and usually endeavour to put on a false impression and outward façade. They hardly prove good friends or partners, or for that matter relatives or mates. They change too quickly and without any tangible reason. Restless and romantically inclined they are children of whims and dreams.

Health and Ailments
Though giving the impression of a big man, the Lunar type is not endowed with any considerable measure of energy or stamina. Lymphatic by temperament, he is unable to stand either hard work or long hours of continued application of energy. He is in fact constantly conscious of the need for preservation of energy, and is anxious about health and well-being all the time. He is apt to suffer from nervous fears, usually appertaining to matters concerning health, and in extreme cases can be given to hallucinations and acute forms of anxiety.

He seems to be predisposed toward intestinal disorders and rheumatic complaints. Female Lunarians have a tendency towards womb and bladder troubles.

The Mount of Venus
At the root of the thumb, there is a large padded formation, whose boundaries extend from the thick crease at the base of the thumb, along the Lower Mount of Mars, and then within the semi-circular Life Line right up to the place where it terminates, meeting the First Bracelet and forming an angle with it. When the Mount of Venus is firm, large and with a central apex, it assumes the rôle of the predominant mount. Its owner is generally said to be of Venusian type.

Physical Features
The Venusian is usually just above medium height, though tallness is hardly his distinctive attribute. He is endowed with a

graceful shape, tends to be handsome and attractive, and generally gives the impression of beauty. There is an element of feminine charm about him. His complexion is white, with a tinge of rose or pink, and is soft and clear. The texture of the skin is fine, delicate and alluring.

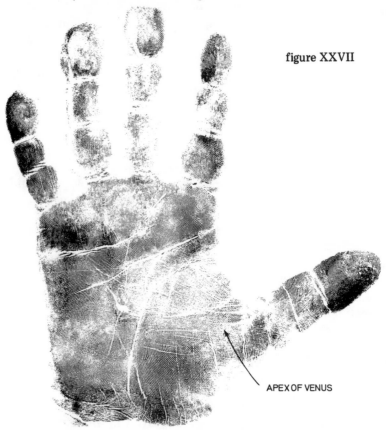

figure XXVII

APEX OF VENUS

His face is round or oval, the cheeks being well formed without obtruding bone structure, and quite often dimpled. His forehead is high, the brow arched and inclined to be narrow. He owns beautiful, well-defined curved eyebrows, with silky abundant hair. Each one is separate and forms an attractive arch.

He has certainly a fine crop of hair and does not grow bald even in later years. The hair is usually dark and plentiful. His eyes are large, almond shaped, clear and beautiful. They have a tender seductive look about them. They in fact give the feeling of voluptuous gentle stimulation. The eyelids too are fine and delicate.

His mouth is small, though the lips tend to be red and thick, the lower one dominating. His teeth are white and arranged in handsome rows. The chin is dimpled, plumpish and oval. He has small gracefully formed ears and his neck tends to be fleshy, impressive and majestic. The shoulders are full and gracefully broad. His arms are fairly plump and his hands are white, soft, and of fine texture. The fingers usually are tapering and the thumb is small.

His legs are shapely, graceful and attractive with high hips which are round and well formed. He certainly has an attractive gait, his feet being small with an arched instep. His impression as a whole is that of grace, attractiveness and sweet tenderness. In both the sexes these are the distinctive features of the Venusian type.

Psychological Features

His most important feature is fellow feeling and love of humanity. He is affectionate, sympathetic, likeable and fond of living and sharing life and its good things. He hates to cause any harm or emotional injury to anyone. He is not all that ambitious though he loves to live to a comfortable standard. Capable of sacrifice, he endeavours to respect the feelings of others and obviously becomes popular. When he falls in love, he is capable of durable devotion and is steadfast and sincere.

He loves all that is fine and goes for perfumes of delicate nature, music that appeals to the heart, and surroundings of beauty. He also loves scenic beauty. Though sensually disposed and though the opposite sex attracts him strongly, usually he listens to the one on whom his affections centre and is strongly influenced by that individual. In order to please the person concerned, he would endeavour to do ambitious things and make good in life. When cheated or humiliated in love he suffers great anguish and yet, in spite of intense personal pain, he is capable of forgiveness. He loves peace, and cannot stand any form of dissension, dispute, or disharmony around him. He in fact is truly sweet and naturally kind.

When devoted to any form of art or creative pursuit, he is able to excel in it and, through his medium, is able to reach the hearts of people. As an artist, he is the intricate creator of delicate beauty and things of taste and lasting charm. He instinctively stimulates the human heart and appeals to genuine emotions by his imagery, thereby attracting attention.

The bad Venusian is liable to be morally currupt and give way to pleasures of the senses. He tends to be a debauchee and betrays a strong inclination towards moral depravation, usually going to the extreme.

Health and Ailments
In matters of health the Venusian is generally strong and healthy and usually maintains physical fitness. He is, however, inclined toward venereal diseases and repercussions of emotional frustrations. Due to his rather voluptuous bearing he is open to love intrigue and suffers from disappointment in love, and this can take a toll of his health and wellbeing. Also excesses associated with his sex life do tend to bring about health problems resultant from dissipation and divitalisation.

THE MOUNTS OF THE HAND

General Characteristics

Pure Mount type is undoubtedly rare; however, when found, it does conform in all its essential characteristics. In practical life, one comes across a varying degree of variations of the pure type, consisting of fleshy elevation and displacement of each Mount of the hand. These have to be individually considered.

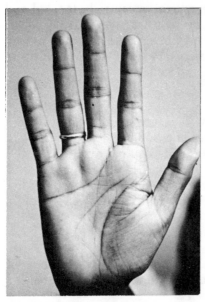 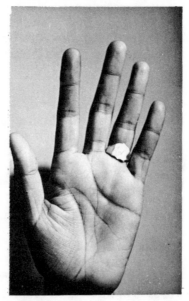

The physiological aspect of the Mount — that is, the fleshy formation — generally, when centrally located and well developed, indicates excellent aptitudes and the most constructive characteristics of the type. When the mount is flat or underdeveloped, it points to negative characteristics and paucity of energy potential. Excessive development, showing accentuated protuberance in the case of any mount, is indicative of abnormal ingredients.

When all the mounts are good, the individual is full of life, energy and can prove to be exceptionally capable and talented. When these are missing or bad he is not likely to show any great qualities of heart or head.

The disposition of the mounts is also important. When a mount is displaced it betrays a certain imbalance.

The Mount of Jupiter
The physiological aspect of a mount, that is to say, its elevation irrespective of its apex, is important and has a special significance. The one based at the root of the index finger is called the Mount of Jupiter, and, as already stated, is associated with such attributes as ambition, pride, social sense and religious consciousness. When the mount is centrally located and well developed it shows the most constructive characteristics. The index finger also goes by the name of the finger of Jupiter and shares the characteristics associated with the Mount at its base.

Good Mount of Jupiter
When the Mount of Jupiter is well placed and developed, there is a healthy love of display, gaiety and honour. The owner is also a lover of nature. He is always inclined to participate in social and public activities and usually can speak well and impressively. Fond of good living and comfort, he is somewhat inclined to seek flattery. However, he is endowed with a personal charm and usually can win his way in life.

Excessive Mount of Jupiter
An excessive development of the Mount is a symbol of arrogance, tyranny, and ostentation. He loves his pleasures and will stop at nothing to gain his selfish ends.

Low Mount of Jupiter
When the Mount is low or absent, its owner is apt to be idle, given to egoism and usually unable to have a real sense of personal dignity. He is also inclined toward irreligious propensities. He is usually lacking in decency and can be vulgar and rather degenerate.

The Mount of Saturn
The padded formation beneath the second finger is called the Mount of Saturn. Prudence, balance and meditation are the qualities associated with it. The second finger too is known as

the finger of Saturn and partakes of the characteristics peculiar to the Mount.

Good Mount of Saturn
When the Mount of Saturn is centrally located and well developed, it endows a wholesome ingredient of prudence and caution. However, there is a leaning toward fatality, and the owner tends to accept that what will be will be. There is also a strong tendency toward the occult sciences and he is apt to be sensitive about little things. Love of solitude and a quiet kind of life seem to be his salient features. He is also liable to be timid.

Excessive Mount of Saturn
This mount is extremely rarely over-developed: however, when excessively high, it shows sadness, morbidity and extreme love of solitude. The owner is liable to be ascetically inclined and at times there is a tendency toward suicide.

Low Mount of Saturn
When the Mount is low or absent, it is indicative of a vegetative existence. The owner is unmoved by any strong feelings and lives in a kind of fear and foreboding. He neither sparkles nor is good company. He in fact tends to spread gloom and lack of sense of life or enjoyment.

The Mount of Sun
The elevated miniature fleshy bulge below the third finger is called the Mount of the Sun or Apollo. It is associated with brilliance, fame and artistic aptitudes. The third finger is called the finger of Apollo and shares the same attributes.

Good Mount of Sun
When the Mount of Sun is well developed and centrally located, it reveals an individual whose prevailing taste is essentially artistic. Aesthetic aptitudes do tend to rule his life. Potentially its owner is capable of achieving glory, success and brilliance of fortune. He is of potential genius, and usually tends to enjoy affluence and wealth. He is endowed with grace, confidence in his own talent and is a lover of beauty.

91

Excessive Mount of Sun
If the Mount is over-developed, it betrays love of wealth and the goods of this earth, and a great leaning toward extravagance, luxury and display. Its owner tends to be envious, quick tempered, vain and boastful. Unfortunately such people have a very high sense of their individual greatness and always complain of being unrecognised and unappreciated by their fellow creatures. They certainly have a strong feeling of being far superior to others.

Low Mount of Sun
When the Mount is low or absent it shows lack of appreciation and indifference to anything artistic. Its owner is too materialistically inclined and is usually dull and without culture or enlightenment.

The Mount of Mercury
The pad below the little finger is given the name of the scribe of the heavens and God of speed, Mercury. It is associated with science, speed and expressional technique. The little finger shares its name and attributes.

Good Mount of Mercury
When the Mount of Mercury is centrally located and well developed, its eminence reveals science, intelligence, eloquence and promptitude in thought. It also indicates potential for commerce and industry, love of the occult sciences and of course speed and travelling.

Excessive Mount of Mercury
When the Mount is developed excessively it is an ill omen. It is a mark of cunning, theft and treachery. Its owner tends to be deceitful and pretentious. A charlatan, he takes to dishonesty in occult matters, and is essentially superstitious. He is able to hoodwink people with his deft and pretentious façade and is what one would like to call a trader for his own benefit in human weakness, though always by devices and means which are crooked and never above board.

Low Mount of Mercury
When the Mount of the Mercury is low or absent, it betrays lack of aptitude for either business or matters appertaining to science. There is no sense of enterprise, no high intellectual talent, nor scientific potential. The mentality is poor and rather ordinary.

The Mount of Mars Negative
Situated below the Mount of Mercury is another fleshy pad on the percussion of the palm. Its boundaries are determined by the two main horizontal lines that cross the palmar surface. The one nearer the fingers is the Line of Heart and the other in the middle of the palm is the Line of Head. This is the Negative Mount of Mars.

The palm is divided into two halves by the well-marked vertical line known as the Fate Line. It begins close to the wrist and, crossing the palm, ends below the base of the middle finger. The thumb side is known as the positive half and the percussion side as the negative half. Since the mount is located in the negative section, obviously it is known as the Negative Mount of Mars.

Good Mount of Mars Negative
This is associated with such attributes as power of resistance, courage, stamina, etc. When the mount is well developed, it endows calm courage and innate potential to maintain excellent control of temper. Its owner is capable of a great deal of staying power and does not yield to force of circumstances easily. When essential he can show resignation and can be generous and magnanimous.

Excessive Mount of Mars Negative
When the Mount is excessively developed and encroaches on the palm it indicates fury, violence and cruelty. Such a person is defiant, insolent, inclined to exaggerate and lascivious.

Low Mount of Mars Negative
When the mount is low or absent, it certainly is a mark of cowardice, and its owner tends to be rather childish and never seems to grow up. Hasty and lacking in stamina or power of resistance, he tends to yield to any pressure too easily and

obviously can hardly make worthwhile progress in life.

The Mount of the Moon
Below the Negative Mount of Mars, along the percussion, is
another rather large fleshy elevation. Its boundaries are
determined by the percussion of the hand on one side and the
wrist line on the other. From around the mid point of the first
wrist line, it seems to bulge into the palm, extending to touch
the Mount of Mars. It covers a large area in the palm surface.
This is the Mount of the Moon. It is generally associated with
imagination, mysticism and travelling besides other attributes.

Good Mount of the Moon
When well developed, it reveals rich imagination, chastity and
poetry of the soul. Its owner is inclined toward the mystical and
shows love of solitude, though he feels restless and would like
to travel. He is introspective and usually inclined to be silent.
There is a certain love of leisure and most probably an
inclination to be resigned and given to abstract thinking.

Mysticism attracts him and usually some form of clairvoyance or mediumistic attribute is innate in him. Intuitive and
sensitive, he seems to be capable of prophetic dreams which
usually come to pass.

Excessive Mount of the Moon
When the Mount of Moon is excessively developed, it shows a
capricious and irritable character. Its owner is given to sadness,
discontent, and wild imagination. Superstitiously disposed, he is
liable to be given to morbid thoughts and unhealthy
forebodings. His intuitive faculty is of the negative kind and he
usually senses evil things and foresees the advent of tragedies
and crises.

In certain cases, the mount is not necessarily high, but occupies
a large oblong area. Such an excess is indicative of
contemplative resignation and its owner is liable to be given to
complete surrender to the force of circumstances. He does not
seem to show any will power and allows life and circumstances
to rule him.

Low Mount of the Moon
When the Mount of Moon is low or absent it shows coldness, want of imagination and hardly any aptitude for ideas. There is a kind of poverty of soul and the intellect is dull. Its owner is capable of appreciation neither of the aesthetic nor the sensitive things in life. He lives a vegetative life.

The Mount of Venus
At the root of the thumb, in the positive section of the palm, almost opposite to the Mount of the Moon, is another rather large fleshy elevation. This is called the Mount of Venus. It is associated with love, sympathy, time and music, etc. The Mounts of the Moon and of Venus literally occupy the whole of the palm beneath the Head line, practically the most important portion of the hand.

Good Mount of Venus
When the Mount of Venus is well developed, it shows instinctive affection, love and melody, the great moving force of life, grace, admiration and tenderness. Its owner tends to be benevolent, capable of a great love of home and family, and is patriotically inclined. It is usually associated with talented singers, and those who have some love of rhythm and capacity for tender passion.

Excessive Mount of Venus
When the Mount of Venus is excessively developed, thus dominating the whole palmar region, it betrays licence, vanity and a strong leaning toward debauchery. Its owner is apt to be depraved, and shows shameless indolence and thoughtless inconsistency of behaviour. He is usually a bad sort, and causes a lot of unhappiness and disillusion to those who may happen to care for him or be close to him. Unreliable and unstable, he prides himself in his licentious ways.

Low Mount of Venus
When the Mount of Venus is low or absent it shows lack of energy potential, coldness and impotence in love. Selfishly inclined, its owner is wanting in any appreciation for art. In fact, it betrays absence of all passion for living, sharing and enjoying with others. He is apt to become dry and, of course, is

totally devoid of the milk of human kindness. He has no soul for music and is insensitive to the finer things in life.

The Mount of Mars Positive
Above the Mount of Venus and beneath the Mount of Jupiter, along the edge of the palm and encircled by the Life line, there is a small, though distinct, fleshy elevation. This is the positive Mount of Mars. It is usually associated with combativeness and aggressive courage.

Good Mount of Mars Positive
When well developed, it shows active courage, promptness in action and an aggressive approach to things. Its owner is capable of showing an enormous amount of energy in the pursuit of his ambitious objectives, and can not only tackle difficult tasks but is inclined to stimulate and accept a challenge with relish.

Excessive Mount of Mars Positive
When the Mount of Mars positive is excessively developed, its owner shows a defiant manner, as well as a violent, impulsive and explosive disposition. He in fact tends to be cruel, insulting, irritable and given to tyranny. Also there is a strong leaning toward sensuality.

Low Mount of Mars Positive
When the Mount is low or absent there is want of energy potential: in fact, there is hardly any fire in its owner's being, and practically no fighting spirit. Courage is wanting and its owner tends to be rather cowardly and unable to accept any challenge.

DISPLACED MOUNTS OF THE HAND

When a proper assessment of the Mount types has been made, an important point to bear in mind is their placement. If any Mount is displaced it creates changes in the physical as well as psychological aspects.

Jupiter towards the thumb
When the Mount of Jupiter is displaced towards the thumb, it represents family pride. Its owner is liable to be greatly influenced in his behaviour and contact with people by this innate tendency toward consciousness of his family background.

Jupiter toward Saturn
When the Mount is displaced toward the Mount of Saturn it denotes quite a different characteristic. Its owner tends to be self conscious, and this is quite evident in his everyday life and behaviour. His character as a whole is tinged with wisdom and thought. While maintaining his main Jupitarian features, he is able to bring a measure of consideration and wisdom to his life. There is sagacity in his leadership and a deeper sense of morality in his general outlook and behaviour pattern.

Jupiter toward the Head Line
When the Mount is displaced in such a manner that it is close to the Head Line, it denotes a strong streak of arrogance. Its owner seems to think no end of himself and is unable to resist the temptation of being arrogant and domineering.

The Mount of Saturn toward Jupiter
When the Mount of Saturn is displaced toward the area of the Mount of Jupiter, seriousness of disposition is strongly influenced by a quality of hope and dignity. Its owner thus is able to show a firm aspect of self confidence. This usually enables him to make good and sound progress in life.

Saturn toward the Sun
When the Mount of Saturn is displaced toward the area of the Mount of Sun, the owner's more sombre characteristics are

softened and he develops a love of solitude which is healthy and denotes peaceful contemplation.

Saturn toward the Heart Line
When the Mount is so displaced that it is leaning too close to the course of the Heart Line, it is none too good an omen. It takes away warmth and natural affection, and replaces it with a callous disposition. The owner is at best inclined to be indifferent and cold.

The Mount of Sun toward Saturn
When the Mount of Sun is displaced toward Saturn, its owner shows affection for children, and usually takes a fatherly and gentle approach to young ones.

The Sun toward Mercury
When the Sun is displaced toward Mercury, there is love of animate things: however, its owner tends to show care and love for animals rather than children.

When the Mount of Sun is displaced toward the Heart Line, it has a peculiar effect. Its owner seems to be disinclined to be serious and does not care to face any situation which is necessary. He develops a kind of irresponsible attitude.

The Mount of Mercury toward the Sun
When the Mount of Mercury is too inclined toward the Sun and appears to be displaced, it creates a character which seems to be devoid of seriousness. Its owner tends to treat everything with a sense of the ridiculous. There is a kind of unwillingness to see things as they are: he endeavours to see those aspects wherein he may satisfy his sense of the ridiculous. Though not evil-minded, he does tend to be none too conscious of the need of being realistic or sedate.

Mercury toward the Percussion
When the Mount of Mercury is displaced toward the percussion, its owner is inclined to be dashing and courageous. He is neither retiring nor does he shirk responsibility. He in fact shows dauntlessness and quickness in action.

Mercury toward the Heart Line
When the Mount of Mercury is displaced toward the Heart Line it is a mark of ability to rise in times of crisis and emergency. Its owner shows an excellent spirit of reacting to any situation demanding action, taking up a challenge, and does so with a deep sense of conscious need of doing something practical and to thereby remove suffering or chaos.

The Negative Mount of Mars toward Mercury
When Negative Mars is displaced toward the Mount of Mercury, it shows a great fortitude and an undaunted spirit. Its owner is capable of tremendous power of endurance and, usually by sheer dint of staying power, succeeds in his aspirations.

The Negative Mount of Mars toward the Palm proper
When the Negative Mars is displaced toward the palm proper and bulges its head up visibly toward the palmar centre, its passive quality undergoes a complete change. The owner then is able to show an aggressive spirit. Besides maintaining its innate quality of resistance, it also takes on the characteristics of an aggressive and courageous front.

Negative Mount of Mars toward the Moon
When the Negative Mars is displaced toward the Mount of the Moon, it shows some exceptional characteristics. Its owner shows meekness of spirit, tremendous patience, and a tranquil nature. Yet he is endowed with hypnotic power and can truly influence in an unusual manner those he comes into contact with. Usually he is not aware of his power of hypnotism, but he does seem to make a strong and enduring inpact.

The Moon towards Negative Mars
When the Mount of the Moon happens to be displaced toward the Negative Mount of Mars, it reveals active imagination, creative talent, and love of harmony. Its owner shows an inventive ability, and exercises a sound control over his creative and imaginative faculties.

The Mount of Moon toward the Percussion
When it is displaced toward the percussion, it seems to stand

out as a large oblong bulge along the outer palm-edge. When such is the case, it shows an unusual power of imagination; however, its owner seems to unavoidably get involved with ingredients of jealousy or envy, which seem to be the ferment of his power of imagination.

The Mount of Moon toward the Wrist
When the Mount of the Moon is displaced toward the wrist, it is hardly a good sign to have. It is an indication of a wild imagination and its owner is given to day dreaming, passive living, and usually tends to be anxious, and superstitiously inclined.

The Mount of Moon toward Venus
In some cases, the Mount of the Moon is so displaced that it encroaches upon the boundary of the Mount of Venus. When such is the case its owner's imagination stimulates emotionalism and adds intensity to it. Such a person seems unable to discipline his emotional fantasies and falls a prey to them.

The Mount of Moon toward the middle of the Palm
When the Mount of the Moon is displaced toward the middle of the palm, the area known as the plain of Mars, its imagination adds to the aggressive force of its owner, thereby endowing him with a powerful instrument to influence people and situations. He in fact shows a great deal of alert mentality and power of imagination, which help him toward making substantial headway in life.

The Mount of Venus toward the Thumb
The largest Mount of the palm is that of Venus. When normal, it is placed inside the Life Line and under the base of the thumb. In some instances it is displaced toward the thumb, thus forming a large, elevated bulge close to the root of the thumb.

When this is the case, it denotes that emotions rule the will. Its owner seems to be too emotional to allow his cold logic or the power of his will to condition his behaviour patterns. He in fact is too apt to be under the sway of his emotions.

The Mount of Venus toward Life Line
When the Mount of Venus is displaced toward the Life Line it adds fire to the vital forces and the owner inclines toward sensuousness. He in fact seems to be fond of luxury and comfort, and loves the physical to excess.

The Mount of Venus toward Moon
When Venus is displaced toward the Mount of Moon this too is none too good, for its owner tends to be too inclined toward sensuality. Quite incapable of self discipline he goes after sensual pleasures and the like.

The Mount of Venus toward the Wrist
When Venus is displaced toward the wrist, it gives similar results. Its owner tends to be sensuous and seeks all those pleasures that help to satisfy his sexual cravings.

Positive Mount of Mars toward Venus
The Positive Mount of Mars is located just above the Mount of Venus and beneath the Mount of Jupiter. When it is displaced toward the Mount of Jupiter, its owner is capable of courage and power of endurance through sheer pride and personal sense of dignity.

When it happens to be displaced toward the Mount of Venus, his power of endurance and courage is due to affection. He in fact shows ingredients of courage and staying power, the basis whereof is his love instinct. For those he may love he would bear a great deal with fortitude.

Positive Mount of Mars toward the thumb
When the Positive Mars is displaced toward the root of the thumb, the courage evinced is through the power of the will and determination.

The Positive Mount of Mars toward the middle of the Palm
In some instances the Positive Mars is displaced toward the area known as the Plain of Mars. When such is the case, it shows tremendous potential for audacious living. Its owner loves danger and shows combative, battling instincts. He certainly enjoys exciting and dangerous living.

101

LIFE LINE

Origin and end of Life Line

By far the most important line on the hand is the Line of Life. It starts from the inter-space between the forefinger and the thumb, and, encircling the large fleshy elevation at the root of the thumb, tends to terminate at a point where the wrist ends and the third phalange of the thumb stretches outwards, thereby forming an angle. (XXVIII, 1,B-a).

A safe guide to the terminating trend of the Life Line is to follow a well-marked line across the wrist where it begins to merge into the palmar surface (XXVIII, 1a). This line is known as the first line of wrist or the First Bracelet and it is important in connection with judgement of time. (As a rule there are several lines at this place; for purposes of Hand Reading, three are taken into consideration (XXVIII, 1).) Follow the First Bracelet, the one nearest the palmar surface, towards the wrist-thumb angle (XXVIII, 1). It is where this line touches the angle "a" that the Line of Life ought to terminate.

The Long Life Line

In practice, one rarely comes across such a long Line of Life. When of this length it indicates the possibility of living to a very great age, and, if in addition the line is devoid of defective markings, it denotes prospects of reaching around a hundred years or so. In some of the treatises of Hand Reading you are sure to come across a statement suggesting that, from end to end, the Line of Life gives the possibility of seventy years of age. This is an erroneous assumption. Nature's provision for the span of human life is much longer than that.

Index to the Book of Life

The Line of Life represents not only our constitution and vitality, but something more than that. It advocates, according to a certain system of hand study in the Indo-Pakistan subcontinent, that the whole of the general pattern of life can be delineated from the Pollax — the Thumb. It is quite understandable. The thumb covers volition, logic and love, as represented by its top, second and third phalanges respectively (XXVIII, 2). This third phalange is commonly known as the Mount of

102

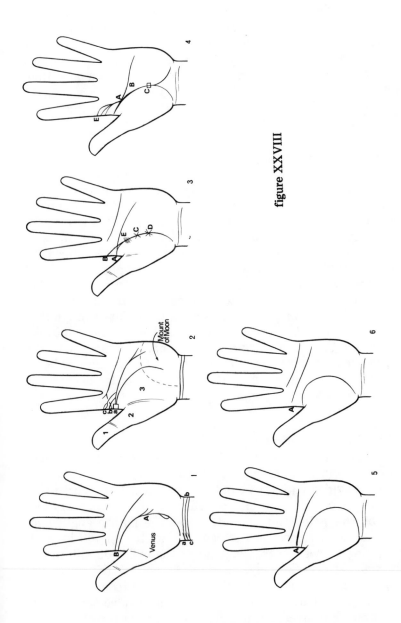

figure XXVIII

103

Venus. The Line of Life encircles this Mount and is sometimes called the Venus Line. From the tip of the thumb to the boundary that the Life Line traces in the palmar surface, there is a great deal that can be gathered about human psychology and constitution, their inter-play with one another, and their manifestation in the form of events. This area may well be considered as being an epitome of the whole hand — an exhaustive index to the book of life.

Delineation of Origin of Life Line
The first aspect of the Life Line to be carefully studied is its point of origin, revealing as it does something unalterable about its owner. It is generally said to begin from the edge of the palm below the first finger and above the thumb. This is roughly correct but extremely misleading. When we begin to seek interpretations with reference to its beginning, it is imperative that we should have some well-defined starting place. It is often stated that when the Line of Life originates from an islanded formation, there is some mystery connected with the birth. The statement is not without truth. But it is the point of origin that has to be fixed, otherwise we are apt to make a serious mistake in interpretation. For example, an islanded formation in the body of the Line, near the start, is liable to be mistaken as being at its origin; in fact, such a mark merely indicates delicacy of health in infancy or early childhood.

The Line of Demarcation
We all know that the lines with which this study of the hand deals are imprinted in the palmar surface, which in its texture is akin to the ridge patterns found on the finger tips — used the world over for tracing criminals. This ridge pattern covers the whole of the palm and extends across the entire length and breadth of each finger on the palmar side. If you will look at the forefinger near the growing end of the nail, you will find a fairly well-defined fine edge or ridge pattern of the finger tip fading out, and a coarser layer of skin coming to meet it from the nail-side back of it. These two, the finger ridge pattern and the coarser skin layer, form a line of demarcation which runs from the growing end of the nail downward to meet the thumb

where it makes an angle with the palm.

At the base of the forefinger you can see a rather heavily marked crease with other somewhat shorter but thickish lines running above and, in some hands, even below it. Mark the point where this crease meets the line of demarcation. In the space between this point and the point where the thumb makes an angle with the palm, you can see the line of demarcation, fairly well-defined and quite visibly traced. A magnifying glass can help you to see it more clearly. Midway between the heavily marked line at the root of the fore finger on one side and the thumb on the other, you will find the origin of the Life Line. The line of demarcation, and no other part of the edge of the palm, is its real boundary. This line of demarcation is most important, as it is essential for accurate dating on the Life Line and is helpful in checking periods on other markings of the palmar surface.

Dating System

As briefly described in the section associated with techniques and terminology, an accurate system of dating is essential for meaningful assessment of times of occurrence of events or changes in life. Without correct timing of events, the value of practical hand analysis can be considerably reduced; and at times it could prove to be the cause of anxiety or have a deleterious effect on the individual.

On the standard measurement, each section indicates a span of ten years. The correct method of its application is fairly simple, though, in particular cases, adjustments may have to be made in the time scale.

The first wrist line (usually tracing its course where the rough skin of the wrist ends and the "fingerprint" ridge pattern begins) is the actual line of demarcation between the wrist and the palmar surface. From the mid-point of the first wrist line up to the centre of the deep crease at the base of the middle finger is the total length of the palm.

A six-inch ruler can be used to measure this length. For the sake of convenience, let us suppose that it is four and a half inches. Its exact halfway point, transposed onto the equivalent point on the Life Line, denotes the fortieth year. In most normal cases this should be fairly accurate.

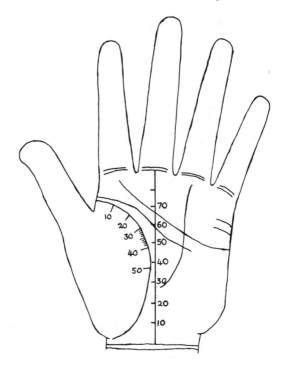

figure XXIX

From this point, four half-inch sections should be marked on the Life Line in the direction of its origin. These can be each subdivided into ten equal sections indicating periods of a single year.

From the fortieth year on, further half-inch sections can be marked, for the fiftieth year, the sixtieth year, etc. Each of these sections can be further subdivided into periods of a year.

Origin — Marks at the Start

If we want to study the circumstances connected with the birth of any person, we must first locate this line of demarcation and then look for the Life Line and how it begins. If it starts as a

106

neat, well-marked and clear line, then birth was in normal, healthy and good circumstances. But when any of the minor markings, such as a square, cross or the like, are found to exist at its origin, then there was something the matter at birth. A square denotes some danger which was averted; a cross is a mark of danger or injury; and an island will point to some mystery around or connected with birth. (XXVIII, 2,a,b,c).

Life and Head Line Joined

In the majority of cases, the Line of Life shares a common origin with the Line of Mentality. These two are often seen to start as if tied to one another. They run across the palmar surface as a single crease for some distance and then depart on their respective courses. The Life Line encircles the Mount of Venus, whereas the Line of Mentality extends in an almost straight direction towards the percussion. When both of the lines begin as one (XXVIII, 3A), it denotes a certain amount of caution and a kind of reticence about the person. If they continue tied to one another well into the palmar region then the person is over-cautious (XXVIII, 4A); there is an element of suspicion and a certain timidity about him. When the two lines separate after the common origin, it merely shows a healthy element of caution, which can prove useful in checking rashness and impetuosity. It is a kind of a brake to the wheel of life (XXVIII, 3A). A strongly tied formation of these two lines is a definite defect; it mars initiative and creates a sensitivity akin to apprehension. Whenever these lines are joined at the beginning, one is sure to find a streak of sensitiveness in the person.

Life and Head Lines Separate

In some hands the Life Line and Head Line are disconnected from one another, with a definite space between them at the outset. The spacing varies: in some hands they are almost touching each other, whereas in others the distance is well marked. When close to one another (XXVIII, 1B), it shows initiative and freedom from apprehensive sensitivity. There is a certain type of daring about such people.

Life and Head Lines wide apart at start

When the space is wider and the lines are well separated, it is a definite indication of impulsive rashness (XXVIII, 5A). Such a distance betrays a somewhat restless nature. There is a kind of reckless bravado about these individuals and they are prone to jump into action without forethought.

Very Wide distance at start
When the distance is very wide, as in XXVIII, 6A, it is an unfailing sign of impetuosity. These are the excitable ones who, due to lack of forethought and restrictive caution, ever tend to create a muddle that is the source of endless trouble for themselves.

Life Line — Starting from Jupiter
Though uncommon, at times, the Life Line starts at a point rather higher up. It begins from the edgeward region of the Mount of Jupiter, the fleshy elevation below the forefinger. When this is the case, the Line of Mentality seems to start at a much lower level (XXVIII, 3B), Jupiter stands for ambition and power and the Life Line, by virtue of its origin there, draws abundantly from these sources of ambition. It denotes an innate and irresistible urge to rise in life. Such individuals are notable for their ambitious cravings for expansion, and the urge from within is so powerful that, as a rule, they tend to succeed very well indeed. Alone, this mark is not a complete guarantee of success, though a great longing and a strong inborn urge to make headway in life do single out a potentially successful individual. In some hands several small but definable lines mark its Jupiterian origin (XXVIII, 4E).

When the Life Line begins high, the length and shape of the first finger, as well as the strength of the Mount of Jupiter, should be noted. If the first finger is strong and outstanding and the Mount of Jupiter is well developed, and rightly placed, the ambitious urge is well fortified and in fact augmented a great deal.

Sweeping Life Line
While encircling the Mount of Venus (XXVIII, 1), the Life Line either sweeps in a large curve through the palmar surface, thereby allowing the mount a larger space and pronounced appearance, or runs in an almost straight direction towards the wrist, thus narrowing the sphere of the mount. When it sweeps

well into the palmar surface, (XXVIII, 5), it denotes a great deal of vitality and strength of constitution. It also shows warmth of affection and breadth of sympathy, the Mount of Venus which represents love in our nature having a fair say in the expression of qualities inherent in it.

Straight Life Line

If the Life Line runs in a somewhat straight direction, it narrows the scope of expression as symbolized by the Mount of Venus (XXVIII, 3). Such individuals lack warmth of affection and, as a rule, are prone to be cold and selfish. There is a definite restrictive tendency in their responses to love life: in fact, it indicates a predisposition towards sterility, particularly in the case of women; if there exists a bow-shaped First Bracelet encroaching on the palmar surface, then the tendency is very much accentuated. This combination has in general been seen in the hands of people who lack the creative urge to be parents. It is not a good combination to have if one aims at matrimonial happiness.

Life Line — Terminating Inwards

The direction that the Life Line takes near its termination is interesting to note. Normally it tends to end towards the wrist-thumb angle (XXVIII, 1A). With such an ending the person is said to be, as it were, home-bound — a person who will always prefer his own country to other lands. Wherever he may travel, he will tend to return home ultimately, bound as he is to his native soil.

Life Line — Terminating towards the Moon

On the other hand, sometimes the Life Line terminates away from the Mount of Venus. It proceeds to, or shows a definite inclination towards the outer edge of the palm where the Mount of the Moon is situated (XXVIII, 2M). Such a termination of this vital line shows a strong urge to be away from home surroundings and native soil. There is an innate restlessness about such people. They are, in fact, constantly urged from within to move farther from home and are inclined to end their days abroad. They travel a great deal and usually settle down eventually in some far-off country.

Life Line — Terminating in a Large Fork

Another common mark that one comes across these days is when the Life Line splits towards its termination and ends in a large fork, with one prong proceeding towards the wrist-thumb angle and the other going in the opposite direction (XXX, 4xy). This shows that the person has great restlessness and a longing for travel and yet at the same time that he is home-bound. In present times, with modern transport facilities and the triumph over space, such a marking is sure to express the urge of the age. Whichever branch is the stronger of the two, will determine the path which its owner eventually chooses.

Life Line — Offshoots

At times you will come across persons who have travelled far and wide, and yet their Life Line terminates towards the wrist-thumb angle. In such cases, if you will follow the course of their Line of Life you are sure to find, at intervals, strongly marked branches shooting out of the body of the line and proceeding towards the Mount of the Moon (XXX, 1t). These are known as travel lines. When a very strong and well-defined branch of this type leaves the Life Line it shows marked restlessness and a craving for travel. I have found that, in general, people with these branches do take to travelling, and that this occurs at the period when such an offshoot leaves the Life Line. It is all the more certain when the Mount of Moon is well developed and is not flabby; a firm consistency of the palm is an additional indication of such an urge to travel.

Travel Lines

Quite often you will notice several horizontal lines which project into the palmar surface from the percussion side. Such lines are marked in the area known as the Mount of the Moon. Look at your hand from the point where the First Bracelet is visible next to the palm at the percussion. Survey the area right up to a spot where the Line of Mentality seems to point its direction of termination. This is the outer boundary of the Mount of the Moon and here will be found these horizontal lines (XXX, 1T). When several such lines are well marked, they

110

tend to intensify the urge to travel; when there is a well-developed Mount of the Moon and when travel lines branch from the Life Line as well, you are sure to find a person who has an innate desire to be on the move.

Life Line — Ending in a Tassel
When the Life Line is long it is not infrequent to notice it ending in the shape of a tassel. A mass of short lines, varying in thickness, seem to shoot out and form a kind of hairy tail (XXX, 6b). Such a formation is uncommon on a short Line of Life. When a tasseled ending is seen it is a mark of diminishing vitality, especially due to advancing years. It is not a good sign to have and, when present, health should not be neglected. It reduces the power of resistance and lays the individual open to ready infection and disease.

Life Line — Minor Marks
A Life Line which is evenly traced, well marked and has a shade of lustre about it, is the type which gives the best indications, but it is a rare phenomenon. I have seldom come across such a line. Living conditions today hardly allow such a healthy life, and the common type of line is the one that is never without some defective elements. These defective markings, as a general rule, are limited to a break in the line, a cross or a star on it and, at times, a square around a portion of it. Islanded formations, cuts and cross-bars, too, are fairly common. Any of these markings are indices of some defective state of well-being.

A Break
A break shows danger to life (XXX, 4b). If it is only present in one hand it is less serious, but if repeated in the other at the same age it is ominous, and can bring one very near to circumstances which may prove fatal.

A Square
It is often noticed that such a break in the Life Line is surrounded by a small, more or less well-defined square (XXX, 4c). This brings in a protective influence. Escape from danger or danger averted is the meaning attached to it; I have verified this formation fairly often. When a square is marked on

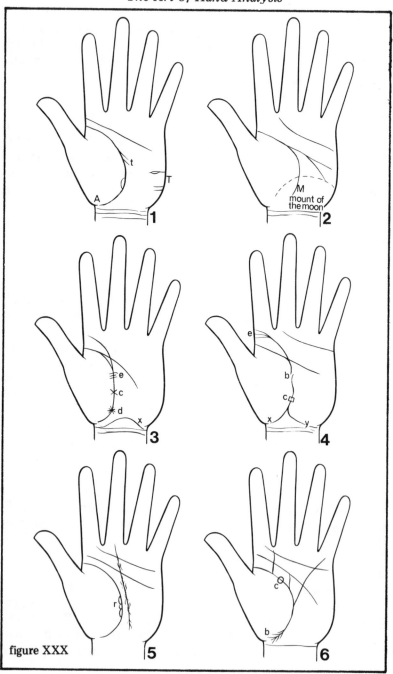

figure XXX

an otherwise good Line of Life, it indicates that a person is liable to pass through circumstances where danger to well-being, and even to life, is not remote.

Accident of Injury
A cross and a star are marks of accidents and threatened injury to life or limb (XXX, 3c,d).

Worries — Ill Health
Cuts and cross-bars are indications of worries that can, and do, create conditions synonymous with bad health. Ill health due to anxiety is the usual prognostication (XXX, 3e).

Internal Defect
An island shows an internal defective state of health (XXX, 1). If a series of islanded formations produce a shape similar to a chain or a rosary with somewhat oblong beads, then it is indicative of a continued delicacy of health which must be attended to without delay. When such an arrangement is present, medical aid must be sought immediately; otherwise it may be too late to bring about normal health conditions (XXX, 5r).

Life Line — Varying Shades of Thickness
In some hands you are likely to see a Life Line of varying shades of thickness. Parts of it will be well-defined and even, others will be thicker and like a heavily-marked crease, and still others will be very thin and feeble looking. Such a line shows uncertain health and a capricious and fickle temperament.

Life Line — Thin
A thin and meagre looking line, with a yellowish hue about it, is an indication of a weak and envious character.

Life Line — Extra Thick
If, in the main, the line is extra thick and carves a big crease in the palmar surface, it adds animality to a person's character and inclines him to violence and brutality. When the colour is red the tendency is accentuated. Such persons are hardly familiar with what is known as self-control, can be easily roused and are

113

E

liable to strike in temper. Yet they are open to suggestion and can be handled to advantage with tact and diplomacy.

Life Line — Circle Thereon
One of the most curious interpretations that I have verified fairly often is the meaning of a circle on the Life Line. It is said to denote danger to an eye. Two circles at the same spot, like two zeros together, are said to be indicative of blindness. I have seen a single circle, but so far have been unable to verify two well-defined, complete circles linked together. A single circle does show some danger to eyesight (XXX, 6c).

Rising Offshoots of the Life Line
During its course, the Life Line normally sends up branches. These are extremely significant and each one of them tells a story with regard to its owner's efforts for worldly success.

A clear well-defined line rising from the Life Line beneath the index finger shows a major ambitious effort for self-development, knowledge and the assertion of individuality — such a branch usually indicates the time of starting school or education. (See the section on the dating system (page 105) for judgement of time.)

Starting below the interspace of the index and second fingers, a strong upward branch reaching the area of the Mount of Jupiter is a mark of achievement through personal contact and endeavour. As a rule this coincides with successful termination of a course of study or training: the owner gets a degree or a diploma from a recognised University or Institution. In some cases, it may mark the end of a period of apprenticeship, leading to a good start of a career, with sound prospects of material reward.

A strong offshoot of the Life Line, reaching the area of the Mount of Saturn beneath the second finger, denotes an important landmark materially. Its owner is able to acquire tangible assets, such as property. Such a mark denotes material stability, increased income and an improved worldly status.

An unobstructed offshoot of the Life Line going towards the root of the third finger, is an extremely good sign to have as it shows brilliant success, wealth or fame. Its owner reaches a point in life when he receives the acclaim of the world.

114

A Life Line branch going to the base of the little finger is also an exceptionally good sign. It indicates considerable success in the field of commerce, industry or science. (XXXI, 1D.)

When an offshoot of the Life Line stops short after it leaves the Heart Line, it reveals a quick short-lived benefit. (XXXI, 2A.)

When an upward branch of the Life Line ends at the Head Line, it shows failure due to stupidity, miscalculation, wrong judgement and lack of proper planning, leading to disaster, the effects of which usually last a long time. (XXXI, 1E.)

Such an upward Life Line offshoot, ending at the Heart Line, shows failure due to emotional causes. Such a person, besides material loss, also suffers heartache which can cast a shadow on his future. (XXXI, 1F.)

When a short upward branch of the Life Line is crossed by a deep line from the area of the Mount of Venus, it is an ill omen. It denotes litigation and usually it portends separation or divorce.

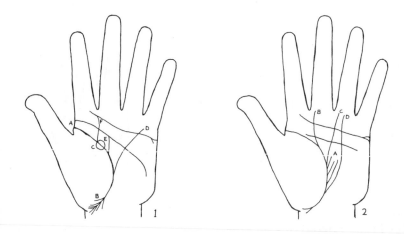

figure XXXI

THE LINE OF HEAD

Head Line — Origin

The major horizontal line, which starts at the same place as the Life Line, is called the Line of Head (XXXII, 1). Beginning between the forefinger and the thumb, on the edge of the hand, it is the most important revealer of one's mental approach to life, career, and the social milieu in which one lives. To a large extent, its formation, character and length are the essential elements which show the potential or otherwise for success, accomplishment and happiness.

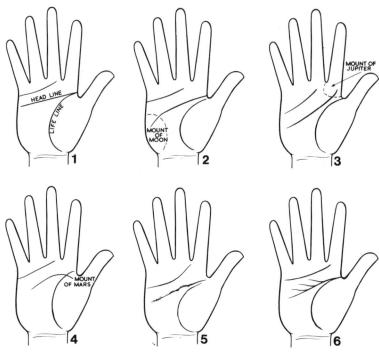

figure XXXII

Head Line Linked to Life Line

When it is slightly linked up with the Life Line at the outset, as already shown in the previous chapter (XXXII, 1), it is a mark of prudence, caution, and a sensible approach to life. Its owner tends to be sensitive and he tends to maintain a balanced, cautious, and rational attitude of mind in all his dealings with others.

When the Head and Life lines jointly cover a short distance (XXXII, 6), it is indicative of a rather sensitive disposition. Its owner is apt to be none too self-reliant, and generally gives the impression of being reticent.

When the tied-up formation of the Head and Life Lines enters well into the palm (XXVIII, 4), it is a mark of extreme sensitivity and self-consciousness. Its owner is usually given to feelings of inferiority and is hardly ever able to be self-reliant.

Independent Start
When the Head Line starts independently (XXXII, 2), it shows a go-ahead spirit and a strong element of self-confidence. Its owner usually displays initiative and enterprise. Energetic and alert, he is often inclined to be theatrical in his behaviour.

Wide Space
When there is a very wide space between the Head and Life lines at the origin (XXVIII, 6), it is not a good indication. It shows lack of self-control, impulsiveness, and a tendency to be foolhardy. Its owner seems unable to practise any measure of discipline and, due to a reckless and imprudent approach to things, usually wrecks his chances of happiness or success.

Head Line — Origin Jupiter
When the Head Line begins higher up in the area of the Mount of Jupiter, and then slopes down to take its normal route, it is an excellent beginning (XXXII, 3). Such a person is endowed with tremendous potential, is naturally disposed to study, learns all about his career, people and the social milieu around him, and can show a relentless effort to achieve success. He has the makings of an outstanding individual.

Head Line — Origin Inside Life Line
When the Head Line drops down at its origin and begins below the Life Line from the Mount of Mars (XXXII, 4), it is an ill omen. Its owner seems to be quarrelsome, explosive, and often lacks consideration for others. He is usually irritable and unable to settle down to anything.

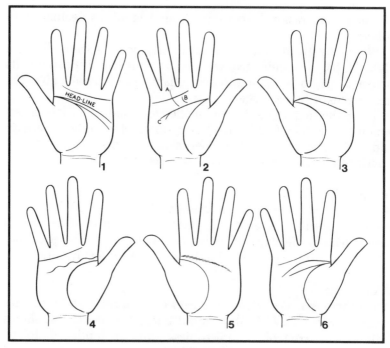

figure XXXIII

Head Line — Straight

While crossing the palmar surface, the Head Line either takes an even and straight course, or tends to be curved. When it is straight (XXXII, 1), it speaks of a practical turn of mind. Its owner tends to be a realist and, due to an element of conventionality in his make-up, may not be quite open to accepting anything new or out of the ordinary. However, once satisfied with the usefulness of something new, he does not hesitate to take to it. He respects tradition and is law abiding. Though none too imaginative, he is a man of his word and endeavours to live with and among people, believing in social co-ordination. In fact, his existence is a very vital element of human society, and he can be seen in all professions, trades, and fields of life.

Head Line — Short

When a Head Line is short, its owner's vision is not large. He likes the tangible and the concrete. He does small jobs, lives a useful but routine life, and abides by the codes and dictates of his own social environment.

Head Line — Long
A long Head Line (XXXII, 1) indicates a high mental aptitude and tremendous foresight of a practical nature. Its owner tends to be a planner, financier, director or executive. He usually has a fine memory and good powers of concentration and visualization. It is a sign of strong individuality and a great capacity for success.

Head Line of Medium Length
Obviously, the character of the owner of a medium-length Head Line would lie somewhere between these two poles.

Head Line — Sloping
When the Head Line curves down towards the Mount of the Moon (XXXII, 2), it speaks of an artistic and creative mind. Its owner attaches more value to things of the spirit than to the goods of this earth. The length and formation of the curve will determine his potential for the artistic and the aesthetic.

When the line is long and curves gently down to the area of the Mount of the Moon (XXXII, 2), it reveals poetry of the soul, rich imagination, and creative talent of an exceptional order. Furthermore, this person tends to be idealistic.

Head Line — Drooping Too Low
It is another matter when the Head Line drops very low (XXXV, 4), for then it is a sign of an over-imaginative mind. Its owner, in fact, tends to live in a world of fantasies and is too apt to be moody and given to melancholic thoughts. He is not quite fit for the rough and tumble of life, and usually gets dejected and lives a despondent and unhappy life.

Head Line — Deep and Clear
When the Head Line is deep and clear, it indicates strong powers of concentration and a good memory.

Head Line — Defective
When islands or indentations mar its course (XXXIV, 2), there is a danger of passing through phases of uncertainty, vacillation, and indecision. Lack of concentration and difficulty in memorizing are also shown by such defective markings.

Head Line — Shallow
A shallow, floating Head Line (XXXIV, 1AC), is a sign of a poor mind and an inability to act with any depth of thought or concentration. Often this person has difficulty in comprehending the meaning of situations in which he finds himself.

Head Line — Upward Branches
Branches which shoot upwards from the Head Line (XXXII, 6) are extremely suggestive indications and show successful use of intellectual powers, bringing about worldly advantages and prestige.

Head Line — Very Short
A short Headline, which barely reaches below the middle finger, is a poor mark to have, for it betrays paucity of intellect, poor memory, and weak powers of concentration. Its owner lives in a small world of his own, and is unable to look ahead or show any ability for constructive planning (XXXIV, 1AB).

Head Line — Flawless — Long
When the Head Line is well marked, has no defects, and clearly defines its course through the palm, reaching the area directly below the third finger, it is a good line. Whether even and straight, or slightly curved, it shows a sound capacity to live intelligently and make one's own way in life constructively (XXXV, 1).

Head Line — Very Long
When a flawless line reaches the area directly below the little finger, it is ideal, for it reveals great strength of mind, excellent powers of memory, ability for deductive and realistic reasoning and, of course, stamina and strong power of will. Its owner is pre-eminently suitable for success through both his inherent talent and his application of energy and level-headedness (XXXII, 3).

120

Head Line — Gently Sloping

Such a long Head Line, gently sloping downward, reveals tremendous creative potential. This person is capable of making an outstanding success in the field of the arts, and usually shines in his specific creative pursuit (XXXII, 2).

Head Line — Edge to Edge

When a Head Line travels across the palm in a straight, horizontal manner and ends at the percussion, it is an undeniable indicator of an excessive intellect, particularly in economic matters. This person is most suited to the worlds of commerce, industry and finance. However, he could be tempted to engage in doubtful practices which involve financial bargaining to his advantage, and most probably he would have an easy conscience about his means to success. He does seem to be able to increase his wealth and rapidly accumulate the goods of this earth (XXXIV, AA).

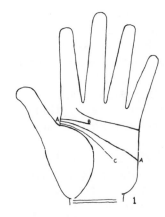
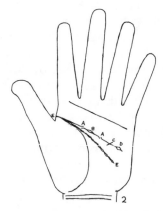

figure XXXIV

Head Line — Double

Although it is rare, one occasionally does come across a double Head Line. In such cases, a sister line seems to accompany the original Head Line, sometimes throughout its course. In fact, it is assumed to be a propitious mark with regard to matters concerning money, inheritance and other economic benefits. The traditional interpretation, that it is a symbol of a large fortune through inheritance, cannot be ruled out; I have come across quite a few instances where this has been the case (XXXIII, 1).

Head Line — Termination

The terminal trend of the Head Line is of great importance. When it ends as a neat, clear line, thinning slightly towards its close, it is normal.

When it terminates in a small neat fork, it indicates descriptive aptitude. Its owner is inclined toward analysis, rationalisation and legal acumen. A persuasive talker, he can "sell" his way through life. (XXXV, 2B.)

If the line forks in such a manner that the parent line continues to run straight towards the percussion, whereas a branch slopes down toward the Mount of the Moon, it reveals an individual who is able to see both sides of an issue simultaneously. It is usually the hallmark of successful lawyers and advocates. Also, it indicates the gift of acting, especially as a comedian. (XXXIII, 2C.)

A Head Line, crossed by a slanting line at its close, is none too good, as it betrays a tendency towards self-deception. Its owner hardly seems to be able to have an objective view of himself. (XXXIV, 2C.)

A Head Line ending in an islanded formation is an ill omen. It shows a tendency toward a diseased mind. Its owner often tends to be brilliant; when the line is long, however, his ideas have a damaging impact on those he associates with. Usually, he is apt to lose his mental balance in the long run. (XXXIV, 2D.)

Head Line — Arched

If, after its beginning, the Head Line ascends in an arch towards the Mount of Jupiter and then gently takes its normal course through the palm, it is of great significance. This individual is endowed with an aggressive and ambitious potential. He is not likely to take "No" for an answer, and in the pursuit of his specific aim he can be tough, and determined. Normally, he achieves his objective (XXXIII, 3).

Head Line — Wavy and Twisted
When the Head Line is wavy and twisted it is an ill omen. Its owner tends to be capricious, unreliable, and unsteady in his character and dealings with people. Avaricious, and inclined to falsehood, he is apt to cheat and steal (XXXIII, 4).

Head Line — Fragmented
A fragmented Head Line indicates both stupidity and a susceptibility to headaches. This person has difficulty in applying himself to anything, falls prey to bouts of lack of memory, and is prone to acute forms of mental anxiety (XXXIV, 2AA).

Head Line — Branches
Branches from the Head Line are significant. If an offshoot goes towards the Mount of the Sun, it is a very exceptional indication. It shows brilliance of intellect which, due to artistic, creative, or literary effort, is bound to lead to fame and fortune. In the hand of a businessman or scientist, such a marking points to exceptional success and prominence, either in industry or invention (XXXIII, 2A).

Head Line — Branches to Heart Line
When a strong upward branch of the Head Line turns towards the Heart Line, it is a sign of a certain coldness in matters of affection. In fact, in matters of love, reason and cold logic will dominate, and this person will usually listen to his head rather than to his heart (XXXII, 6).

Head Line — Breaks and Gaps
Gaps in the Head Line, or clear breaks, are not desirable. They indicate a disappointed passion, which can lead to imbalance (XXXIV, 2AA).

Head Line — Broken Pieces overlapping
When the Head Line is broken in the middle and the two pieces

123

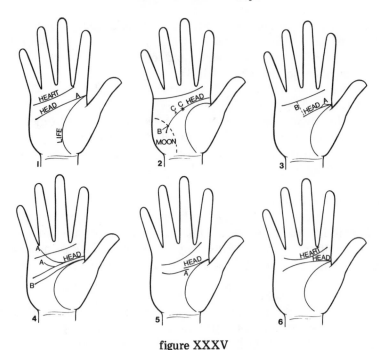

figure XXXV

overlap each other, just below the Mount of Saturn, it is a very significant warning. Its owner is accident prone, and is apt to undertake daring and risky steps. Unless he is able to discipline his over-adventurous impulses, he can meet with great misfortune, and end up with broken limbs. Although he may be fortunate enough to escape mortal danger, he may take quite a long time to recover from his injuries (XXXV, 5A).

Head Line — Island Middle
When the Head Line contains a clear island in the middle, it shows a strong predisposition towards continued headaches, inertia and nervous fatigue. It also gives clues to a hereditary tendency towards maladies which may have a bearing on cerebral fevers (XXXIV, 2B).

Head Line — Islanded throughout
Islanded formations throughout the Head Line speak of a

nervous disposition, tension, anxiety, and headaches. There is always something the matter with the health of the individual, but his ailments are quite curable, with normal attention and medical care (XXXIV, EE).

Head Line — Crosses, Stars
Crosses or stars on any part of the Head Line are none too good, for these show misfortunes which can prove, in some form or another, dangerous (XXXV, 2CC).

Head Line/Heart Line Interspace
Generally, the space between the Head and the Heart Lines should be even, and they should be at a fair distance from one another. When this is the case there is no interference in each other's domain. When the Head Line rises in its course through the hand, and thus inclines towards the Heart Line, it is not a good indication. It shows a tendency towards palpitations, fainting fits and, when the space is too narrow, it also implies asthma (XXXV, 6).

THE LINE OF HEART

Origin and Termination

The Line of Heart begins from the area of the Mount of Jupiter and, travelling below the bases of the fingers across the palmar surface, terminates at the percussion edge, below the root of the little finger (XXXVII, 1A)). As one of the most eloquent signatures of human feelings, it denotes some specific aspects of health and, of course, all those emotional situations which appertain to affairs of the heart.

Idealism in Love

When the Heart Line begins from the area of the Mount of Jupiter it is a sign of idealism in love. Its owner tends to be kind, affectionate and capable of dignity and honour in all matters concerning intimate human relationships. He is, no doubt, apt to put his loved ones on pedestals and naturally expects them to stay there. Liable to be disillusioned as a result of such idealism he has to learn to be moderate in this respect: otherwise he will be badly hurt and, most probably, grow bitter.

Origin Between Index and Middle Fingers

When the Heart Line begins between the index and middle fingers (XXXVII, 1B), it moderates the idealistic elements of the former type and endows the owner with a capacity for balanced sacrifice, steadfast affection and, of course, happy love. This individual, however, tends to live a laborious life. This may be due to a search for personal satisfaction, or perhaps due to the conditions of his life. He does, in the long run, find happiness: and of course can be fortunate in the worldly sense, too.

Origin Below the Middle Finger

When the Heart Line begins below the middle finger (XXXVII, 1B), on the Mount of Saturn, it is not a good augury. Its owner is devoid of higher forms of emotions and in a way heartless. His love is associated with sensual pleasure. Unable to realize the sensitive nature of intimate living, he is not really able to give sincere devotion. He usually lives an uneasy life and, due to lack of tenderness in his being, often fails to understand

126

friendships or affections do not grow into happy relationships. He is cold, selfish, and primarily physical in his approach to matters of love.

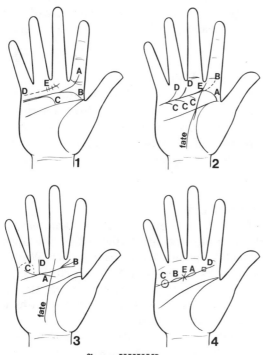

figure XXXVI

Origin Below the Third Finger

Fortunately, it is in rare cases that the Heart Line begins beneath the third finger (XXXVII, 1D). This betrays a poverty of tenderness or love and an inability to feel deeply. Its owner is foolish and, in matters of emotion, almost dead.

From the Edge to the Percussion

In some cases the Heart Line begins from the edge of the palm, between the index finger and the thumb, crosses the entire palmar surface and· ends at the percussion (XXXVII, 2A). It is not a very common mark. Whether it contains branches or is bare, it indicates extreme love, passion, and an innate predisposition towards perfectionism. Its owner feels deeply and

127

unconsciously responds to the slightest variations of mood, stimulus, or emotional atmosphere. Capable of both great ecstasy and deep suffering, he is usually inclined to be unhappy. Jealousy and envy abound in his relationships. There is, in fact, an excess of affection in his nature which can lead to tyranny and possessiveness. He usually ends up an embittered person.

Long and Short Heart Lines
Generally speaking, a long Heart Line shows depth of passion and the other qualities of the heart. A short one diminishes such attributes and, the shorter it tends to be, the colder the disposition grows. In fact, when very short and spare, it reduces its owner to the level of an animal.

Colour of the Heart Line
The colour of the Heart Line is an important feature. When in keeping with the complexion of the rest of the lines, it would indicate a balanced emotional approach to life. When it happens to be pale, it betrays a tendency towards cold sexual urges and usually, when it is long, its owner tends to be given to debauchery, egotism, and not very decent emotions with regard to the opposite sex. A red Line of Heart points to an excess of passion; its owner leans too easily towards ardent love and violence in love and sex. It is a mark of a disposition which is neither balanced nor trustworthy. It is also a bad augury in matters concerning health.

A rosy or even-coloured Heart Line is a good mark to have. Its owner is endowed with healthy love instincts and can prove a good friend and a reliable partner, capable of deep affection, loyalty, and sensitivity in intimate living.

Flawless, Crossing the Entire Palm
A Heart Line which crosses the entire hand, without any off-shoots and extremely bare (XXXVII, 3A), indicates cruelty and malignancy. It is found in the hands of individuals who tend to treat their blood relatives in a most inhuman manner, and who would not hesitate to remove them if they stood in the way of greed or worldly advantages.

Twisted Heart Line
A twisted and wavy Heart Line is also a bad indication. When it assumes a waving formation in the middle, beneath the second finger (XXXVII, 3B), it is usually a mark of usury. Its owner tends to be extremely greedy and takes to the trade of lending money at exorbitant rates, fleecing his victims in any way he can.

Wavy Extremities
When the Heart Line is wavy at its extremities, it indicates a predisposition towards blood ailments. Such individuals are also prone to heart trouble. (XXXVIII, 2B.)

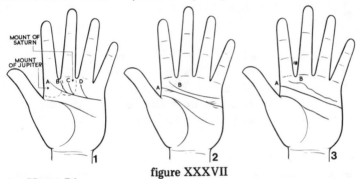

figure XXXVII

Sister Heart Line
Occasionally, a sister line follows the track of the Heart Line pretty well through the whole of the palm (XXXVII, 2B). Such a second line shows tremendous devotion in love or friendship, its owner being extremely loyal and faithful. Excess of emotion and an amorous nature are some of its characteristics. This line also tends to repair any defects in the original Line of Heart and helps to cover negative propensities.

Sign of Great Misfortune
The Heart Line, besides indicating emotional matters, also throws a revealing light on other important aspects of life. This should be carefully borne in mind, for some of the indications do have major significance. For instance, when the Heart Line originates from the third phalange of the index finger it is an ominous start. It denotes great misfortune, and its owner is never able to succeed in any sphere of life (XXXVI, 1A).

129

Heart Line Low at the Start
When the Heart Line drops so low at the start that it reaches close to the Head-Life Line, it shows a person who is too apt to be imposed upon. He is also inclined to be possessed by one he loves, and tends to be restricted in emotional expression. He often chooses a partner who is jealous, possessive and extremely difficult; feelings of being subjected to emotional domination are therefore experienced (XXXVI, 1B).

If the beginning of the Heart Line touches the joined Head and Life Lines, it is not a good augury. In fact, it is assumed to point to the danger of sudden death. Such an indication in no way means that the owner will necessarily die young, or in middle age. It only suggests the type of fatality that is likely to end his life. (XXXVI, 2A.)

Heart Line Touching Head Line Below Saturn
Sometimes the Heart Line stoops to touch the Line of Head beneath the Mount of Saturn. When this is the case, it speaks of a passion which is all-consuming and leads to disaster and, in some cases, fatal consequences (XXXVI, 1C).

Heart Line — Forked Start
When the Heart Line forks at the start and one prong goes to the Mount of Jupiter and the other bends down towards the Life Line, it indicates a strong predisposition towards self-deception in matters appertaining to love and affections (XXXVI, 2AB).

Downward Branches of Heart Line
Downward branches of the Heart Line are marks of disappointments. Each such strong offshoot tells the story of a love or affection which causes unhappiness and pain (XXXVI, 2C).

Heart Line Branch Cutting Fate Line
When a downward branch of the Heart Line cuts through the Fate Line it is a sad mark. It shows that the partner of the owner is likely to pass away. It is, in fact, a sign of widowhood. The time of such an event is calculated by the Fate Line (XXXVI, 3A).

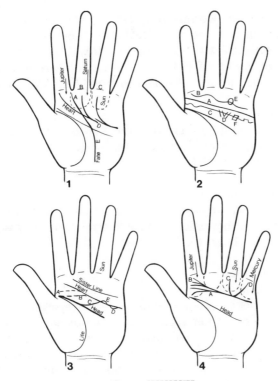

figure XXXVIII

Upward Branches

Branches going upwards towards the bases of the fingers indicate successful friendships, or affectionate associations to the owner's advantage (XXXVI, 2D).

Three Offshoots of Heart Line at Start

When a Heart Line blossoms into three distinct offshoots which rise to the Mount of Jupiter, it is the mark of an individual endowed with spiritual justice. He usually receives honours, wealth and awards. Such a tridentile origin of the Heart Line always leads to fortune, happiness and great honour (XXXVIII, 4B).

Offshoot Toward Mercury

In rare cases, a curved offshoot of the Heart Line progresses firmly towards the Mount of Mercury. Such a mark points to

131

excellent chances of worldly progress and the owner is usually able to build up a sound and sizeable fortune, through steady profits and fruitful activities. However, this does not take place either through games of chance or legacies. There is a definite effort behind such a forward financial trend (XXXVI, 3C).

Broken Heart Line
When a Heart Line is broken in more than one place, there is a tendency toward unfaithfulness. This person is unable to be loyal or constant (XXXVI, 1D).

Defects in Heart Line
When it is cut, or crossed, or contains bars in its course, it indicates deceit, unhappiness in love and misfortunes associated with affairs of the heart (XXXVI, 1E).

Island in Heart Line
When an island appears in the line it is usually indicative of a guilty love intrigue, often due to vanity, rejection, or other similar causes. The owner seems compelled by some inner force to commit adultery and get involved in a rather serious affair (XXXVI, 4A). But if the islanded formation is beneath the Mount of the Sun and there is no emotionally defective indication in the hand, then this mark is associated with eye trouble (XXXVI, 4B).

Circle on the Heart Line
A circle on the Heart Line is usually connected with heart trouble. When several islands also appear there is a tendency towards a nervous heart condition, and its owner should not ignore his well-being with regard to blood circulation, pressure, etc. (XXXVI, 4C).

Square on the Heart Line
When a square covers an area of the Heart Line, it shows that the individual will go through a period when there is a danger of either physical, with regard to the heart, or emotional harm. Such an indication is a good augury, for it helps to protect against possible injury. However, the owner usually goes through a phase of acute tension and apprehension (XXXVI, 4D).

132

Cross on the Heart Line
A cross clearly marked on the Heart Line is a sign of serious sickness, or accident, which can cause a great deal of damage (XXXVI, 4E).

Heart Line Merging into Fate Line
Sometimes the Heart Line is joined to other major lines of the hand. When it merges into a rising Fate Line, which goes towards the Mount of Jupiter and ends there, it is an extremely fortunate mark to have. Its owner will rise to a position of power, prestige and wealth, through affection, love or marriage. He will be greatly admired and loved and will enjoy a life of luxury and happiness (XXXVI, 2E).

Heart Line Giving Rise to Sun Line
When a Sun Line shoots out of the Heart Line beneath the third finger and rises firmly, it is another good sign. Its owner will find a great deal of success and happiness, though late in life, through love and affection. The mature years of such individuals are rich with joy, material wealth and a great deal of personal satisfaction (XXXVIII, 4C).

THE LINE OF FATE

Origin and End

Where the wrist proper ends, the skin ridge pattern forms a line of demarcation with the palm. A bold wrist line usually crosses the area along the entire length of the palm-wrist borderline. This is where the Line of Fate ought to take its origin and, when complete and full, it runs across the length of the palm and terminates beneath the crease below the second finger, on the Mount of Saturn. Such a complete Fate Line is extremely rare (XXXIX, 1A).

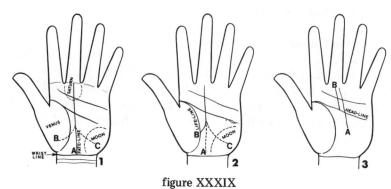

figure XXXIX

The Fate Line shows the vicissitudes of fortune, the material changes, events and happenings associated with career and life work. It also symbolizes the material wealth, or otherwise, of its owner. Psychologically, it is a very important revealer of human character.

Origin First Bracelet

When it has its origin at the First Bracelet and extends to the top of the palm, ending just below the middle finger, it indicates an exceptional fate. Its owner is endowed with unusual force of destiny and rises to a high position. He has, in fact, the makings of a great leader, a ruler, or a captain of industry. He usually achieves great distinction and wields a tremendous power to shape the destinies of his fellow beings. For good or evil, he tends to be a force to be reckoned with (XXXIX, 1A).

134

The Line of Fate

Origin Close to Wrist
When the Fate Line starts early, close to the wrist, and is clear in its course, its owner grows conscious of responsibility at an early age; circumstances seem to involve him in situations where he has to shoulder burdens, either his own or those of near ones. However, this consciousness enables him to develop an awareness which can later prove effective in the conduct of his affairs, in the days when he is struggling for success (XXXIX, 2A).

Origin Life Line
When the Fate Line begins from the Life Line it reveals a destiny which, for the individual's success and happiness, has to depend on personal merit. In point of fact, its owner endeavours to be a self-made man, and, by determined application of his energy and talents, he is able to make the kind of headway which makes him the envy of those around him. He learns the technique of the mastery of his fate. He does not depend on chance, but instead plans his life and career, making the right use of his potential. However, he is helped to start off by his family (XXXIX, 2B).

Origin Mount of Venus
If it starts inside the Life Line, from the Mount of Venus, the Fate Line describes a very different type of destiny: its owner's life is dictated by his family. His wordly possessions, his career and his life work, all seem to be ruled by his family; he is literally unable to liberate himself from the situation into which he was born (XXXIX, 1B).

Origin Plain of Mars
Sometimes the Fate Line is missing in the lower palm and then seems to appear suddenly in the middle of the hand, in the area of the Plain of Mars. Such a start denotes a long period of struggle, uncertainty and difficulties before any measure of security is achieved. Its owner goes through phases of depression and anxiety. However, once he begins to stabilize, he builds up material assets and truly shapes his destiny. He owes his success to no one and, with the advent of better days, reveals a sound quality of self-confidence. In fact, he is able to apply his hard-earned lessons to useful ends (XXXIX, 3A).

Origin Mount of Moon

When the line of Fate begins from the area of the Mount of the Moon and rises flawlessly to the Mount of Saturn, it certainly indicates a unique destiny. Its owner is endowed with qualities which appeal to the public and has the makings of a successful public career. There is a kind of star quality about him and he is usually able to influence people. Whether in the field of entertainment, politics, industry, or arts, he stimulates the imaginations of others, who become his devotees, followers, or admirers. He has what is known as emotional appeal. Usually he is able to influence members of the opposite sex forcefully and is helped by them in his career. He is, however, inclined to be capricious and temperamental, and often theatrical. He is, in fact, a born actor. Usually he makes a success of his life and work (XXXIX, 2C).

Origin Mounts of Venus and Moon

Rarely, a Fate Line begins as a large fork, one prong embedded in the Mount of Venus and the other in the Mount of the Moon. The owner of such a line faces a great struggle in the pursuit of his ambition. He seems to be spurred towards an objective by his great love, but is hampered by his own wild imagination. In fact, he labours hard yet his dedication and imagination seem to cause him great spiritual disruption. However, if the line extends flawlessly to the base of the middle finger, he is ultimately able to achieve his ends, though not without tremendous hardship and persisting inner conflict (XXXIX, 1BC).

Origin Head Line

A Fate Line beginning from the Head Line, though extremely rare, is at times a significant indication. When clear and reaching the area of the Mount of Saturn, it is symbolic of success through intellectual acumen but not, of course, before middle age. Its owner, though a late starter, tends to accomplish a great deal materially and makes his maturer years adequately successful and financially secure (XXXIX, 3B).

Revealing Termination

The Fate Line not only significantly indicates some specific aspects of human destiny by its origin and manner of beginning, but also reveals something important in the way it terminates and the area in which it ends.

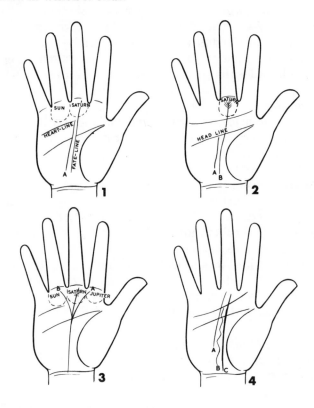

figure XL

Natural Point of Termination
The natural point of termination of the Fate Line is the area beneath the second finger, the Mount of Saturn. When it ends there, without any marked deviation either way, it suggests a destiny which, due to careful planning and steady application, enables its owner to accumulate adequate material assets and to enjoy the winter of life in comfort and contentment. As long as it reaches its natural terminal point regardless of its origin, this line points to a secure old age (XL, 1).

Termination on Head Line
A Fate Line which ends abruptly on the Head Line is not good
(XL, 2A). Its owner persistently makes blunders and errors of
judgement of considerable magnitude; the course of his life is
strewn with misfortunes of his own making. In such a case, a
thorough investigation of the various other palmar indications is
essential in order that he may discover the error of his ways.

Termination on Heart Line
In some instances the Fate Line ends abruptly at the Heart
Line. This is certainly an ill omen for it shows that, due to some
affliction of the heart, whether it be physical or psychological
(the causes have to be detected from other aspects of the hand),
its owner is inwardly compelled in such a manner that a change
of situation, unfortunately adverse, is liable to lead him toward
disaster. His course of destiny is emotionally disrupted, perhaps
because of a broken love affair, family affection, or other
similar causes. He seems to be going unavoidably towards a
course of action which will lead, inevitably, to unfortunate
consequences. With such a sign, the owner tends to dwell
constantly upon unhappy ideas, usually due to love troubles,
and often passes day after day despondently (XL, 1A).

Termination Mount of Saturn
In some cases the Fate Line ends in the area of the Mount of
Saturn in small branches which look like a bushy tail. A neat,
clean termination reveals intelligent planning and adequate
provision for the future. However, when it ends in a multiplicity
of offshoots, the concentration necessary for the use of intelligence is disrupted; and its owner is inclined to scatter his
energies, to not make use of his intelligence and to spend his old
age in difficult circumstances. His cardinal difficulty seems to
be lack of foresight and intelligent planning (XL, 2B).

Recurring Obstacles
Another bad sign is a Fate Line which ends clearly in the area of
the Mount of Saturn but is cut by a few distinct transverse lines.
Its owner is bound to come up against recurring obstacles in
everything he undertakes. Misfortunes seem to dog his footsteps
all the way (XLI, 2F).

The Line of Fate

Termination Third Phalange of Middle Finger
A Fate Line sometimes crosses the Mount of Saturn and enters the third phalange of the middle finger. This is an unusual ending and tends to indicate an exceptional destiny, whether it be for good or evil.

Termination Toward Jupiter
When the Fate Line gently, though firmly, curves towards the Mount of Jupiter and ends there it denotes a successful realization of one's ambition, and often a brilliant career. It is also associated with those rare but brilliant marriages that seem to be the extraordinary destiny of a chosen few (XL, 3A).

Termination Mount of Sun
At times it deviates from its natural terminal point and ends in the area of Mount of Sun, beneath the third finger. Such a termination indicates an innate love of the arts or riches; the owner tends to devote the whole of his being towards the cultivation of literary or artistic talent, and usually applies his talents fruitfully. He is sure to be recognized in due course and generally makes his mark in his specific field of interest (XL, 3B).

Course of Fate Line
The course of the Fate Line through the palm reveals the path of its owner's destiny. Any changes, obstructions, or offshoots indicate significant events along the path of life. When the line is clearly and deeply embedded in the palm, it shows a constructive outlook, an ability to concentrate on work, and an interest in career and the goods of the earth. Such a person has a strong, stable disposition, values material assets and is willing to work hard for them (XL, 4C).

Wiry and Thin
If the line happens to be wiry and thin, as if floating on the surface, its owner lacks grit, stability and stamina. Apt to be capricious and changeable, he never seems to make any sizeable headway in life (XL, 4A).

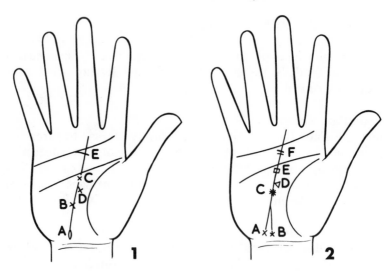

figure XLI

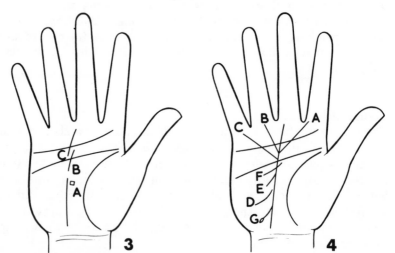

Wavy and Irregular

When the Fate Line is irregular and wavy throughout its entire course, it betrays a fickle disposition and want of steadfast purpose. Its owner tends to be of irregular habits, disagreeable and rather quarrelsome. Unable to attend to anything constructively, he loses interest quickly and looks for something else. It is rare that he makes any dependable progress in life (XL, 4B).

Dominating Other Lines
An unusually deep Fate Line, dominating the other palmar markings, is hardly a good sign. Such an ill-balanced line indicates an inner conflict, persistent nervous strain and deep anxiety, all due to the fact that its owner seems to be compelled by force of circumstance to continue on a path which is completely opposed to his taste, interests and inner requirements. His nervous fatigue and anxiety make him a very apprehensive individual, who seems to have neither peace of mind, nor any form of pleasure in living.

Origin An Island
When, for instance, a Fate Line emerges from a well-formed and distinct islanded formation, close to the wrist, it reveals a personality which seems to be under the shadow of some mystery or fear. Usually assumed to be the sign of a mystery at birth, the unwary hand analyst considers it to be a mark of illegitimacy. Whatever the circumstances associated with the owner's birth, it can certainly be taken to be a mark of some unknown element in his being which seems to make him feel alien to those around him. He labours under some social fear and is apt to be at a psychological disadvantage in his relationships with his fellow men. (XLI, 1A.)

Loss of a Parent
A clear cross on the Fate Line, close to its start near the wrist, is usually indicative of the loss of an older member of the family, most probably a parent. The early days of this individual, therefore, are often bereft of some essential affection, and he grows up with a sense of something wanting in his formative years. (XLI, 2A.)

Formidable Obstacle
When, however a cross is found along the course of the Fate Line, it indicates a formidable obstacle, followed by a change, usually unforeseen. When the cross fills a gap in the Fate Line, it certainly points to a most critical change in the destiny of its owner. The ensuing psychological repercussions can prove to be quite lasting and often change the person's outlook, in a rather negative manner. He is not likely to regain his former balance quickly. (XLI, 1B.)

141

Major Change of Situation

When a cross is placed alongside the Fate Line, but is still attached to it, it has a completely different significance. This marking indicates a major change of situation, area of living, or work. Such a change brings with it new contacts and conditions, and necessitates a certain degree of re-orientation. It usually helps to stimulate some dormant potentials. In some instances, the individual tends to reach out for a serious, religious, or philosophical understanding of life and its vicissitudes, and is able to find inner consolation in so doing. (XLI, 1D.)

Major Disaster

A star at the outset of the Fate Line is rather unfortunate, for it tells of some major disaster during childhood, such as loss of fortune to one's parents. This often shadows the individual's early life and in some instances leaves traces of fear, suffering and pain in the unconscious. When the star is seen on the course of the Fate Line, it always indicates misfortune, reverses of position, and losses. This usually happens without any previous warning and takes its owner unawares. (XLI, 2BC.)

Military Success

A triangle, when situated next to the Fate Line on the Life Line side, has a very curious significance. When found on the hand of a soldier, it reveals a military success. In the case of an ordinary civilian, it usually pertains to some fight in which he is able to combat successfully. (XLI, 2D.)

Mark of Protection

A square, anywhere on the Fate Line, is a mark of protection. When found in the middle of the line it is a sign of warning: its owner, during that phase of his life, is liable to undertake activities which can involve him in heavy financial loss or disaster; however, he is able to avoid any serious calamity. When a square is marked along the Fate Line, either on the side of the Life Line or the Mount of the Moon, it shows protection from danger, either at home or while travelling. (XLI, 2E.)

A Serious Change

A break in the Fate Line is always a mark of a serious change in

142

life and career. When the break exists in such a manner that the broken ends overlap each other, it indicates that the individual has himself inaugurated the change, after prolonged deliberation. Such a change does not involve loss or, for that matter, any financial difficulty. (XLI, 3BC.)

Unfortunate Occurrences
Cross bars signpost unfortunate occurrences. If the bar is stronger than the Fate Line, it shows a very difficult and disturbing situation. (XLI, 4F.)

Major Step Forward
An upward branch of the Fate Line is a sign of promise. If its direction is towards the base of the forefinger, it points to a major step forward on the road to the owner's ambition. It endows power, prestige and the goods of this earth. (XLI, 4A.)

Intellectual Success
When it points towards the base of the third finger, wealth and success are a result of intellectual pursuits. This is an extremely favourable indication in the hands of those associated with literary or artistic concerns. (XLI, 4B.)

Success in Science or Industry
When such a branch goes towards the little finger, great success in the fields of science or industry is sure to crown the efforts of its owner. (XLI, 4C.)

Marriage of Great Advantage
When the Fate Line, while going on its normal course, is supported by a well-formed and ascending line, originating from the Mount of the Moon, it is an extremely exciting and interesting indication. It shows a strong and advantageous impact of a person of the opposite sex on the individual's life, material fortunes and character. Usually it is a mark of a marriage which brings great worldly advantage, as well as being happy, stimulating and lasting. (XLI, 4D.)

Union or Marriage
When a distinct line curves upwards from the Mount of the

Moon and merges into the Fate Line, this, too, is indicative of rewarding union and marriage, though it does not necessarily bring any material advantages with it. (XLI, 4E.)

Heart-breaking Romance
When such an upward line intersects the Fate Line, thereby cutting across its course, it is none too good an augury. No doubt, it shows romantic encounter; however, the person in question is attracted by an ulterior motive. He or she makes use of the material position of the owner of this marking, shows love only for the duration; when the object of this specious relationship is accomplished, the owner is left disillusioned and heart-broken. Such a mark can have a very disturbing influence on the psyche of its owner. (XLI, 4F.)

Strong Emotional Ferment
One of the interesting features of such lines of influence from the Mount of the Moon is that, however they terminate in connection with the Fate Line, they do tend to create a strong emotional ferment in the owner. He is never quite the same after the line has effected its influence, and usually comes alive and begins to find a new meaning to life.

Submissive Partner
When the Influence Line is weaker than the Fate Line, then the spouse is submissive and usually falls into line with the ideals and ways of the owner. When it is stronger and deeper, the owner is generally ruled by the partner; however, matrimonial harmony does seem to be well maintained.

Islanded Influence Line
One of the rather unfortunate marks in connection with an Influence Line is when it begins from a neat little island. The owner of such a mark marries someone who brings misfortune and suffering, though in many ways he may be made happy by the closeness of his relationship with the partner. (XLI, 4G.)

Painful Affair of the Heart
One of the most unfavourable indications in connection with the Fate Line is a deep, firm branch of the Heart Line cutting

across its course. It is a sign of a painful affair of the heart, which tends to injure its owner's worldly position and can prove drastic with regard to his financial situation. In the case of married people, it is usually indicative of the death of a partner, a death which leaves the spouse without adequate source of income or security. (XLI, 1E.)

Time on Fate Line

When judging any of the changes and markings along the path of the Fate Line, it is essential to work according to a time schedule. Time on the Fate Line is calculated from the first wrist line upwards and should be marked with spaces indicating ten year's span.

As explained in the chapter on the Life Line (see page 105), there is a necessity for an exact technique of dating events. A similar standard of measurement can be applied to the Fate Line.

Starting from the mid-point of the first wrist line, half-inch sections should be marked up to the mid-point of the crease beneath the middle finger. The first section denotes the period between birth and the tenth year, and, if subdivided into ten equal sections, will indicate the first year, the second year, etc. Measured beyond this, further half-inch sections denote the twentieth year, the thirtieth year, etc., on the Line of Fate.

In a similar manner, the same standard measurement can be applied to the Line of Sun. In this case, however, the dating should be from the point on the first wrist line directly in line with the mid-point of the crease beneath the third finger, which is the normal termination point of the Line of Sun.

F

THE SUN LINE

Origin of Sun Line
One of the most fascinating and promising indications in the human hand is the Line of Sun. Its place of origin is close to the wrist; from there it should cross the palmar surface vertically and reach close to the base of the third finger, where it should end. However, such a complete line is almost non-existent. The Sun Line usually begins from other areas, and varies in significance according to its origin. (XLII, 4A.)

A Good Sun Line
If good and sound in essence the Sun Line, irrespective of its origin, reveals innate potential for success, fame and distinction. In fact, without its presence it is unlikely that real reward and its enjoyment are truly possible.

Glorious Life
When the line originates close to the wrist, and flawlessly proceeds to its point of termination beneath the root of the third finger, it foretells a glorious and extremely exceptional life. From early childhood its owner enjoys those unique privileges which, besides riches, distinction and social position, provide excellent scope for intellectual development and the capacity to rise in life and maintain an enviable position. Such an individual is endowed with a razor-sharp mind, and a love of art; he is sure to distinguish himself in some field or another and is never likely to be without honour and prestige. (XLII, 4A.)

Origin Inside Life Line
When the Sun Line begins inside the Life Line, in the area of the Mount of Venus, and rises firmly, it is usually a fortunate sign. Such a person is helped by relatives at the outset of his life and career, and is able to forge ahead with promise. This is in fact a mark of success in art and literature, as well as an indication of a great and brilliant fortune. This lucky individual is able to learn with facility and use his knowledge effectively towards reaching a measure of success which can be truly unusual. (XLII, 3A.)

146

Origin on Life Line
A Sun Line which has its origin at the Life Line points to a person who, although undoubtedly aided by relatives in his initial success, achieves distinction later in life through personal merit and endeavour. Such an individual usually rises above his parents and makes a mark in his chosen field. (XLII, 2A.)

Origin Mount of The Moon
When the Sun Line begins on the Mount of the Moon, close to the wrist, and reaches the base of the third finger, it denotes a certain success due to the help of influential people, especially those of the opposite sex. The owner of this line is endowed with the ability to make an impact on people, is a born actor, and often has a good deal of sex appeal. He tends to stimulate the imagination of those with whom he comes into contact and generally manouevres situations to his personal favour. His fields of success can be the stage, acting, poetry, literature, or related arts. (XLII, 2B.)

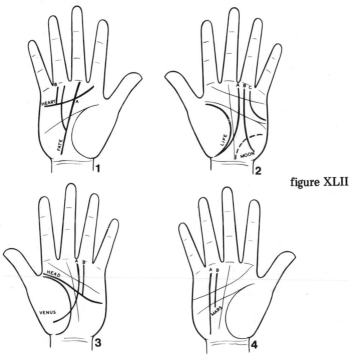

figure XLII

147

Origin Middle of the Palm

A Sun Line which begins from the middle of the palm, the area known as the Plain of Mars, is associated with struggle. When it begins thus and reaches the base of the third finger, its owner does achieve success, but only after a great deal of hard work, serious set-backs and without any outside help. He is truly the architect of his own good fortune, and as such his success is built on solid foundations and proves to be lasting. (XLII, 4B.)

Origin Fate Line

In some instances, the Sun Line begins from the Line of Fate, and then moves forward to end at the base of the third finger. When well-marked and clear, it is a very fortunate indication. Its owner is able to achieve success in whatever field or type of work he chooses. This is all the more certain if his efforts are in the arts. He in fact has an innate aptitude for the world of art and can achieve not only material success, but a good — and often excellent — reputation. This kind of Sun Line is the hallmark of earned success in a chosen career. (XLII, 1.)

Origin Between Head and Heart Lines

In some cases, the Sun Line begins between the Head and Heart lines, from the percussion side, and curves up to reach the area of the base of the third finger. This is an interesting sign, for it shows an aggressive approach to the problem of success. Its owner is literally undaunted in his search for fame and fortune, and usually shows that kind of stamina and acumen which assist him in the achievement of his desires. He is sure to see his dream come true. (XLII, 2C.)

Origin Head Line

When the Sun Line begins from the Head Line, it is an excellent indication for devotion to art or search of renown. Its owner is endowed with a relentless determination and is able to put his heart and soul into the effort for success — in art, literature, or poetry — and would aim at nothing short of glory. He would be interested only in pursuits which would allow him to achieve celebrity or fortune, preferably long-lasting. (XLII, 3B.)

However, he would owe his success to no other factor than

his own brains and inherent merit. This marking certainly points to a brilliant mind.

Origin Heart Line
A rather interesting feature is a Sun Line which begins from the Heart Line. It shows, in all cases, success and happiness late in life. Its owner is able to find financial security and protection from any kind of material want in the winter of his life.

Yet in matters of art, music etc., it is not quite as good an augury. It indicates that its owner is liable to be influenced by an affair of the heart, and that this will divert him from wholehearted devotion to whatever art he may be associated with. It is likely that he may make something of it, but not that kind of real success which proves outstanding. (XLII, 1B.)

Success in Different Fields
Although the Sun Line does indicate worldly success, glory and wealth, it does not point to outstanding achievement in every sphere. In the hand of a businessman, a good Sun Line will indicate that type of brilliance of mind which enables its owner to devise ways and means of making money and fortune; in the hands of a writer or an actor the same sign would show brilliant application of talent to accomplish fame and fortune.

A Short Sun Line
When the Sun Line starts near the wrist but stops short after its beginning, as in XLII, 4A, it shows that although the early part of the owner's life and career may display a certain brilliance, he is not able to maintain his success and comes to very difficult days.

Sun Line Stopping at The Head Line
A Sun Line that stops at the Head Line (XLIII, 1B), reveals tremendous handicaps and the wrong application of talent, however brilliant, which leads to disaster in the search for fame or fortune, whichever the case may be. Such a person needs a very cool and careful scrutiny of his methods and technique and in almost all the cases a complete change of outlook and application of mind and energies before he is able to avoid disastrous consequences of his ill-directed efforts.

149

Sun Line Stopping at The Heart Line
When the Sun Line ends at the Heart Line (XLIII, 2B), its owner, despite a great deal of potential for success, is unable to achieve anything worthwhile due to the emotional aspect of his life.

Thin Sun Line
When the Sun Line is very thin (XLIII, 3A), although a certain amount of potential for success is there, the quality is poor.

Thick Sun Line
When very thick (XLIII, 3B), there is a lack of refined talent, though its owner is capable of success and distinction. In point of fact he is able to make an impact through rough art — aggressive, though uncultured, talent.

Fading Sun Line
At times the Sun Line starts well, then fades away and, after an interval, starts again (XLIII, 4A). This shows a period of success, then obscurity and struggles without reward and then, again, brilliant success. If the second part goes up to the Mount of the Sun, it indicates lasting and durable results.

Mark of a Scandal
An island (XLIII, 1C) in the body of the Sun Line is an ill omen. It is a mark of scandal, ill-repute and loss. During the period marked by the island, its owner experiences humiliation, suffering and financial losses.

Mark of Jealousy
A bar crossing the Sun Line (XLIII, 2A) is a significant indication. It always points to the fact that the brilliance of the owner has directly or indirectly stimulated envy or jealousy in a person who will attack his position, fortune or name. If the line is thin, the owner will be able to brush off the interference; if heavy and strong, he is sure to come to harm. Many such lines would suggest that there is something in the psychology of the individual which tends to elicit enmity and anger in those with whom he comes into contact. He should examine his motives and behaviour patterns carefully otherwise he is bound to come up against many adversaries and much suffering.

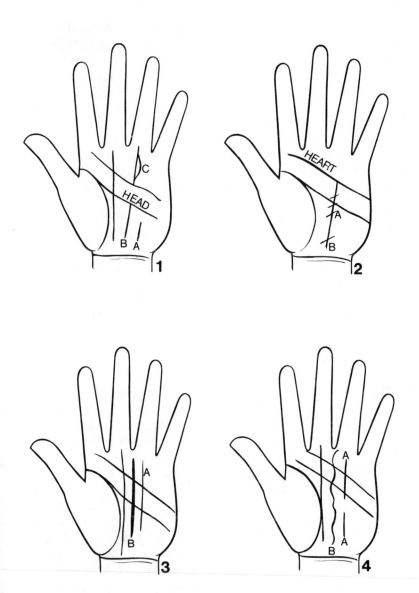

figure XLIII

A Wavy Sun Line

A wavy Sun Line (XLIII, 4B) indicates the uncertain and erratic application of talent. Its owner is sure to be brilliant but quite incapable of steady application of his gifts. He usually goes through ups and downs and most probably, never sits down to think seriously about why he undergoes such vicissitudes.

Fame and Brilliance

If a clear, un-indented Sun Line, starting from the area close to the wrist and reaching the Mount of the Sun, is accompanied by a Head Line which is exceptionally long, straight and deep, and reaches the edge of the palm, the owner is inclined to be absorbed in the acquisition of wealth (XLIV, 1AA).

His brilliant talent is applied with a singleness of purpose and all his energies, contacts, and efforts are fruitfully spent in a well organised and thoroughly planned manner to make money. He does not aim at mediocre, comfortable living, but aspires to achieve wealth and outstanding financial fortune; he does in fact seem to amass assets of tremendous value. There is nothing haphazard or undisciplined about him. He works hard, studies his projects diligently and leaves nothing to chance.

Speculative Interests

With a long Head Line reaching the lower part of the Mount of the Moon such a Sun Line is then a strong inclination towards taking big risks (XLIV, 1B). Speculative interests are indulged in and if the third finger happens to be as long as the middle one (XLIV, 1aa), the owner tends to be an incorrigible gambler, although a fortunate one. Although he may at times lose heavily, he often engages in speculation and gambling as a profession and in the long run does make a success of it.

Pecuniary Success

At times a hand with a long clear Sun Line also has a branch from the Head Line which curves upwards and merges with the rising Sun Line. This is an excellent indication for pecuniary success, due to the owner's intelligence (XLIV, 1C).

Major Financial Loss

If the Head Line branch cuts through the Sun Line the owner

suffers a major financial loss and disaster through miscalculation and wrong judgement. He in fact comes to harm through his own monetary blunders (XLIV, 1D).

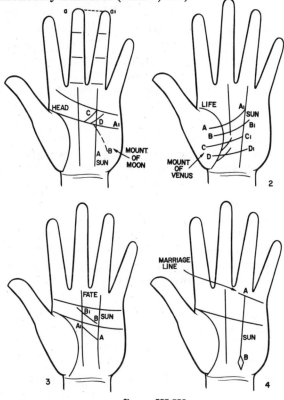

figure XLIV

Money From the Family
When a long, deep Sun Line is touched by an upward curving line from the Mount of Venus (XLIV, 2AA1), it is an interesting indication. This is a mark of money coming through the owner's own people or family, albeit after a great deal of hardship and incessant struggle.

Loss Through a Close Relative
When a similar influence line from the Mount of Venus cuts through the Sun Line then financial loss is incurred, and that too through a close relative (XLIV, 2BB1).

153

Lawsuit With a Relative
At times an Influence Line from the Mount of Venus can be seen cutting a branch of the Life Line and proceeding to touch or merge into the Sun Line (XLIV, 2CC1). Such a combination of markings shows a lawsuit with a relative, which the owner wins after a good deal of worry and anxiety. This proves materially beneficial in the end. If, on the other hand, the Sun Line is cut, the owner loses the lawsuit to the relative concerned and also suffers a heavy financial loss (XLIV, 2DD1).

Mutually Beneficial Partnership
When the Sun Line is joined by a clear branch to the Fate Line it indicates a partnership which is sure to be materially advantageous and emotionally harmonious (XLIV, 3AA1).

Disastrous Partnership
If, unfortunately, the Sun Line offshoot cuts through the Fate Line, though the partnership will be entered into with a great deal of hope and promise, it will prove disastrous for the owner. With such a combination of markings it would be most unwise to entertain any idea of partnership (XLIV, 3BB1).

Loss and Unhappiness Through Marriage
When a brilliant Sun Line is cut and stopped by a Line of Marriage, it is an extremely unfortunate mark. The owner often enters into a marriage which proves unsuitable and, due to emotional unhappiness, loses his position and reputation and suffers a set-back from which it is difficult to recover (XLIV, 4A).

In some cases, this situation arises due to an emotional entanglement which speaks of disgrace. Irresistible temptation clouds the intelligence of the owner and as a result he loses prestige, position and name.

Success Through a Guilty Love Affair
When a long clear Sun Line begins from a clear and well-defined islanded formation the owner is virtually started on the path of success by a guilty love affair. He can look forward to a brilliant career and the kind of success which may make him the envy of those around him (XLIV, 4B).

THE LINE OF HEALTH

Origin and End
The Line of Health is not a common indication and, when found in a hand, it tends to run a short course. Its normal place of origin is close to the Life Line and the Rascette. When long and clear it terminates on the Mount of Mercury at the base of the little finger. When thus present it reveals health awareness. Its owner tends to be health-conscious and is inclined to guard his own well-being. There is, in most instances, a tendency towards apprehension, and he seems to reach out for remedial measures at the slightest sign of indisposition (XLV, 1A).

Health Line Absent
Quite often the Health Line is absent from the hand, and when this is the case it is indicative of a positive approach to matters of health. People who lack this line tend to enjoy a steady physical and emotional condition.

A Long Life
When this line begins close to the Rascette and is not in any way joined with the Line of Life, it shows good health, a capacity for enjoying life, and prospects of longevity. Usually its owner lives to quite an advanced age (XLV, 4)

Origin Mount of Venus
When the Health Line begins on the Mount of Venus and, crossing the Life Line, proceeds on its course, it is not at all a good sign. It denotes a predisposition towards distention and stomach complaints; its owner tends to suffer from palpitations, which seem to recur at different intervals. He is inclined to have a very sensitive digestive system, and anything can trigger off the complaint which usually leads to techeacardia (XLV, 2A).

Twisting Health Line
When it happens to cross the palmar surface in a twisting manner, it is a sign of a propensity towards biliousness, indigestion and liverish complaints. Its owner is never too well,

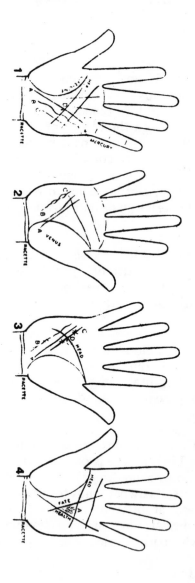

figure XLV

and because of that often suffers from anxiety and tension. There is, however, nothing seriously wrong with his constitution and if he were to adhere to a careful routine of living and regular habits, he could maintain a steady disposition and pretty good health (XLV, 1B).

Thin and Wiry Health Line
If the Health Line is poorly marked or rather thin and wiry, it is a definite clue to the need for physical care. Its owner is apt to suffer from poor health, though not necessarily a particular disease (XLV, 1C).

Mark of Longevity
When it happens to cross the palm undisturbed and reaches the Mount of Mercury, it is a mark of longevity; this person is sure to live to a ripe old age. Though conscious of the necessity of looking after his health, he does not seem to overdo it. He believes in precaution, and usually looks after himself (XLV, 1A).

Origin Life Line
When it originates from the Life Line, close to the wrist, it is not altogether a good sign to have. It shows a tendency towards fainting fits and, in some cases, digestive trouble, which may lead to palpitation (XLV, 2B).

Cross With the Head Line
An unusual significance is attached to the clear Line of Health which forms a distinct cross with the Head Line in both hands. This has been considered a sign of talent for the occult, and its owner is naturally disposed towards the study of, and deep interest in, occult sciences (XLV, 1C).

Cross in the Area of Mount of Moon
But when such a cross of the Health and Head Lines is formed by a drooping Line of Head, in the area of the Mount of the Moon, it is a different matter. Then it shows excitability, and its owner is apt to have an overly sensitive imagination. He needs to control his mind and, unless he does so, is liable to suffer from hypersensitivity, heated imagination, and may be given to all sorts of unhealthy fantasies (XLV, 3D).

Triangle With Head and Fate Lines
Another mark of an aptitude for the occult occurs when the Health Line forms a clear triangle with the Line of Head and the Line of Fate. This person is sure to show a gift of intuition, and can be good in the field of mediumistic work. Clairvoyance is likely to be his right line of development (XLV, 4A).

Islanded Health Line
When the Health Line is islanded and poorly marked, it is a definite sign of physical trouble. Its owner is very apt to fall prey to chills and ills, and should endeavour to look after his digestive system (XLV, 2C).

Broken Health Line
When the line is cut and broken it is evidence of stomach troubles (XLV, 3B).

Mark of Sterility
A cross or a star on the Line of Health, particularly at the point of its crossing the Head Line, is usually considered to be a sign of absence of family. I have found this marking in the hands of people who seem to be sterile (XLV, 3C).

Yellow Health Line
Colour is important in connection with this line. When it appears to be pale and yellow it is usually an indication of liverishness and bilious complaints. Its owner tends to suffer from internal troubles.

Success in Science or Industry
Quite often there is a clear and distinct line which is an offshoot of the Life Line, and which goes towards the Mount of Mercury. This is found in the hands of those people who are capable of great success in the field of science or industry. The Line of Health should not be mistaken for this marking. It requires a good deal of practical understanding of the lines before one is able to distinguish between the Line of Success in Industry and the Line of Health and it is essential to bear in mind that such a mistake can easily be made.

THE LINES OF MARRIAGE

The horizontal lines that are marked on the percussion of the Mount of Mercury, beneath the crease line at the root of the little finger and above the Heart Line, are commonly known as the Lines of Marriage. Traditionally, each such line of union is supposed to indicate a deep emotional bond which usually assumes the form of marital status (XLVI, 1AB).

More Than One Emotional Link

It is rare to find a single line of union in any given hand, and the presence of several lines suggests that the owner is potentially capable of forming strong emotional links with more than one member of the opposite sex. The formation, location and strength of each line will give the nature, time and duration of such an attachment (XLVI, 1). Usually, the most salient Line of Marriage shows marital status. This would point to the one who really matters and, ultimately, sways the heart to an extent that life-long partnership can follow (XLVI, 1B). A clear, deep and straight line is an ideal formation. It denotes depth of feeling, loyalty and durability in a happy matrimonial relationship.

Short Marriage, Long Marriage

When a Line of Marriage is short, the influence is short lived, whether it pertains to a liaison or marriage, though the emotional impact would be quite strong (XLVI, 1A). When the line is long and bold, the union lasts longer. When is crosses the percussion and covers the whole of the Mount of Mercury, it is usual to consider it as a mark of a legal bond. Such a line is firm, clear and straight (XLVI, 1B).

The Unmarrying Type

When the Line of Marriage curves upward, it reveals an interesting character. Its owner does not seem inclined to marry. He is quite willing to form a liaison and enjoy the fruits of a close relationship, but would take to his heels at the slightest suggestion of a matrimonial tie-up (XLVI, 1C).

159

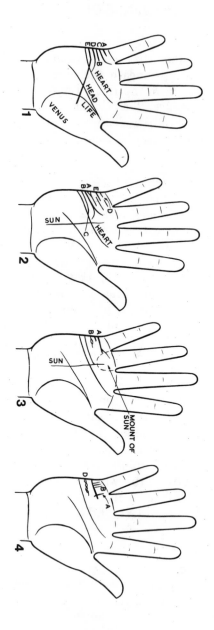

figure XLVI

Partner Lives shorter
When the downward sloping Line of Marriage touches the Heart
Line, the partner is liable to suffer from a prolonged period of
ill-health before passing away (XLVI, 1D).

Mark of Divorce
A drooping Marriage Line which crosses the palmar surface, cuts
the Life Line and ends in the area of the Mount of Venus is an
ill omen. Such a mark denotes divorce as the outcome of a
painful and broken marriage (XLVI, 1E).

Forked Start of Line of Marriage
When the Line of Marriage is forked at the start, it is a mark of
separation from one's beloved, due to either circumstances over
which neither partner has any control, or prolonged absence
abroad. If the Line is undisturbed after the fork, then marriage
assumes a healthy and fruitful pattern which tends to be
durable and close (XLVI, 2A).

Terminating in a Fork
In some instances, the Marriage Line terminates in a fork. This
is a mark of separation and if one of the prongs touches the
Heart Line, divorce takes place and is in the owner's favour
(XLVI, 2B).

Brilliant Union
When a straight and deep Marriage Line sends out an upward
branch which enters the area of the Mount of the Sun, it is an
extremely desirable mark: it speaks of a brilliant union, which
brings not only great happiness but material success and worldly
position in its wake (XLVI, 3A).

Union with a Wealthy Person
Likewise, a Marriage Line curving up to merge with the stream
of the Sun Line is a sign of a union with either a famous or a
wealthy person, obviously to the subject's advantage
(XLVI, 3C). When the Marriage Line cuts the Line of Sun,
however, such a union would be a misalliance (XLVI, 2C).

161

Loss of Worldly Position
A Marriage Line which droops downwards to cut through the Sun Line brings ill-fame and loss of prestige and worldly position (XLVI, 2C).

Mark of Separation
A broken Marriage Line clearly showing a gap where the break takes place is none too good an augury for it betrays elements which cause a break in the relationship. It is usually a mark of separation or divorce (XLVI, 2D). However, if the break occurs in such a manner that the broken ends overlap then it indicates that, although a separation takes place, it is sure to be followed by a reunion which will prove lasting and durable (XLVI, 2E).

Opposition to Marriage
In some cases, a clear Line of Marriage seems to be cut by a firm line from the base of the little finger. Opposition to the intended union, either by relatives or others, is usually foreshadowed by this marking (XLVI, 4A).

Marks of Children
Thinly formed lines touching the Marriage Line from the side of the base of the little finger have a different meaning. Such lines indicate potential issue: the strong ones are usually the male children, the lean ones female children (XLVI, 4B).

Guilty Intrigue
An island in the body of the Marriage Line is not a desirable sign to have. It certainly causes pain and suffering, for it stands for betrayal or a guilty intrigue against the owner (XLVI, 3B).

Great Sexual Urge
Several tiny islanded formations in the Marriage Line are marks of a great yen for sexual pleasures which inevitably leads to dissipation and impotency in the end. The owner of such a mark is unable to resist any temptation of a sexual nature, usually gathers ill-fame and is prone to venereal diseases as well (XLVI, 4D).

THE LINE OF INTUITION

Uncommon Mark
One of the unusual markings in the human hand is the Line of
Intuition. Its presence is extremely significant with regard to
interests that pertain to the occult, the mystical and all
divinatory techniques.

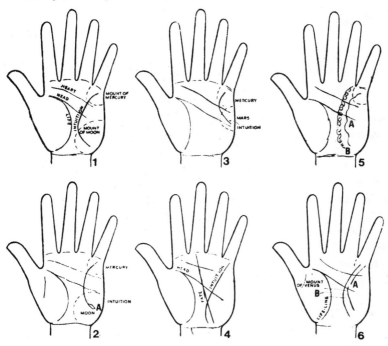

figure XLVII

Origin and End of Line of Intuition
When it is normal, it should originate from the lower area of the
Mount of the Moon, close to the obtuse angle formed by the
upper wrist line and the Life Line. It then traces its course
through the palmar surface in a slanting manner, proceeding
towards the base of the little finger, and ends in the area of the
Mount of Mercury (XLVII, 1).

Gift of Intuition and Prophesy
When the Line of Intuition is well defined, deep, clear and without defective signs, and runs its course undisturbed, it reveals a fine quality of sensitivity. Its owner is endowed with a rich imagination and an exceptional potential for clarity of vision.

He has a profound gift of intuition, which enables him to foresee the shape of things to come accurately. His dreams have prophetic content and his presentiments tend to unravel the unknown.

Disciplined Mediumship
Such gifts have spontaneity of expression, though they seem to be none too consistent. However, if their owner undergoes proper development and training, he can cultivate a form of disciplined mediumship and reveal a sustained talent for clairvoyance, clairaudience and other forms of reliable extra-sensory perception.

Interest in Divinatory Techniques
This person usually devotes himself to a specific branch of the occult arts and achieves a degree of unrivalled mastery therein, naturally shining in his field of interest. Through conscious application of the tenets of the acquired technique he brings accurate and revealing results, but it is also certain that his innate gift of seership works in an inexplicable manner which makes his prophetic utterances more emphatic, astonishing and bewilderingly correct.

It is a sad thing when such a good Line of Intuition is marked, for then his dreams, prophetic revelations and mediumistic aptitudes are likely to remain dormant and only spasmodic expressions of his gift can be expected. Without rigid discipline and essential training he will never be able to use his unusual potential fully or in a constructive manner. He is given to hunches and instinctive moments of revealing the truth.

Gift of Eloquence
A good Line of Intuition also endows the owner with a gift of eloquence and a taste for literature. He has a talent for facility of expression and a natural understanding of the proper use of

words. However, he usually limits his investigations to the region of the unknown.

Literary Genius
Such a line is often marked in the hands of intellectuals of merit, especially those who are pre-eminently associated with the spoken or written word. It is in fact the mark of an orator of note or a literary genius.

Control of Intuition
In certain cases, instead of beginning from the lower area of the Mount of the Moon, the Line of Intuition takes its origin from the upper area of the Mount of the Moon. Such a start alters the basic character of its owner. He is not satisfied with a spasmodic expression of his prophetic gift, but rather endeavours to learn to control his intuitional faculties. He develops a command over his gifts and can make use of them at will, having gone through an arduous disciplinary process. By nature he is inclined towards effective and determined application of his potential and is obviously a man of exceptional will power.

Strong Hypnotic Power
One of the unusual qualities of such a Line of Intuition is a strong hypnotic power. Its owner usually makes constructive use of this ability and is able to make a dramatic impact with it. Such a person can excel in the fields of politics, public speaking, law, psychiatry, entertainment and literature.

Disturbing Presentiments
When the Line of Intuition begins from the small fleshy elevation at the edge of the palm known as the Mount of Mars and curves upwards to terminate in the area of the Mount of Mercury, beneath the little finger, it is not a very good mark. This shows an ·intensity of nature as well as an over-abundant imagination. Its owner is not well equipped with any ability to really keep these tendencies under control and can be given to occasional expressions of violence. He often has disturbing presentiments and his prophetic dreams and visions are apt to be of a violent and drastic nature. He usually proves to be a prophet of doom and never seems to have any visions of hope or dreams of glad tidings. (XLVII, 3.)

Terminating on Upper Mount of Mars
When the Line of Intuition begins normally but ends in the area of the upper Mount of Mars, it is a welcome indication. This individual has a great control over his imagination and is able to exercise his power of intuition with exceptional constructiveness. He also possesses a tremendous potential for the hypnotic technique. He usually makes a great impact on those with whom he comes into contact, and tends to set new trends of thought and behaviour. His forceful personality makes its presence felt and, being essentially a man of goodwill, he has a magical effect on people in creating hope and optimism in their hearts. (XLVII, 6.)

Gift of Prophecy
When the Line of Intuition is without flaws and forms a small neat triangle with the Lines of Fate and Head, it is most revealing. A triangle shows a natural aptitude for the occult, and when thus formed it heightens this innate potential. Endowed with a tremendous gift of seership, its owner can unfold a gift of prophecy and foresight which can be truly great and often without equal.

He is usually a man of intellect and his gift of intuitional powers works hand in hand with his exceptional brains, with the result that he reaches great heights in his field of interest or endeavour. He uses his faculties consciously and with great determination, rather than depending on his innate potential alone. He seriously endeavours to master some specific occult art and, having done so, applies it in an effective and conscientious manner. He prefers to be a prophet of hope rather than one of doom. He certainly makes a success of his life and work. (XLVII, 4.)

Wavy Line of Intuition
When the Line of Intuition traces a wavy course through the palm, it betrays a twist in the owner's psychology. It in fact shows an eccentric, dubious and whimsical nature. Restless and discontented, he lives an uneasy life. Obviously those who happen to be closely associated with him also suffer because of his unsteady, unreliably restive and twisted psychology. (XLVII, 5A.)

Originating from an Island
When the Line of Intuition, otherwise clear and deep, begins from an islanded formation, it is a definite sign of an exceptional potential for clairvoyance. Its owner can be a very successful medium and often demonstrates a quality of seership which is extraordinary.(XLVII, 2A.)

Mark of a Sleep Walker
Such a mark, however, also points to a person who is inclined towards somnambulism, and is liable to become a habitual sleep walker.

Formed Like a Rosary
When the Line of Intuition is formed like a rosary, with many islands joined together, it betrays a disordered imagination. Its owner is given to forebodings of an evil nature and has an unhealthy imagination. He has a nasty habit of frightening people by his accurate, spontaneous visions of doom and destruction. (XLVII, 5B.)

Broken Line of Intuition
A break in the course of the Line of Intuition should be carefully noted. This means that the owner is endowed with an intuitional gift, but it tends to be defective and cannot be relied upon; it works in fits and starts and not always accurately. His own nature, like his gift, tends to be unstable. He can prove to be somewhat disturbing: at times he can be very correct and at other times completely off the mark. (XLVII, 6A.)

Family Opposition to Occult Interest
If the Line of Intuition is cut by clearly defined lines that originate in the area of the Mount of Venus, or from the Life Line, it tells an interesting story. Their owner is deeply inclined towards the occult and prophetic techniques; however, his relatives and members of his immediate family would seriously oppose his pursuits of the unusual. In most cases he does not succumb to these pressures but instead takes up the challenge, learns some specific occult technique, and demonstrates mastery and excellence therein. (XLVII, 6B.)

THE GREAT TRIANGLE

Formed by Life, Head and Health
The Great Triangle in the palm is formed by the three major Lines of Life, Head and Health. In some cases, the Health Line may be missing and the Line of Intuition, running in a slanting fashion across the palmar surface, constitutes the third line (XLVIII, 1).

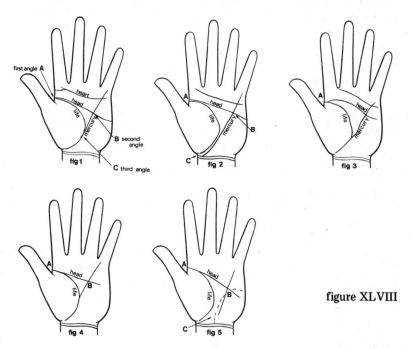

figure XLVIII

Spacious and Large
When the Great Triangle is large and spacious (XLVIII, 2), and formed by regular, good lines it is an excellent sign to have. The Line of Life indicates good health, the Line of Head adds intelligence and power of reason, and the Health, or Mercury Line points to active intuition and mental awareness. Thus formed, its owner is noble, audacious and generous by disposition. He aims high and demonstrates active, constructive and

thoughtful application of energy potential to achieve his aspirations. His most prominent characteristic tends to be a well-balanced disposition.

Ill-Shaped Triangle
When the Great Triangle is ill shaped, and formed by irregular and poorly traced lines, its owner tends to be lacking in balanced character and is unlikely to do work of high calibre (XLVIII, 3).

Narrow Triangle
When the lines are positioned in such a way that they make the triangle narrow, it is a sure sign of pettiness. This person tends to be mean, avaricious and fearful. He is rather cowardly and can turn tail at the slightest intimidation (XLVIII, 4).

The Upper Angle
The angles of the Great Triangle need special examination. The upper angle, also called the first, is formed by the junction of the Life and Head lines. When this is sharply pointed and clearly defined, as in XLVIII, 1A, it speaks of sound caution, common sense and a nature which is given to refinement.

A blunt angle (XLVIII, 3A), formed by a short Head Line or any other cause, shows lack of fine intellect, a slow, dull mind, and a tendency towards uncouth instincts.

Materially Insecure
When the Life Line is joined to the Head Line deep into the palmar surface and the angle seems more blunt than it should be (XLVIII, 4A), its owner tends to be rather apprehensive and materially insecure. As a result, he acts out of fear and poverty and is so concerned with his own material well-being that he tends to be unmindful of other people's feelings and is liable to encroach upon their privileges. He is neither self-confident nor courageous.

Life and Head Lines Separate
When a blunt angle is formed by the Life and Head lines being separated (XLVIII, 2A), it shows a go-ahead spirit, independence and audacity.

169

Too Wide Angle
When the angle is too wide, and the lines well separated, it shows a reckless disposition. Its owner can be foolhardy and is liable to take impulsive, risky steps.

The Second or Inner Angle
The second, or inner angle is formed by the junction of the lines of Head and Mercury (or Liver). When it is sharp and well defined it denotes a potential for longevity, as well as a good intellect. Its owner has an active mind and displays brilliance in the application of his mental energies (XLVIII, 1B).

Very Sharp Angle
A very sharp second angle (XLVIII, 4B) is none too good to have, for it indicates a nervous disposition which can be the source of health problems. Its owner is liable to be erratic and is not very controlled in his reactions.

Extremely Nervous Disposition
When the angle happens to be obtuse (XLVIII, 5B), due to the downward curve of the Head Line and a Health Line which takes its origin from the Mount of the Moon close to the percussion, the owner is liable to have an extremely nervous disposition. He is given to very quick changes, abrupt reactions and, of course, is highly inflammable and without self-discipline.

The Third Angle
The third angle is formed by the junction of the lines of Life and Liver, close to the wrist. When it happens to be sharp and clearly defined it reveals a tendency towards neuralgic complaints and fainting fits. It also shows a predisposition towards palpitation of the heart (XLVIII, 1C).

Mark of Active Living
When the Lines of Life and Liver come close to one another but do not join, it shows a good potential for active living and sound health (XLVIII, 2C).

Deceit and Faithlessness

If the third angle is very obtuse, leaving a large space between the Lines of Life and Liver, it shows a strong tendency towards deceit and faithlessness. Such a person can hardly be trusted and is inclined to cheat, take advantage of others, and prove disloyal (XLVIII, 5C).

THE QUADRANGLE

Table of the Hand
The Quadrangle is the area of the hand between the Heart and Head lines, excluding the Mounts of Jupiter and Negative Mars. This is also known as the Table of the Hand (XLIX, 1).

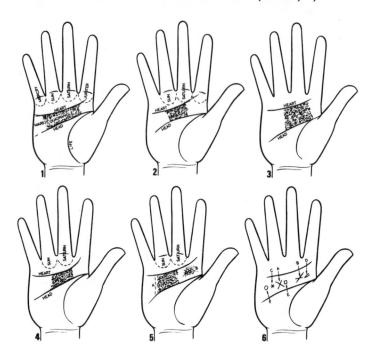

figure XLIX

Regular Quadrangle
When the lines of Heart and Head are traced along their proper places and are engraved in the palm clearly and without flaws, then the Quadrangle is regular, well proportioned and graceful. Such a Quadrangle indicates a just and honest character, generosity and clarity of mind and sound powers of judgement. Its owner is loyal and sincere by nature. He is also endowed with a steadfast and calm disposition (XLIX, 1).

172

Psychological Imbalance
However, when the Quadrangle is missing, it is a sign of psychological imbalance and usually some misfortune is experienced by the individual concerned.

Too Wide Quadrangle
When the Quadrangle is too wide throughout its length, it reveals an independent disposition. However, the owner does not seem to be endowed with caution and as a result is apt to make serious mistakes of judgement. He is none too willing to listen to others and usually will think and act according to his own views and ideas. Spontaneity and bravery can often be seen in his behaviour (XLIX, 3).

Honest and Straightforward
When the Quadrangle is well proportioned throughout, but becomes wider as it approaches the percussion, it is a good indication, for it shows an innate capacity for honesty and its owner tends to be straightforward, wise and firm (XLIX, 5A).

Careless About Public Opinion
The relative width of the Quadrangle under the Mounts of Saturn and Sun is of great importance. When the Quadrangle is wider under the Mount of Saturn than beneath the Mount of Sun, the individual is inclined to be careless about what others may think of him (XLIX, 2). In fact, he seems not quite concerned about his reputation.

Careful About Public Image
When the space is comparatively wider under the Mount of Sun than below the Mount of Saturn, the owner is rather sensitive about public opinion. He is careful about his public image and endeavours to create a good impression (XLIX, 5).

Narrow and Self-Centred
When the lines of Heart and Head are too close it makes the Quadrangle narrow, and thus irregular. This is an indication of narrowness of character; its owner tends to be mean and deeply self-centred (XLIX, 4). If this is the case, it should be carefully observed as to which of the lines is the cause of the narrowness.

173

If the Heart Line is placed low, then the narrowness is due to the cold, calculating head which dominates the individual's heart (XLIX, 4). On the other hand, if the Line of Head rises towards the Heart Line and causes narrowness (XLIX, 2), the feelings dominate the head; the owner tends to be lacking in any clarity of vision or logic, and seems blind to reality. His narrowness is due to excess of emotion and want of sound judgement.

Calm and Steady
The Quadrangle covers a vital area of the palm, and therefore any indications within the area are important and should be closely scrutinised. When no unusual minor marks or criss-cross lines exist, the owner tends to be calm and steady. He is generally a genial and a reliable person.

Restless and Irritable
When hair lines, criss-cross lines, or other defective markings appear in the body of the Quadrangle, inner calm is disturbed and the owner is apt to be restless, irritable, and hypersensitive to outside stimuli. Not quite self-contained, he is given to worry and impulsive reaction (XLIX, 5B).

Aptitude for the Occult
When a clear, independent cross exists in the centre of the Quadrangle, touching none of the main lines, it is known as the Mystic Cross. This marking indicates an aptitude for occult studies and metaphysical interests; the owner has the makings of an adept (XLIX, 6A).

Excitability and Haste
A cross which is poorly formed (XLIX, 6B), whether it be under the Mount of Saturn or any other place, is not a good augury. It shows great excitability and its owner is liable to be hasty, over-sensitive, and unwise in his reactions. He can't really be trusted and is unable to control his impulses or feelings. Usually he seems to make a mess of his life.

Brilliant Career
A star (XLIX, 6C), is usually an indication of some outstand-

ing success, and when it appears under the Mount of Saturn it points to brilliant achievements on the pathway of destiny. Its owner usually enjoys an illustrious career. If the star is found under the Mount of Sun, the individual is artistically inclined and will achieve great fame in some field of art or literature. If otherwise interested, he will be known for his wealth and worldly success.

Success in Science
When the star is placed directly under the Mount of Mercury, its owner can achieve brilliant success in science. Such a star is also seen in the hands of those who rise to great heights due to eloquence or business acumen.

Research and Scientific Study
If a well-shaped triangle exists in the Quadrangle it is an indication that its owner is endowed with some unusual aptitude for research and scientific study. He usually undertakes interests which pertain to the unveiling of secrets, and deals with problems of everlasting values (XLIX, 6D).

Lack of Self Control
A regularly-formed and small square in the Quadrangle, when independently placed, shows lack of self-control. Its owner is quick-tempered, but this is due to neither malice nor ill will. Its owner in fact is kind hearted and generous (XLIX, 6E).

Eye Trouble
A clearly-formed circle in the Quadrangie is an ill omen, for it points to eye trouble. Its owner would be well advised to watch his sight and not take any risks in this connection (XLIX, 6F).

THE GIRDLE OF VENUS

Origin, Course and Termination
One of the revealing indications regarding emotional make-up
and individual reaction mechanisms concerning psycho-physical
aspects of love is the semi-circular line known as the Girdle of
Venus. It takes its origin from the area of the palmar edge
between the roots of the index and middle fingers, gently slopes
downwards and then, forming a semi-circular arch beneath the
Mounts of Saturn and Sun, curves upwards to terminate in the
palmar area between the third and fourth fingers (L, 1).

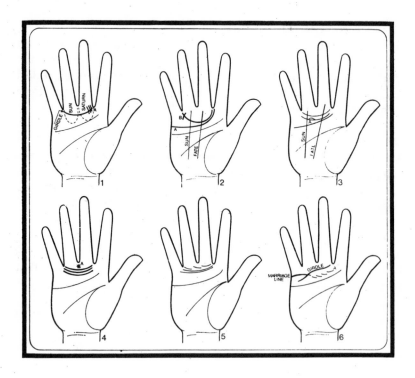

figure L

Symbol of Aesthetic Sense

When flawlessly formed it is a symbol of sharp aesthetic judgement, sensitivity, and innate capability for wholesome emotional response. This person is capable of healthy reaction to the opposite sex, irrespective of whether he is stimulated by physical allure or intellectual charm. He is likely to be enthusiastic, spirited, and vibrant, but it must be noted that he can also be variable in response; it is for this reason that he is liable to be indiscreet and flirtatious in love.

Generally Fragmentary

Such a complete and well-formed Girdle of Venus is not a very common phenomenon. In the majority of hands it is generally marked in a fragmentary form, broken and piecemeal.

Danger of Loss

When the lines of Fate and Sun are normally marked but the Girdle of Venus is so firm, strong and deeply ingrained in the palmar surface that it gives the impression of cutting through these lines, almost dominating them in its course, it is none too good an augury. Such a formation is a warning, for it points to real fear of loss or attack on its owner's worldly fortunes and assets — and that, too, by those he happens to love and care for. Close friends, lovers, and mistresses are some of the persons who could be tempted to deprive him of his material belongings, money and even prestige. He has to maintain an alert eye on those around him if he cares to safeguard his assets and possessions (L, 2A).

Talent for Literary Work

On the contrary, when the Girdle of Venus is much thinner and looks like a wiry bow, and the lines of Fate and Sun appear to be more prominently marked, it shows a predisposition towards aesthetic pursuits and a talent for literary work. This person has an exceptional sensitivity, a good wit, and intelligence of quite a high order. He can also respond to love stimuli in a fine and rather sensitive manner (L, 3).

Multiple Girdle of Venus

In some cases a double or a triple Girdle of Venus is seen in the

177

G

hand. This is none too good, for it betrays a strong predisposition towards love of the physical as well as a persistent attraction to the pursuit of the usual vices. Such individuals do not stop at seeking satisfaction of their sexual urge, but also tend to look to drugs, stimulants and similar agents to heighten their pleasure (L, 4).

Life of Vice
When the double or triple Girdle of Venus is poorly marked and also contains breaks in its course, the owner seems to be on an eternal quest for strange and vicious pursuits of a sexual or allied nature. A slave of his base nature, he indulges in impure pleasures and usually ends his days in most unfortunate and depraved circumstances. Psychologically he is imbalanced and his moral values tend to be so distorted that, unless he is given prolonged psychiatric help, he is sure to be doomed. Usually he is resentful and anti-social and unwilling to be helped. Obviously he seems pre-conditioned to live a life of vice and come to an unhappy end (L, 5).

Terminating Beneath Mount of Mercury
An unusual formation of the Girdle of Venus is at times observed when, instead of ending between the third and the little fingers, it proceeds to terminate beneath the root of the little finger, in the area of the Mount of Mercury (L, 5). Such an indication has a variable significance. When all the main features of the hand are sound and constructive, it speaks of passion and ardour in the pursuit of individual objectives. Its owner would show a great deal of potential for hard work, have an alert intelligence and, of course, reach his aims through constructive application of his energy potential.

A Bad Character
On the other hand, when the other features and markings indicate a bad character, the owner of this Girdle of Venus is strongly inclined towards love of intemperance, lasciviousness, and, of course, all the allied ills. He can be given to deceit, theft, falsehood — in fact he would stop at nothing to satisfy his base and compelling passions. His need can be terrifying, and can assume dangerous proportions. One feels quite unsafe in his

company and should, in fact, keep away from him as much as possible (L, 3A).

Cutting Line of Marriage
When the Girdle of Venus extends so far towards the palmar edge that it cuts through a firm Marriage Line, it is far from being a healthy sign, especially when the Marriage Line is longer than normal and the Mount goes beyond the region of the Mount of Mercury (L, 6). The acute emotional imbalance which this indicates is so pronounced that its owner betrays a hysterical disposition and is by nature unstable. Erratic and unreliable, he never seems to be able to show a balanced approach to matters concerning love, sex or intimate life. He is too apt to blow up and his excitability is such that he tends to charge the emotional environment with disruptive hysteria. He has a very unnerving and frightening impact on those around him and can conjure up fears, tensions, and eruptions that can be truly soul-destroying. Woe betide the individual whose ill fortune it may be to marry him. He can never be subjected to any discipline, nor would he allow any one near him to live a balanced or contented life.

Fragmentary Girdle of Venus
When the Girdle of Venus is formed by fragmentary ray lines, dim, thin and superficial in character, it should be carefully noted. It shows a tendency towards hysteria, depressive instincts and negative disruptive influences. If it happens in the hands of a child special care can help and with proper handling the defect can be eliminated. When in the hands of an adult, it is certainly a bad sign. Such an individual is plagued by imbalance, fear and tension. However, psychological care can often help to remove this nervous apprehension (L, 5).

Islanded Girdle of Venus
A well-formed island in the body of the Girdle of Venus is none too good a mark to have. The owner is exceptionally sex-minded, and is ever open to pursuit of and indulgence in the immoral relationships which seem to form his milieu. Emotionally eruptive, he is never able to resist temptation and can go to

179

extreme lengths to satisfy his sex urge. Such an island also points to the danger of venereal disease and usually the owner contracts it in one of its forms. Unfortunately, his presence in any social set-up is always a prelude to serious disruption, jealousy and conflict (L, 3A).

Star in Girdle of Venus

A star in the body of the Girdle of Venus is also an ill omen, and if it happens to be marked across a double or triple formation it is all the more dangerous. This, too, betrays an irresistible urge for sex and there will be little discretion or selection involved in the choice of a mate. Obviously this individual is usually landed with an almost incurable form of venereal disease. He is unable to keep away from the opposite sex and is quite unmindful of passing on the infections he contracts during his relationships with different, usually immoral, members of the opposite sex.

He is a menace to society and is apt to be dangerous: he can be cruel if thwarted, and always brings untold misery and unhappiness to those close to him (L, 4A).

Flirtatious and Fickle

When short, sharp vertical lines cross the Girdle of Venus close to its start, it is an interesting symbol. The owner tends to be flirtatious and rather easily tempted into an intimate relationship; however, he is too fickle to form a lasting bond. Quite charming and nice when he wants something, he likes the company of the opposite sex and tends to collect quite a few lovers around him. He is neither faithful nor inclined to form a good marriage partner (L, 1A).

Loss Due to a Member of Opposite Sex

When a clear, short bar cuts the Girdle of Venus beneath the third finger it reveals that the owner may suffer a loss due to members of the opposite sex. This would come about through indulging in intimacies with the wrong type of individuals. He is too inclined towards impure pleasures and unable to have a clean and morally sound relationship. He seems to walk towards his own doom, with his eyes wide open. (L, 2B.)

THE RASCETTE

Wrist Lines
Where the coarse skin border of the wrist ends and the actual
skin-ridge pattern of the palm proper begins, in all normal cases
a deep, clear line firmly crosses the wrist area from side to side.
This is known as the First Wrist Line. Parallel to this, other
similar lines cross the wrist area; these are usually known as the
Second and Third Wrist Lines. All the three lines are technically
called the "Rascette"

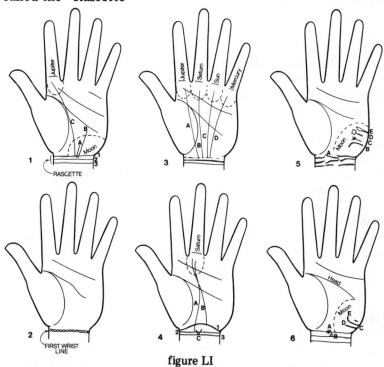

figure LI

Potential Longevity
Collectively, when well marked and without defective signs,
they are assumed to be marks of good potential longevity, each
one of them suggesting around 25 to 30 years. However, if any
of them contains defective indications, the potential for length
of life is proportionately abbreviated.

181

First Wrist Line
The First Wrist Line is of paramount importance. A clear, deep one endows a strong constitution, fit health and good prospects in the individual's life.

Chained First Wrist Line
When the First Wrist Line assumes the form of a rosary and contains islands throughout, strongly giving the impression of a chain, it speaks of a life of hard work over the years. However, its owner does finally achieve success, and without doubt his efforts are crowned with affluence, comfort and leisure in old age. (LI, 2.)

Sign of Dissipation
If the First Wrist Line is disfigured, colourless and poorly formed it is a sign of dissipation. Its owner tends to be extravagant and incautious, contributing all the while to his own misfortunes. (LI, 5A.)

Bow-Shaped Wrist Line
A curious formation of the First Wrist Line is seen at times when it curves upwards like a bow into the palmar region. This is significant as it reveals a strong predisposition towards internal trouble; in female hands it has particular relevance to the generative system and child-bearing. Obviously it is not very conducive to having a family. When accompanied by other defective markings it can be considered a mark of sterility, though in no case can this be assumed when the formation exists on its own. (LI, 4.)

Magic Bracelet
When all three Wrist Lines are well formed the Rascette is usually referred to as the "Magic Bracelet", pointing to great fortune and happiness in life. Certainly they work as a charm.

Marks of Journeys
A clear, well-defined line which proceeds from the Rascette to end in the area of the Mount of the Moon denotes a journey, either by land, sea or air. When such a line goes across the Mount of the Moon, it points to an important trip to a far-off

land. Each line ending in the Mount of the Moon area is symbolic of a particular journey. (LI, 1A.)

A Successful Journey
A fine, clear line rising from the Rascette, travelling across the ball of the thumb, and ending in the Mount of Jupiter, beneath the index finger, is certainly indicative of a long and a successful trip. Its owner is sure to achieve the object of his travel. (LI, 3D.)

Fortunate Sea Voyage
When such a line traces its course across the Mount of the Moon, and then proceeds to end in the area of Jupiter, it is a mark of a long sea voyage, culminating in good fortune and the achievement of one's ambitions. (LI, 1C.)

Hazardous Journey
A similar line from the Rascette which crosses the palmar surface and ends beneath the middle finger, in the area of the Mount of Saturn, speaks of a rather hazardous journey. (LI, 3C.)

Sinister Mark
When two such lines co-exist, and cross each other close to their termination, it is a sinister mark. Their owner is unlikely to return from one of these long journeys. There is a sad element of misfortune in undertaking these travels. (LI, 4AB.)

Distinction Abroad
A clear, fine line beginning from the Rascette and ending beneath the third finger in the area of the Mount of the Sun is a very fortunate sign. Its owner will acquire great reputation and prestige through his association with men and women of distinction during his sojourns abroad. In point of fact, it is these distinguished foreigners who first seem to recognize his true genius, which his native people then immediately begin to acclaim. (LI, 3C.)

Wealth Through a Journey
A fine, well-marked line starting from the Rascette, crossing the

183

palm in a slanting manner and ending in the Mount of Mercury below the little finger is a sure sign of sudden wealth. Its owner usually gains fortune either during travel or in connection with a distant journey. (LI, 3D.)

Vain and Deceitful
A break in any of the Wrist Lines is an ill omen. It is a mark of a vain, deceitful individual who, due to his evil intentions, digs his own grave. (LI, 5A.)

Angle on the Rascette
An angle in the body of the Rascette is the sign of an unusual inheritance in old age. Promotion, honour and money form the essential constituents of this belated legacy.

Inheritance
A star in the middle of the First Wrist Line is also an interesting indication of inheritance, however the owner does not have to wait till very late in life for its arrival. (LI, 4C.)

Triangle in Rascette
A clear triangle in the Rascette is yet another indication of a large inheritance and exceptional good fortune, not necessarily unexpectedly. It certainly elevates the individual's status and endows him with great material advantages. (LI, 6B.)

Travel Lines
Between the First Wrist Line and the Head Line there are a number of lines which enter the Mount of the Moon from the percussion side. These are known as the Travel Lines. (LI, 5,6.)

A straight line across the percussion into the Mount of the Moon shows a safe journey and a satisfactory one. It can be by sea or land. When the travel line turns upward at the end it shows good results; when such a line turns downwards, the journey ends in failure. A cross at the end of the travel line denotes it will end in disappointment, and when the line ends in a square, the journey will be fraught with dangers, but the individual will be protected against them. If the travel line contains an island it indicates that the trip will end in a bad way and the aim for which it is taken will never be realized. (LI, 5B, C, D, E; 6D, E.)

THE UNUSUAL MARKINGS

There are some rather unusual markings in the human hand which besides the obvious major Lines of Heart, Head, Life, Fate, Sun, etc., have a special place and significance of their own. When any one of these exist, it is essential to make note of the same, as each one of them has a far-reaching effect on the life and psychology of its owner.

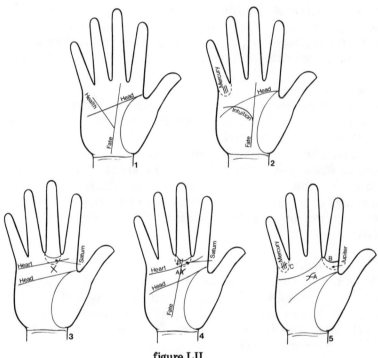

figure LII

The Small Triangle, the Mystic Cross, the Solomon's Ring, the Ring of Saturn and the Medical Stigmata are the more outstanding ones in this series.

The Small Triangle
The Small Triangle is formed by the lines of Fate, Head and Health. When all these Lines are without defective signs and the

185

triangle is well shaped and regular, it is symbolic of certain basic and lasting characteristics. Its owner is predisposed towards the occult and takes a serious interest in esoteric phenomena. Endowed with the spirit of inquiry and research he approaches occultism as a science. He endeavours to take up a specific branch of the occult and studiously proceeds to master the laws governing its technique and make a practical use of this knowledge. (LII, 1.)

Uncanny Gift of Divination

In some instances, the Line of Health is missing and a clean Line of Intuition forms the third part of the Small Triangle, but this is extremely rare (LII, 2.). It reveals an exceptional aptitude for the occult sciences, and points to an uncanny gift of divination.

The Mystic Cross

In the space between the lines of Head and Heart, below the middle finger, a clear cross is sometimes engraved in the palmar surface. It is usually in the area under the Mount of Saturn and is unattached to any other line. This is known as the Mystic Cross. When well-defined, large and clear (LII, 3), it speaks of an intense longing for a mystical way of life. Its owner has the makings of a true seer or an occultist of great merit. As a rule, he acquires an exceptional degree of efficiency in the art of divination.

Church Dignitaries

When a clearly-defined Mystic Cross is engraved in the palm in such a manner that its prongs touch a strong, unbroken Fate Line, it relates to church dignitaries and religious leaders of distinction who lead a fortunate life due to their position in ecclesiastical matters (LII, 4).

Superstitious Practices

When the Mystic Cross is ill-formed, with uneven prongs, it is none too good an augury. It betrays a lack of a true sense of the mystical and a leaning towards superstitious practices. (LII, 5).

The Ring of Solomon

The Ring of Solomon forms a semi-circle across the Mount of

Jupiter at the base of the forefinger. When normal it begins from the edge of the palm about halfway between the Life Line and the crease at the base of the finger. It arches gently upwards and terminates at the interspace between the first and the second finger (LII, 5B).

It is an unfailing symbol of inherent aptitude for the occult and the technique of divination. Its owner is predisposed to study all that pertains to the nature of man and his destiny in the days to come. It is usually a predictive symbol. From time immemorial, it has been known as the mark of the deft hand analyst. When the Ring of Solomon is complete and really sound, the practitioner shows an exceptional degree of accuracy in both his psychological assessment of personality and prognostication for the future. He can be expected to reach an enviable success in his chosen career, whether it be hand analysis or another branch of the occult sciences.

The Ring of Saturn

The Ring of Saturn is marked below the crease at the base of the second finger. When normal, it forms a half circle around the centre of the Mount of Saturn (LII, 4B). This is also the natural point of termination for the Fate Line.

It is an established law of hand reading that any sign or line barring the course of a major line is a disruptive influence and hinders its natural fruition. If a Ring of Saturn is marked against the current of the Fate Line, material security in old age is hampered.

Whenever I have noticed this mark it has betrayed something defective about the psychology of the owner; in fact I have never seen this mark in the hands of successful people. Those who own it seem to have something wrong with their individual psychology.

The Medical Stigmata

The Medical Stigmata (LII, 2) is a composite sign. Below the base of the little finger, three to four deep slanting lines are crossed by a clear distinct line. This denotes an innate aptitude for the medical profession, particularly for surgery.

187

THE MINOR MARKS

The minor marks undoubtedly have special significance and as a rule are harbingers of far-reaching changes associated with the life and psychology of their owners. A great deal can be learned from a close scrutiny of these small signs. When a minor sign is located in the area of a mount it emphasises the characteristics associated with that elevation; when it appears on a line, it denotes major changes and events.

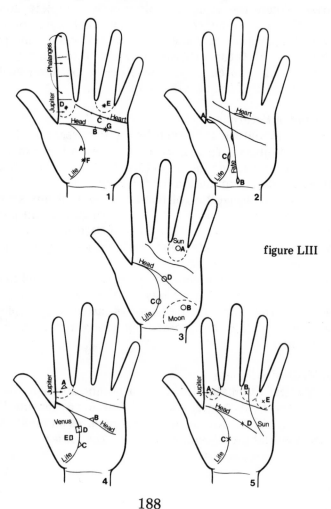

figure LIII

The Dot
A Dot or a Spot is a deep indentation in the skin, either in the area of a mount or in the body of a major line. It assumes various colours, of which white, black, blue and red are important.

As a rule a Dot denotes a malady or illness, often of nervous origin, but the white dot in connection with certain lines is an exception. When a white dot is found indented in the Heart Line, it is indicative of a conquest in love; if marked on the Head Line it denotes an invention or a discovery, probably of a scientific nature. (LIII, 1B, C.)

The Island
An Island is a harbinger of misfortune and denotes either a weakness or a loss. It is generally observed in the body of a line though it is sometimes found marked in other areas of the palm.

When the Life Line originates from a well-defined island it suggests some mystery associated with birth. It denotes the same thing when the Line of Fate begins from a distinct islanded formation. (LIII, 2A.)

An island marked along the course of the Life Line speaks of a period of illness. When the Line of Head contains an island, it points to a weak mind. If the islanded formation is near the Mount of Mars, it indicates evil thoughts. On the Line of Fate an island speaks of loss, uncertainty and even disgrace associated with the material aspect of life, but when it is found on the Line of Sun it is a sign of scandal and disrepute which tends to prove socially disastrous.

The Circle
The Circle is a comparatively rare sign. When found on the Mount of Sun it is extremely propitious as it then points to the advent of glorious success. When it is found on the Life Line it denotes a malady which I have often observed to have a bearing on eyesight, and if found on the Line of Head it threatens blindness. (LIII, 3A, C, D.)

A circle on the Mount of the Moon shows danger of drowning. (LIII, 3B.)

The Triangle
The Triangle is a fortunate sign; as an independent mark it is generally found in the areas of the mounts of the palm.

Its location on the Mount of Venus is particularly interesting: this is usually found in the hands of those who show calculation in love. In fact its owner reveals a shrewd sense of material values and tends to use love as a basis to make a fortune.

When the Triangle is found on the Mount of Jupiter it denotes diplomacy. It is a sign of love of mysticism when found on the Mount of Saturn, and artistic inclinations when found on the Mount of Sun. It is a mark of political talent and acumen when it is found on the Mount of Mercury.

The Square
The Square is an auspicious mark and is generally known as a sign of preservation. It is associated with the major lines and serves to protect the owner from a defective indication. When found on any line, it adds to its power.

When, for example, the Life Line is broken, it denotes danger to life and health; however, if a Square covers the break it protects life from harm.

It is unwelcome in one position and that is when it is found on the Mount of Venus rather close to the Life Line. In such a case it points to confinement either in prison or in conditions resembling imprisonment. (LIII, 4E.)

The Cross
As a rule the Cross is an unfavourable mark; it is observed on the mounts and the lines of the hand.

There is one exception, however, and that is when it is found on the Mount of Jupiter. Thus located, it speaks of a deep, happy love affair which normally culminates in marriage. (LIII, 5A.)

When a Cross is found on the Mount of Saturn it shows evil aspects of mysticism; on the Mount of Sun it betrays errors in the pursuit of art; on the Mount of Mercury it denotes dishonesty; and on the Mount of Venus it indicates a fatal love affair.

When a well-marked Line of Sun is found to have a distinct cross associated with it, it denotes wealth and worldly position. This is extremely rare.

The Star

The Star is usually a fortunate mark. When it is found on the Mount of Jupiter, it denotes gratified ambition, honour and distinction. If marked on the Mount of Sun, it is a sure sign of wealth and riches. (LIII, 1D, E.)

MINOR MARKS ON INDEX FINGER

Index — 1st Phalange

Minor marks are of exceptional importance if they are marked on the various phalanges of the fingers. The most usual signs include: a vertical line, a cross, a very definite and clear star, a short distinct triangle, a rectangle or square, a circle — complete and without defect —, an island and a grille. Obviously, some of them have rather sinister meanings and others have far-reaching and propitious indications.

If we try to locate these signs in the segments of the fingers, we should start with the first finger and its first phalange. This phalange is associated with social consciousness, idealism, spirituality, and all that pertains to higher values in the moral and perfectionist sense. It is also connected with occult sciences, theology, metaphysics, and magical arts.

A Vertical Line

A definite and clear vertical line on this phalange is an exceptionally good indication of an individual who leads an active life, possesses a deep sense of religion, and is able to express spiritual exaltation in everyday life. He tends to influence those around him by his own behaviour patterns, which are always highly moral and spiritual (LIV, 1).

Mark of a Cross

A cross, clearly formed, is not altogether a good augury. As a straight line gives aptitudes for development and expression of spirituality, a cross disturbs, creates imbalance, and obviously leads towards fantasies, visions, and those superstitious and probably irreligious ideas which have a negative — and often satanic — impact on others (LIV, 2).

Sign of a Star

A star is a very rare mark, and in order to be complete it must have at least five neat, well-defined radii. It is an exceptionally fortunate indication and denotes an event of tremendous importance in the life of the individual. This change in the course of one's life is often accompanied by material or spiritual

192

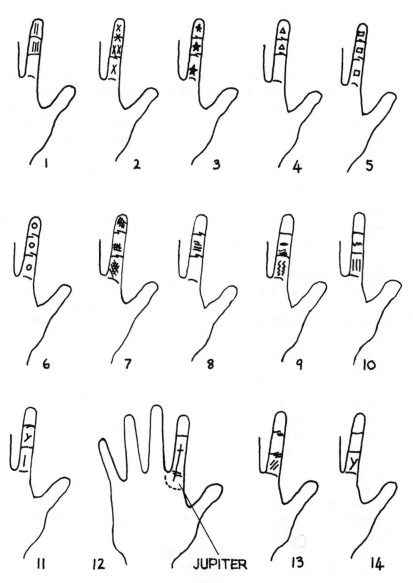

figure LIV

rewards (LIV, 3).

A Clear Triangle

A cleanly formed, neat little triangle, though not so very common, is a very, very interesting and revealing mark. Any triangular formation indicates an inborn aptitude for theological, occult, or magical studies. Obviously, when it is marked in the first phalange of the index finger, its owner is unconsciously drawn towards pursuits which have theological, occult or spiritual significance. This person tends to devote a lifetime to the study of and specialization in one particular field. As a result, he achieves some outstanding results and receives recognition for his contribution to that specific area (LIV, 4).

Sign of a Square

A rectangular shape in the first phalange of the index finger, usually known as a square, is a very interesting mark to have. A square is normally associated with protection from harm. This area of the finger has a tendency towards dangerous visions, fantasies, implication with magic and the occult. Obviously, the precariousness of these borderline interests could lead such an individual to fall prey to fears and tensions, and a well-formed square provides a very definite protection from the results of extremism. When thus protected, he will maintain and remain well within the precincts of moderation. (LIV, 5).

Mark of a Circle

A circle is not a very common thing to see in the first phalange of the index finger. When found, it is always indicative of a triumph in terms of faith. Such an individual can show very great religious faith and even in the most odd, awkward and dangerous situation can get through because of his faith in the deeper things of life. Although he is a man of intelligence, perception and critical understanding, whatever the circumstances and difficulties he may have to face, it would be his deep conviction that would always enable him to conquer rather than yield to any temptation or fear. A circle in fact will allow him to become the master of any situation (LIV, 6).

An Islanded Formation

An island which is a leaf-formed formation in the first phalange is not too good a mark. It has some unspiritual and unsavoury moral significance about it, and the owner is liable to undertake activities of a dubious nature (LIV, 8).

Sign of a Grille

The worst form of indication in the first phalange, however, is what is known as a grilled formation. Fine, clear lines cross each other in the upper phalange of the first finger and assume the shape of a grille. This indicates the zeal of the fanatic. Its owner is narrow-minded and completely limited to strict adherence to the form and ceremony associated with the religious codes of behaviour. He has no sensitivity to the inner meaning of religion, nor does he go beyond the outer symbolism. For him the symbols become God and he does not look beyond the ceremony for the meaning of the tradition. His zeal and fanaticism is so conditioned that if he were to see anyone not strictly following the so-called tenets of the religion, he would not hesitate to undertake steps to persecute the so-called non-believer. His inflexible fanaticism can often lead him to acts of violence or actions which are of an illegal nature; he would, because of his zeal, be quite willing to endure imprisonment. He often gets so disgusted with those he sees around him that he escapes to a convent or retreat and cuts himself off from normal life (LIV, 7).

2nd Phalange of Index Finger

The second phalange of the first finger is associated with ambition, aspirations and a sense of purpose in life. Minor marks in this area must be most critically and carefully observed.

Vertical Line

When a clear, vertical line is marked on this phalange, it is an exceptionally brilliant indication. It is the mark of a noble ambition, incessant effort to achieve one's objective, and a manipulation of people and situations in order to be successful. Such an individual becomes well known and respected. (LIV, 1).

195

Horizontal Line
On the other hand, a horizontal line, or a transverse cross line, in this area is not a very good indication. Though the individual would endeavour to reach out for his objectives, there is something oblique in his character and he may not hesitate to use deceptive means to accomplish his aims. Unfortunately, it renders him somewhat unreliable (LIV, 9).

Wavy Lines
Confused or wavy vertical lines in this area do not augur well. They indicate a strongly ambitious disposition, but these aspirations are apt to be unworthy in character. As a matter of fact, their owner is an exceptionally disturbing influence in his social group and can but prove to be a very unhealthy element of society. With such indications it would be unwise to cultivate any friendship, business association, or intimate relationship with the individual (LIV, 10).

Slanting Fork
A forked line, somewhat slanting, with a fork ending towards the upper part of the finger, is none too good a sign either. It suggests that, in spite of the ambitious endeavours and high aspirations of its owner, he is bound to meet with ill success. It could lead to misfortunes and unhappiness; the individual, due to some twist in his character, is likely to create circumstances which would never allow him to be healthy or constructive in the pursuit of his objectives (LIV, 11).

A Cross Mark
When a clear cross is marked on the second phalange it indicates tremendous literary success. If it is located in the middle of the phalange, it has a way of stimulating a positive response in those who are in a position to patronize creative and literary works (LIV, 2).

Cross at the Joint
Rarely, one comes across the formation of a clear and distinct cross at the joint of the first and second phalanges. It is supposed to be the sign of sudden literary success which will produce exceedingly good results, both materially and in

196

matters concerning name and recognition. Its owner usually becomes a distinguished man of letters and receives many honours (LIV, 2).

Star Mark

A five pointed star, clearly defined, is not a common sign to have. It is a mark of true chastity, nobility of character and an impeccably pure life. Such an individual is saintly by nature; he lives a life of great moral and spiritual stature. Usually such individuals are considered to be saints, and people flock to them (in spite of their limited contact with the world) to receive their blessings, help and cures (LIV, 3).

A Triangle

A triangle neatly formed in this section has a very unusual significance in the field of foreign service, diplomacy and political acumen. As a matter of fact, it endows a tremendous capacity for influencing public affairs; its owner is usually well known, shines in political negotiations, and becomes a man of distinction in the affairs of the world (LIV, 4).

A Square Mark

A rectangle is also indicative of great ambition, strength, and determination. Its owner reaches out towards very high goals and makes a headway which could be the envy of those around him. But he is intelligent in manoeuvring around situations, and in such a manner that he is able to achieve results without creating enmity, envy or any form of negative reaction (LIV, 5).

A Circle

Occasionally, a neat, clean circle is also found in the second section of the first finger and is supposed to be a mark of success which brings fortunate circumstances and rewards.

This particularly applies to an artist who reaches the hearts of the people with the message and eternal value in his work, and is remembered for this long after his death. (LIV, 6.)

A Grille

A grille is not a good mark to have in this area, for it is a mark of a crook and its owner tends to cheat, deceive and be generally unreliable. He is hardly an asset to society and could create a tremendous amount of complication, misunderstanding, and difficulty for those with whom he associates (LIV, 7).

A Line from Jupiter to 2nd Phalange
In some cases a clear vertical line is seen to rise up from the area of the Mount of Jupiter and enter into the second phalange. This is quite an interesting and unusually good indication. It gives that nobility of character, strength of ambition, and high aspirations which lead to great honours and a life which is distinguished as well as enviable. Such a mark is found in the hands of people who, through personal merit and honourable deeds, are able to bring themselves before the public, communicate with the community, and act for the good of all concerned (LIV, 12).

Third Phalange
A Vertical Line
Usually it is most unlikely to have a straight, clear line in this phalange, but when it does exist it is an indication of substantial and constructive importance: it endeavours to correct the disposition towards too many worldly and physical needs. Avoiding gross habits, its owner is able to live a more sensible life, in which moral values have a proper say (LIV, 11).

Multiplicity of Wavy Lines
Unfortunately, a multiplicity of wavy lines adds to the predisposition towards matters which are not quite virtuous. The fact is that its owner is so tempted by the so-called good things of life that he is liable to lose his self control. He is unable to maintain his position in life. This form of wavy formation has to be clearly defined in order to accentuate the evil propensities, and therefore should be carefully watched. Lines which are less well defined point to an individual who is not so easily tempted, although the danger is still there (LIV, 9).

Multiplicity of Vertical Lines
In certain cases, three or four vertical lines seem to be clearly

198

marked in the third phalange of the first finger. These are indicative of ambitious inclinations in several areas and undoubtedly their owner is able to make headway in each line of interest. The main trend of the owner, however, is to go after riches and the goods of this earth. He does become a man of considerable affluence, and lives a life of comfort: if there are supporting marks in other parts of the hand he acquires great wealth. He is able to work relentlessly. This is a mark of an individual who shows a tremendous capacity for success (LIV, 10).

Cross Lines
Cross lines on this phalange of the finger have a peculiar significance. They show prospects of a legacy, benefits, and gains. Though such an individual does tend to come into a great deal of money, these lines also show a strong inclination towards self-indulgence, and the owner seems unable to resist such a temptation. Intemperance is one of the things which can attract him, and he may be exceptionally fond of good and rich food. Naturally, in due course of time, he is liable to suffer from problems connected with the digestive system and stomach. Being rich and entertaining, he has a tendency to show off.

He usually endeavours to interest people in his wealth, but instead of making a constructive and a good impression, he seems to defeat his own purpose.

Usually, he proves a poor host, for although he spends money and goes out of his way to please people with all he has to offer, he creates a sense of envy or jealousy in others. He has an unfortunate habit of looking for flattery and appreciation, and is always fishing for compliments. It would be a wise thing for such an individual to live his own life, form a circle of friends who really understand his weaknesses, and who are willing to forgive his vain nature; if he can do that, he will be able to live very comfortably and without creating any great animosity in the minds of those with whom he associates (LIV, 13).

Forked Line
A semi-vertical line forming a fork on the upper side is an extremely unusual mark, and when this is found it should be

very carefully noted. It is the sign of an ambitious individual who is inclined to make large-scale plans and would look for the spectacular and out of the ordinary. It is, however, unlikely that he will achieve his very high ambitions, for he is apt to miscalculate and over-reach himself. Unless and until he is able to discipline his great ambitious urge and live constructively, he is liable to come across major losses and can be very unfortunate and miserable (LIV, 14).

A Cross Mark
In some cases, a clear cross is marked on the third phalange, and in this case its owner shows vulgarity, an unhealthy disposition, and unreliability. His characteristics are such that he could prove to be the source of sorrow and unhappiness to others, for he has tempting ways of seducing people into wrong channels. He is rather a poor lot; he lives an immodest life, and usually gets a bad name (LIV, 2).

Star Sign
A clearly-engraved star is, fortunately, an exceptionally rare sign. It is indicative of accentuated immodest instincts. Its owner could be terribly shameless and immoral; his character as a whole is that of a person who is really despicable (LIV, 3).

Square Sign
A square, however, is quite a welcome indication and, when found here, helps to diminish the despotic instinct. Although he is inclined to dominate others, and could prove to be harmful to society, the presence of a square definitely checks his evil instincts (LIV, 5).

Circle Mark
The circle is the best mark to have in this area, for it is indicative of success in one's chosen field. Its owner is likely to show a great deal of tenacity of purpose and is capable of reaching his objectives in a constructive manner (LIV, 6).

Grilled Formation
The worst mark in this area is a grilled one. Any formation of crisscross lines which is clear, and looks like a grille, is

altogether an unhealthy mark to have. It is indicative of immoral instincts, love of physical indulgence and corruption. Its owner is inclined towards crime, and has such persuasive and tempting ways that any association would lead those close to him towards a life which is rather degrading, shameful, and directly or indirectly involved in criminal activities (LIV, 7).

MARKS ON THE SECOND FINGER

The Middle Finger
The middle finger is known as the Finger of Destiny and is usually associated with mysticism and love of solitude. It is also concerned with exact sciences and, in specific cases, agricultural pursuits, mathematics, etc.

The evil tendencies associated with it are egotism and greed.

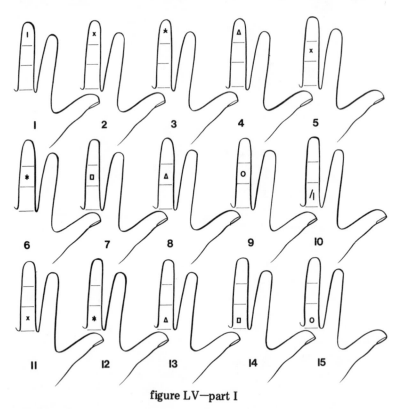

figure LV—part I

First Phalange
The first phalange, however, has a bearing on prudence, superstition, and melancholy. In point of fact, a person with a prominent first phalange is prone to show a desire for self-destruction.

202

A Vertical Line
Minor markings in this first phalange have a specific significance and should be very carefully observed. A clear, straight, vertical line accentuates the tendency towards self-destruction and escape from reality. Too often its owner is possessed by inner ferment and fears which betray a lack of hope and an extreme pessimism. When he is in the throes of despondency he is inclined towards a suicidal attitude of mind. Rarely, however, does such a person take his own life. He tends to isolate himself from society and broods intensely, even over little things (LV, 1).

Several Vertical Lines
A multiplicity of vertical lines in this area is also a very unfortunate indication to have. This person doesn't seem to have any faith in anything and is dominated by a death-wish. The more he thinks about it, the less he finds to make life worth living. He gets too involved within and lacks balance and hope (LV, 16).

Wavy Lines
A multiplicity of wavy lines in the first phalange of the second finger is another unfortunate indication. These indicate that the individual is given to a twisted mind and usually falls prey to a succession of events which could prove to be ultimately fatal. However, he does not seem to be able to discipline himself, or use his intelligence to help him towards an escape from his unfortunate end (LV, 17).

Mark of a Cross
A cross clearly defined in this area is not a very welcome mark to have. It points to a disturbed moral balance, and a person who is unable to follow the right path. He has faith in neither the divine powers, nor human beings; nor is he willing to accept any moral code. Unfortunately, he is devoid of feelings for others and respect for social and moral obligations; quite unconsciously he rebels against all that is good, honest or spiritual. As a result his life becomes a series of events which incorporate crime, immorality, superstition, and even suicidal tendencies. Usually he lives a very unhappy life and, because of

203

his behaviour and his innate tendencies, other people do not want to have anything to do with him. He is deeply imbalanced and in moments of acute despair could take his own life (LV, 2).

A Star Formation
In certain cases, a clear star formation is noticeable in this phalange. This points to an unusual destiny. The owner seems to be born to play some rôle of importance in the affairs of his time, directly or indirectly, which has very far-reaching effects. He inevitably gets caught up in a web of circumstances over which he has no control and, occasionally, his own life is in danger. Neither can he disengage himself from these situations; he truly becomes an instrument of events which can lead to destruction, rebellion, or revolution — anything which is of long-term importance to the society in which he lives (LV, 3).

A Triangle Mark
When a clear triangle is observed in this area one should be extremely careful about associating with the individual in whose hand it is indicated. There is a tremendous amount of magnetism in such an individual which, unfortunately, enables him to seduce the innocent, the unwary and the pure towards a life of immorality and intemperance. Usually, he is unable to discern that he is acting in this manner (LV, 4).

A Square Mark
A mark of a square in this phalange shows an interesting character: its owner seems to escape the effects of his own evil deeds and, although he is inwardly drawn towards acts of immorality, he is able to avoid going to the extreme. This forms the basis of some protection for him. However, he is not always able to feel safe or, for that matter, acceptable to society and has to live a life of fear, anxiety and tension (LV, 18).

A Circle Sign
A circle is a very rare sign in this area, and if it happens to be clearly defined and well formed, it gives very good results. Its owner leans towards mysticism and is able to develop his inner potentials in such a way that he can become an enlightened

individual. He is also able to avoid any temptations of superstition, melancholy, or imbalance with regard to his ethical and spiritual approach to life. It is one of the very best marks to have, as it is a sign of success, hope and spiritual endowment (LV, 19).

The Grille
The mark of the grille in the first phalange is considered to be very ominous. Its owner has no capacity for judgement of right and wrong and enjoys unethical pursuits. He is liable to sexual diseases, indulges in intemperance, and has a precarious mental balance. Yet he does not seem to mend his ways, and feels that he is entitled to seek physical pleasures in his own way. He often reaches such a point of desperation that he seriously considers suicide as an alternative to life as he knows it. Such an individual can be helped by long psychiatric treatment or intense indoctrination of moral values in his early years. (LV, 20.)

The Second Phalange
After a study of the minor marks on the first phalange of the second finger let us proceed to examine the various symbols engraved in the second phalange of the middle finger. This segment of the finger is important and any mark therein, when clearly defined, is liable to have a strong effect on the psychology as well as the trend of the life of the individual.

A Vertical Line
When a clear distinct vertical line is engraved on the second phalange of the middle finger, it denotes wisdom, understanding, and a deep knowledge of metaphysical, spiritual and esoteric matters. Usually, its owner shows a predisposition from early days towards such pursuits which will enrich his mind and give him prudence and spiritual elevation. The sign is a rare one and, when found, points to an individual who is endowed with insight and the capacity for revelation. (LV, 21.)

However, if such a line extends into the third phalange on one side and the top phalange on the other, it has a completely different significance. Instead of wisdom its owner is inclined towards folly, stupidity, and a lack of understanding. He never seems to realise the impact his behaviour makes on others and, unfortunately, keeps repeating foolish mistakes. Ultimately, he finds himself in awkward isolation condemned by those around him. (LV, 22.)

Cross Lines
Cross lines in this section of the finger are not a good augury. The owner of such markings is most unwilling to learn anything, tends to be stubborn, inflexible, and lives in a state of ignorance. He usually lives in pitiable circumstances and, since he has no intellectual acumen, is unable to make any real progress. A multiplicity of such lines adds to his ignorance and makes him even more inflexible. (LV, 23.)

Thick Cross Line
Sometimes a very thick cross line which looks like the lead of a pencil is engraved in this area. This is a mark of fatality and is associated with poison or lethal drugs. A dark coloured dent of a similar nature usually proves dangerous and a blue marking is also indicative of death by poisoning. (LV, 24.)

A Cross Mark
A clear and well defined cross in this phalange is an interesting though rather dangerous mark. Its owner has a speculative, adventurous spirit about him and seems drawn by uncertain situations which spell danger. Quite impulsively, he gets mixed up with things, people and conditions which are none too safe. Obviously, he is liable to suffer. (LV, 25.)

A Star Sign
A well formed star found here is none too good. It has a catastrophic effect on its owner, probably involving a criminal act. He seems to be incapable of avoiding circumstances which could lead to his death. A blind force seems to goad him into such a situation. (LV, 6.)

A Square Mark
A well-marked square in this section of the finger has quite an extraordinary significance. Usually the square is a mark of protection, but, when it is engraved in this area its owner is apt to fall a victim to circumstances which unavoidably lead him towards his death. (LV, 7.)

A Triangle
The most interesting and promising mark in this area is that of a well defined, clear triangle. It speaks of special aptitude for the occult sciences. This person studies diligently, and is usually able to achieve distinction and success. He is capable of a deep insight into human affairs, psychology and, in certain cases, the destinies of nations and countries. A very rare sign indeed, an enviable mark of the seer and the master of the occult. (LV, 8.)

A Circle
A very neatly formed circle here is also an exceptionally good indication and, like the triangle, shows great success in the field of the occult. Its owner is endowed with exceptional potential for insight into human life and destiny, and endeavours to cultivate and master some of the occult techniques whereby he is able to foresee the shape of things to come. He achieves a prestigious status in his field. (LV, 9.)

A Grille
A grille here is an unfortunate sign to have. It is an omen of ill-luck and it points to a predisposition towards diseases, especially of nervous origin. When such a mark is present, its owner should avoid anything which might produce nervous fatigue or agitation. With care, such an individual can shield himself from unnecessary ailments and live a fairly balanced life. (LV, 26.)

Third Phalange

A Vertical Line
A vertical line, well defined and of clear visible formation, is indicative of success which is associated with a military career. Its owner shines on the battlefield and achieves glory through skill, audacity, and military strategy. Usually he rises to a great height and becomes famous for his exploits in battles and wars (LV, 27).

Oblique Line
In some cases such a deep, clear line is marked on the third phalange in an oblique manner, which is not altogether a good

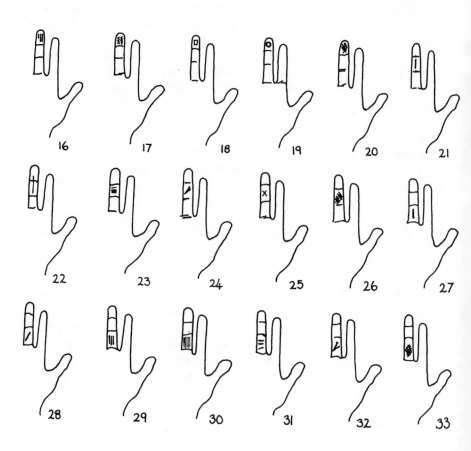

figure LV—part II

sign to have. It reveals a brave and skilful soldier who certainly distinguishes himself in war; during his act of bravery, however, he usually meets his death. Posthumous fame and awards seem to be his destiny (LV, 28).

Multiplicity of Lines
A multiplicity of clear and well defined lines in this section of the finger is quite exceptional and reveals an individual who is inclined towards a career associated with mining. In the process, he unearths mineral wealth, makes a fortune and no doubt gets known for his talent in so doing (LV, 29).

When a multiplicity of vertical lines in this area gives a confused picture, it has a completely different significance. Their owner is apt to be given to melancholic ideas, depression, and extreme forms of anxiety. Unfortunately, he never seems to acknowledge any ray of hope, even in the best of circumstances, and is usually a glutton for self punishment (LV, 30).

Cross Lines
Another bad indication is cross lines in this section of the finger. They denote misfortune: their owner avoids reality, takes to solitude, and is usually abandoned by his friends and relatives. He seems to live a wretched, lonesome life and probably does not find any meaning in it (LV, 31).

Slanting Fork
When a slanting line forks at its upper end in this phalange the owner seems to have a natural dislike for others and usually shuns their society; naturally, he is avoided and disliked by others. He, too, suffers from the ill effects of loneliness and in some instances this is aggravated by his conscious knowledge of being intensely disliked and avoided (LV, 32).

A Cross
A well defined, clear cross in this area is hardly ever found in a male hand. But when it is clearly imprinted in a female hand it indicates a marked tendency towards sterility and its owner is not likely to have any children. There is either an internal inability to conceive or some form of operative impotence (LV, 11).

209

H

A Star

A star, with clear and well-defined radii, is fortunately a rare sign; when present, it is associated with an act of murder. It does not necessarily mean that the owner is either a murderer or a victim of murder. However it does suggest direct or indirect involvement in a dangerous situation where an act of murder may take place (LV, 12).

A Triangle

A neatly formed triangle is not a good indication to have here, in spite of the fact that it usually shows an aptitude for science and a talent for diplomacy. Its owner seems disposed towards wicked pursuits, and uses his exceptional abilities in such a manner that he sets into motion a chain of events which will prove the cause of his ultimate undoing (LV, 13).

A Square

A square in this area betrays greed and merciless pursuit of the goods of this earth. Its owner is apt to be terribly miserly and would not hesitate to perform illegal or immoral acts to satisfy his craving for material possessions and money (LV, 14).

A Circle

A circle in this segment of the middle finger denotes an unusual potential for natural sciences and philosophy. Without doubt, this person is able to achieve great proficiency in his field of research. As a rule he is considered to be an authority, and deserves the prestige which he gains through a great deal of hard work and application of his energies (LV, 15).

A Grille

A grille formed by criss-cross lines betrays an unusual and unfortunate character. Its owner is terribly miserly and, due to his love of money, he tends to become suspicious and apprehensive of other people. He develops a kind of protective instinct which leads towards a peculiar form of insanity associated with miserliness. Such an individual is his own worst enemy and in spite of being affluent he lives a miserable life indeed (LV, 33).

MARKS ON THE THIRD FINGER

First Phalange
The first phalange of the third finger is associated with idealism and an artistic nature.

A Vertical Line
A well-defined vertical line marked in this area is indicative of the extremist in the pursuit of beauty; its owner can show complete devotion to his pursuit of an idea, so much so that he is unable to see realities. This usually makes him an eccentric. He is capable of creating things of unique character and beauty (LVI, 1A).

Multiplicity of Lines
Three or more clear-cut lines marked in this phalange are an interesting combination. There is a great deal of innate genius in their owner, but he is unable to show any deep devotion or application to his ideas. Usually his behaviour and his creative imagination incline him towards mental imbalance. There is a kind of multiplicity in his approach to things (LVI, 2A).

Cross Lines
Cross-lines in the first phalange of the third finger are none too good either, for they point to unconscious elements in the nature of their owner which create obstacles to his artistic work. This leads to a very deep and disillusioning frustration. The tendency is so strong that this person keeps repeating errors of judgement and is unable to create things of beauty. He becomes so terribly disappointed with himself that he can easily begin to show signs of a serious mental imbalance. (LVI, 3A.)

Sign of the Cross
A clear and a definite cross in this section of the finger shows devotion, chastity and a total submission to all that is artistic. There is a high degree of sensitivity in its owner; he easily becomes excited, and reacts to beauty with such passion that he is not able to maintain an equilibrium. There is no doubt about

H*

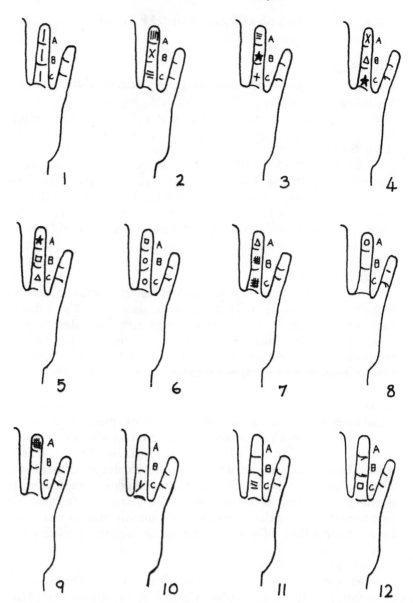

figure LVI

his genius and he could create objects of distinctive beauty and unrivalled imagery (LVI, 4A).

Star Mark
A star with five clear radii distinctly defines the mark of a genius. Its owner shows a love of splendour and beauty, and can make a tremendous impact with his originality and creative work. Very exceptionally zealous and intensely occupied in his pursuit of the ideal, he is liable to wreck his nerves, health and sometimes the balance of his mind. However, he is no doubt capable of setting a new trend in his field of art and usually creates masterpieces for posterity (LVI, 5A).

A Square
In some cases a rectangular formation, clearly defined, is marked in the first phalange of this finger. This is a mark of protection against error; its owner is able to apply his genius and talent to the pursuit of his ideal in a sane and balanced manner. His creative aspirations produce works which are of real beauty, distinction and artistic brilliance (LVI, 6A).

Triangle
When a neatly-formed triangle is marked in the first phalange it shows quite a different aptitude. In fact its owner studies beauty as a science and endeavours to pursue his aspirations in an orderly, systematized manner (LVI, 7A).

A Circle
A clear, neatly-formed circle is, of course, a rare mark to have in this section of the third finger. It is indicative of brilliance and outstanding, though unexpected, success in the field of art. Indirectly it is a sure signpost to a genius who is apt to be recognised in his life time. When discovered, he creates a tremendous impact in the artistic world (LVI, 8A).

A Grille
A grilled formation in this section of the third finger is a most unfortunate mark to have. Its owner, though talented, is given to inner distortion and imagery of unhealthy artistic value. His creative efforts usually bring forth artistically unacceptable

specimens; they betray his inner imbalance and disturbed imagination (LVI, 9A)

Second Phalange

Vertical Line
A neat, clearly-defined vertical line in the second phalange of the third finger is quite an exceptional indicator of great prospects of recognition. Its owner is brilliantly endowed with talents which can make a mark in his specific field of interest. He becomes famous and is sure to be known for his creative or inventive genius (LVI, 1B).

Slanting Fork
Sometimes a slanting forked line is observed here: this is not a very good indication. No doubt some talent may exist in its owner, but he seems to be very much divided in his efforts and is unable to concentrate on any creative project. This means he is unable to achieve any distinction or constructive reward. Such a forked line, in fact, is a mark of barren talent which is unlikely to bear any fruits (LVI, 10).

Cross Lines
Occasionally several cross-lines are found in this section. These are none too good, for they are indicators of a jealous nature and nonexistent talent in any field of art or endeavour. Their owner is liable to come up against a great deal of frustration and unhappiness, since he seems to think that he has an un-recognised talent (LVI, 11).

Cross Mark
When a clear, well-formed cross is marked here it indicates tremendous envy and conceit. Its owner believes that he is endowed with unrevealed genius and is convinced that he should be recognised for his talent. He is so conceited that he endeavours to give battle to those who are truly famous for their genius. He competes with them with a rather venomous envy and, since there is no chance for his own success, always comes across great unhappiness and disappointment (LVI, 2B).

Marks on the Third Finger

Star Sign
A neatly-formed star with clear radii is a welcome sign of talent of an exceptional nature. Its owner is endowed with real merit and achieves distinction, fame and success. Usually this comes rather suddenly, though he may have worked for years before he made his mark (LVI, 3B).

A Triangle
A neatly-formed triangle in this area, though rare, is of exceptional value. Its owner endeavours to look deeply into the mysteries of art and its spiritual significance. He approaches his work in a scientific manner and yet his devotion implies a search for the spirit and the divine essence hidden behind the artistic technique (LVI, 4B).

A Square
A square, properly formed, is an interesting and revealing mark. It points to innate talent, but its owner seems to restrict himself to a certain special type of work and interest. And this self-imposed restriction does not allow the full blossoming of his true genius. However, within the precincts of his specialization, he does succeed. Those who study his creative works and can see the limited nature of his output will probably be grieved that he had not allowed himself a fuller expression (LVI, 5B).

A Circle
A well-formed and neatly engraved circle in this area is, without the least shadow of a doubt, a mark of great success. It not only gives tremendous material reward and recognition to its owner, but also brings with it a sense of satisfaction (LVI, 6B).

A Grille
A grilled formation indicates a most envious professional disposition. Colleagues of this person usually try to avoid him and, if they are unable to do so, seem disinclined to communicate with him. Unfortunately he is never able to find a remedy for his deadly envy, suffers a great deal, and in the end grows bitter and resentful (LVI, 7B).

Third Phalange

Vertical Line
A clear vertical line here is an exceptionally good indicator of personal happiness; its owner usually enjoys a fruitful sense of living (LVI,1C).

A Cross Line
When a cross-line or multiplicity of cross-lines is found to exist here, it gives completely opposite results. The owner is unable to find personal happiness or success, and lives a life of misery (LVI, 2C).

Cross Sign
A clear cross here is also none too good a sign, for its owner is apt to undertake activities and sponsor ideas which not only interfere with his ambition and work, but lead to severe frustration. He is likely to grow bitter and live an unhappy life (LVI, 3C).

A Star
A star, clearly formed, shows vanity, great love of flattery and lack of a constructive attitude towards life. Usually its owner is unable to maintain his sense of balance and in the long run faces a great deal of unhappiness and misery (LVI, 4C).

A Triangle
A triangle on this phalange shows skill and talent in building one's own image. This person is able to make a good impression on others, but has the tact and discretion to prevent himself from appearing vain or overblown (LVI, 5C).

A Square
A square is a protective mark, helping the owner to avoid the consequences of his urge for vanity and flattery. He is unconsciously inclined to use his desire for appreciation in a very careful manner (LVI, 12).

A Circle
The circle in this area is an exceptionally propitious indication;

it speaks of affluence, success, and recognition (LVI, 6C).

The Grille
A grille in this section of the finger is an ominous mark, as it denotes poverty and an envious nature. Since its owner is not at all disciplined and is liable to show his rather unfortunate jealousy, he tends to create conditions and circumstances which bring him humiliation. He lives a miserable life and ends his days in very unfortunate circumstances (LVI, 7C).

MARKS ON THE LITTLE FINGER

First Phalange
The fourth finger is associated with skill, love of science and business acumen. Its first phalange is associated with idealism, science, love of eloquence, and study.

Vertical Line
A clear vertical line on this phalange shows powers of eloquence and aptitude for effective speech. A leaning towards the occult, and potential for intuition, are also strongly indicated (LVII, 1A).

Cross Lines
A cross-line or multiplicity of such lines unfortunately betrays an empty talker, a liar who is also prone to be a thief (LVII, 3A).

A Cross
A well-marked cross in this area shows a gift for prophecy and exceptional eloquence (LVII, 4A).

A Star
A clear star indicates strong potential for being a successful speaker who is able to make a tremendous impact on his audiences (LVII, 5A).

A Triangle
A neatly-formed triangle is indicative of an innate aptitude for the occult sciences, and its owner is naturally endowed with psychic faculties (LVII, 6A).

A Square
When a square is clearly formed here, the individual is able to use his expressive talent in an exceptionally sound commercial manner and is usually able to make a great success of himself (LVII, 7A).

A Circle
A clear, well-formed circle on this phalange is certainly an

218

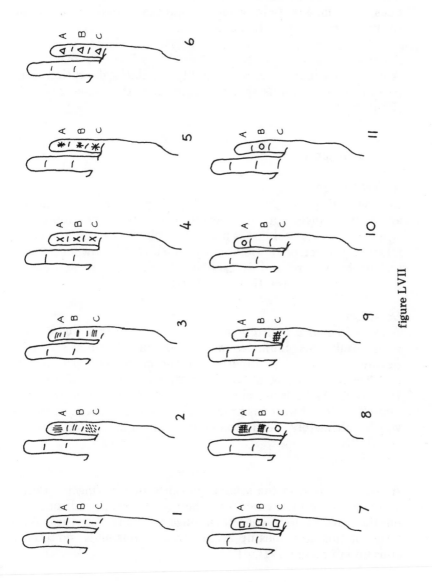

figure LVII

219

indication of an exceptional potential for success. Its owner does well in any field where eloquence and decisive public speaking are essential (LVII, 10).

A Grille
A grille is an indication of an ability for skilful deception. This person leans towards black magic and the baser instincts (LVII, 8A).

Second Phalange

A Vertical Line
The second phalange of the little finger has a bearing on aptitude for invention, science and technological developments. When a clear, vertical line is marked herein, it is a sign of natural talent in the scientific field and in research. The owner is often serious by nature and is capable of making a great deal of headway in his chosen field (LVII, 1B).

Cross Lines
A cross line or a multiplicity of cross lines in this area do not bode well; this indicates an inclination towards scientific research, but there is something in the individual's psychology that seems to bring about frustrations and lack of success. Unfortunately he is not always able to discern the causes within himself which thwart his progress; he keeps on making mistakes which ultimately lead to much unhappiness and failure (LVII, 2B).

A Cross
A clear-cut cross in the second phalange of this finger is rather an unfortunate indication for it betrays a strong predisposition on the part of its owner to indulge in shady activities. As a result of this he comes up against tremendous odds and usually ends up in prison (LVII, 4B).

Star Sign
A well-formed star on this phalange is quite unusual, and when it is found it is a mark of notoriety. Its owner tends to be a

sharp operator and because of his rather nefarious activities and associations with notorious people he is liable to create situations which are scandalous. He usually gets caught in his own trap and suffers because of his ill-doings (LVII, 5B).

A Triangle
A well-formed, small triangle in this area is a mystic symbol, and denotes an innate potential for the occult (LVII, 6B).

A Square
A square here is not altogether a welcome indication. Its owner seems inclined towards a negative use of his intelligence; because of the abuse of his wit and scientific ability, he obstructs his own prospects of success or happiness. He often ends up in the hands of the law, and has to spend quite a time in prison (LVII, 7B).

Small Circle
A well-formed, small circle in this section of the little finger indicates not only success and honour in the fields of science and industry, but also prospects of affluence and unusual achievement in the owner's chosen field (LVII, 11).

Grilled Formation
A grille is not altogether a welcome mark here. Its owner makes exceptionally silly mistakes in the conduct of his affairs and, instead of using his capabilities in the right way, he is disposed towards blunders which can easily send him to prison. Unfortunately he rarely realizes what he is doing (LVII, 8B).

Third Phalange
The third phalange of the little finger is associated with talent in business. When evil indications are marked therein, its owner inclines towards sharp practices and is given to a thieving disposition.

A Vertical Line
A vertical line clearly and strongly marked in this area is an indication of a born deceiver; this person cannot resist the temptation of indulging in theft (LVII, 1C).

Wavy Lines
Several confused or wavy lines are sometimes observed here and
when this is the case the owner is an incurable thief and a liar.
His lot is miserable, unhappy and difficult (LVII, 2C).

Cross Lines
One or more cross lines in this area aggravate the temptation to
steal and lie. Its owner is an habitual thief and trickster, always
looking for chances of depriving others of their belongings. He
uses very clever devices to achieve this (LVII, 3C).

A Clear Cross
A well-formed cross in this part of the finger is also none too
good, for it takes away the ability to distinguish between right
and wrong. This individual is predisposed towards a life of crime
and, because of his immoral activities, comes to an unfortunate
end. He cooperates with his so-called friends in acts of theft and
deception and usually gets caught in the long run (LVII, 4C).

Star Sign
A clear-cut star, however, is a mark of a tremendous ability to
be eloquent and to make an impact on those with whom one
comes into contact. This person is a persuasive talker and can
usually succeed in his aspirations. His capacity for new ideas
and his ability to work with other people form the basis of his
success (LVII, 5C).

Mark of a Triangle
A clearly-formed triangle in this area is quite exceptional; when
found, it is a mark of a true diplomat. It indicates a high degree
of intelligence, a capacity to negotiate with people, tact, a
convincing manner, and of course tremendous talent for solving
intricate problems. Its owner is well fitted for handling the most
difficult tasks and is usually able to perform his duties in an
excellent manner. He is not inclined to allow others to take
advantage of him, nor does he like to put others at a disadvantage. But if his interests do clash with those of another
individual, he is quite able to work round the situation and no
doubt succeed in the preservation of his own interests
(LVII, 6C).

222

Square Sign
A square, when formed clearly in this area, is rather an interesting and to some extent mystifying indication. It in fact reveals some mystery associated with the life of the individual. Such a person is difficult to understand and usually proves quite inscrutable in his behaviour and his dealings. He is mysterious and secretive; it is very difficult to say whether his motives are good or evil (LVII, 7C).

A Circle
A well-formed circle shows a tendency to plan undertakings which may be enterprising and adventurous, but these seem to pertain to criminal activities such as theft. However, its owner is not necessarily an active operator (LVII, 8C).

A Grille
A grilled formation situated in this area is the worst indication one could have. It betrays an incurable thief who is also an extremely foolish one. He is an habitual liar and tends to steal constantly but he does not use a great deal of intelligence in the pursuit of his objectives. Because of his stupid mistakes he normally gets caught and punished. He is a small-scale criminal who is in and out of trouble pretty well all his life (LVII, 9C).

MARKS ON THE THUMB

First Phalange
Now that we have examined the minor marks on the different segments of all the fingers, we will conclude by the examination of these important signatures in the two segments of the thumb.

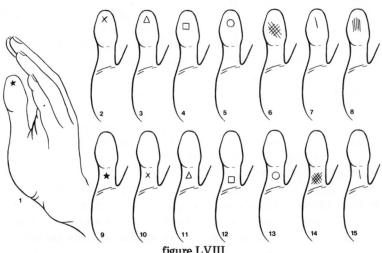

figure LVIII

A thumb, of course, individualizes the person, and though it only contains two phalanges it is articulate and of great importance. Its first phalange is associated with the power of the will and determination.

Vertical Line
A clear, vertical line in its first phalange is a welcome indication, denoting exceptional determination. Its owner is capable of great deal of stamina, and can apply his energies in a manner which reveals persistence, tenacity, and purposefulness (LVIII, 7).

Even as many as three vertical lines are considered to be fairly sound and do tend to add to the owner's will power.

Multiplicity of Lines
However, a multiplicity of lines in this regard would indicate a diffusion of energies and lack of concentration, thereby

224

diminishing the capacity for determined action (LVIII, 8).

A Cross Line
A cross line in this section is a mark of obstacles, and if there is a multiplicity of such lines great obstacles are likely to cause frustrations, difficulties and disappointments.

Cross Sign
A clear-cut cross is none too good a sign to have for it is usually considered to be the mark of an individual who is inclined to be unchaste, disloyal and without moral values (LVIII, 2).

A star Mark
A star, well-formed, is also a sign of immorality and its owner shows a predisposition towards acts which go against the accepted codes of morality, religion and social behaviour. In point of fact, the individual can be of a loose character and given to evil instincts (LVIII, 1).

A Triangle
A clearly-formed small triangle here is exceptionally rare; when found, it reveals unusual powers of concentration, especially in the pursuit of scientific work. Its owner has the makings of highly sound researcher, with a tremendous capacity for determination and application of his energies. He usually succeeds and makes a name for himself (LVIII, 3).

A square
A clearly-defined rectangular shape in this section of the finger is indicative of intense concentration. The person is inclined to be single-minded in the pursuit of his aspirations and unfortunately he usually develops a self-centred attitude and can be unmindful of the feelings of others. He is liable to a tyrannical disposition and, probably quite unaware of this defect, continues on his path absorbed in his own thoughts and devoted to his own cause (LVIII, 4).

A circle
A circle is an unusually brilliant sign, and when found on the thumb's first phalange it shows great ability for steadfast

application in the pursuit of one's aspirations. It is considered a mark of great triumph in the owner's specific field (LVIII, 5).

A Grille
A grilled formation in this section is none too good an augury, for it indicates that the owner is in danger of death caused by his partner. This stems from matters relating to unfaithfulness and immorality (LVIII, 6).

Second Phalange

A Vertical Line
The second phalange of the thumb is associated with logic and reasoning, and when a clear-cut vertical line is present it is a certain indicator of sound power of reasoning. It adds to the powers of analysis, rationality and logic of its owner (LVIII, 15).

Multiplicity of Vertical Lines
If there is a multiplicity of vertical lines here, in other words more than three, then intelligence and analysis are likely to suffer and the individual becomes more quarrelsome and diffuse.

Cross-Lines
A cross-line or a multiplicity of cross-lines when clearly defined betrays a lack of logic and common sense. The owner is susceptible to false reasoning and self-deception.

A Cross Mark
A clearly-formed cross in this section is indicative of a person who is easily influenced by others. In point of fact, unless he is on his guard he is liable to be corrupted by those of a firmer mind who can direct his energies in any way they like (LVIII, 10).

A Star Sign
A star formation in the second phalange of the thumb, is also a bad mark to have; its owner is endowed with a good disposition, and is basically kind and compassionate. However, he is unable to distinguish between good and bad persuasion and generally falls into the web of other people's intelligent manoeuvring.

226

This usually leads him into troubles from which he cannot easily extricate himself (LVIII, 9).

A Triangle
A definite and well-formed triangle is an exceptional mark, for it is a sure sign of philosophic talent and an aptitude for scientific work.

Its owner tends to be serious-minded, inquisitive, capable of research and constructive progress. With diligent use of his intellectual powers, he usually attains status and prestige in the field of his academic interests (LVIII, 11).

A Square
A square shows a very firm power of the reasoning and exceptionally strong logical faculties. There is a tendency for this person to be stubborn, which means that he quite often defeats his own purpose (LVIII, 12).

A Circle
A well-formed circle is a mark of exceptional logic which leads to sure success. In point of fact its owner triumphs in life through reason and logic (LVIII, 13).

A Grille
A grille in this section is none too good to have for it is a mark of dishonest application of logical faculties, and its owner is liable to use deceptive reasoning to achieve his ends. Though endowed with a sharp mind, this person is unfortunately not quite able to use it in a healthy or moral manner (LVIII, 14).

MARKS ON THE MOUNTS

The Mount of Jupiter
Ascending Line
An ascending clear and definite line found on the mount of
Jupiter (LIX, 4E) enhances its most favourable characteristics.
When uncrossed and strong it is a symbol of success in the field
of ambition, socially, materially and in general.

Cross
A cross located in the region of Jupiter (LIX, 1F) is a very good
sign of a happy union.

Star
A star on Jupiter (LIX, 3F) is considered to be a most
favourable sign. It shows satisfied ambition, honour, happiness
in love and a sudden elevation in life. It is one of the most
propitious signatures of predestination for great things, and
unexpected distinction and the accomplishment of fondest
ambitious dreams result from it.

Triangle
A triangle on Jupiter (LIX, 4F) shows aptitude for diplomatic
astuteness. Its owner is endowed with subtle political acumen,
and can prove exceptionally clever in the art of diplomacy.

Square
A square on Jupiter is, as elsewhere, a protective mark
(LIX, 3F). Its owner is endowed with a kind of sober and
prudent approach to his ambition. He is able to show a sound
sense of discipline, and usually reaches his objective calmly.
Without being intoxicated by his success, he is able to maintain
just pride, grace and essential humility.

Grille
A grille on the mount of Jupiter (LIX, 3E), however, is a
defective mark. When present it betrays domineering spirit,
vanity and tendency toward loose morality. Its owner is also
given to exaggeration and superstition. None too stable or

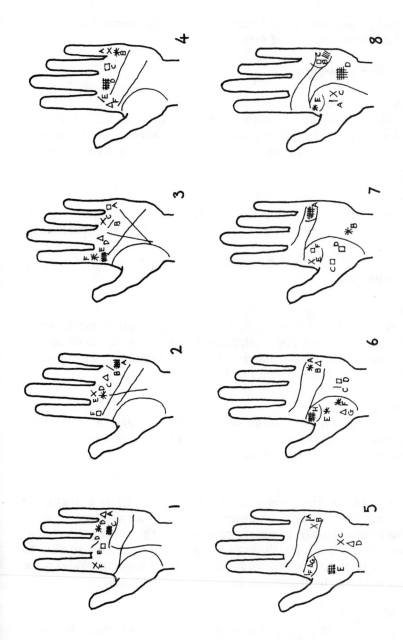

figure LIX

229

socially balanced, he is bound to come up against frustrations, unhappiness and loss of face.

The Mount of Saturn

Ascending Line
A clear, straight ascending line on the mount of Saturn (LIX, 1D) is a symbol of great good luck, success and happiness. If there are two clear upward lines they too indicate success and good fortune.

Cross
A cross on the mount of Saturn (LIX, 2E) is not a good sign. It shows a tendency toward the use of the occult sciences for evil ends.

The cross here is also considered to be a symptom of possible childlessness.

Star
A star on this mount (LIX, 2D) is an unfortunate mark. When clear and well defined, it shows a danger of incurable disease. It is also found in the hands of serious criminals, who usually suffer the ultimate penalty of the law.

Triangle
A triangle on the mount of Saturn (LIX, 3D) is a revealing symbol of innate aptitude for the occult. Its owner is well versed in some of the mystic or occult arts.

Square
A square on the mount of Saturn (LIX, 1E) is a fortunate symbol, as it indicates preservation from some great fatality. When such a mark is clearly engraved in the mount, its owner, though liable to go through some danger to life, is able to escape fatal consequences. Nature in its own way provides some escape from any hazardous situation that may arise.

Grille
A grille on the mount of Saturn (LIX, 4D) is an unhappy omen. Its owner seems to be unlucky throughout the entirety of his

life, and to suffer miserably in his old age. It is also seen in the hands of those who happen to be imprisoned: though not necessarily evil, they do through sheer bad luck seem to go through suffering and confinement.

The Mount of Sun

Ascending Line
A clear, well-defined ascending line on the Mount of Sun (LIX, 3B) is a very welcome sign, as it indicates good fortune, glory and wealth. Its owner is capable of achieving great success and fortune through brilliant application of his talents in his career.

Cross
A cross, clear and definite, is a bad mark on this mount (LIX, 3C). It betrays blunders in the pursuit of art or success. Its owner usually seems to lack a balanced approach to his objective.

Star
A star on the Mount of the Sun (LIX, 1B) is a mark of fame; though only after hard work and grave and risky situations. Though it indicates wealth, it does not however, indicate happiness. There is some peculiar shadow of an ominous nature which seems to lour over its owner's life and fortune.

Triangle
When a triangle is marked on the Mount of Sun (LIX, 2C), it announces the application of science to art, leading to well-deserved success. Its owner is of a high artistic calibre.

Square
A square, clear, well-defined and independently formed on the Mount of Sun is an excellent mark (LIX, 4C). It serves as a true protective influence and helps its owner to achieve tremendous artistic success. At the same time it induces sober business ability which enables him to escape from the ill effects of the intoxication of success.

231

Grille
A grille on the Mount of the Sun (LIX, 1C) is a veritable symbol of vanity and paucity of talent. Its owner seems foolishly to feel that his talent is not recognised, though he is hardly endowed with any worthwhile aptitude for art or success. He is usually inclined to be mentally unbalanced.

Mount of Mercury

Ascending Line
A clear, definite ascending line on the Mount of Mercury (LIX, 2B) is rare: however, when present, it is a symbol of unexpected though distinctive good financial fortune. It also indicates some exceptional business or scientific potential.

Cross
A distinct, well-formed cross in the Mount of Mercury (LIX, 4A) is not altogether a good sign. It denotes a strong predisposition towards dishonesty, and a deceptive nature. Its owner, though shrewd and cunning, is too easily tempted toward kleptomaniac acts.

Star
A star on the Mount of Mercury (LIX, 4B) reveals remarkable talent for misappropriating other people's ideas, goods or projects; in fact, whatever is available. Its owner can be a thief and a rascal — a thoroughly dishonourable person.

Triangle
A triangle on the Mount of Mercury (LIX, 1A) is indicative of the adroit diplomat and skilled politician. Its owner is extremely astute and clever in manoevring situations to his own advantage. Alert and well informed, he is usually evasive and outsmarts others.

Square
A square on the Mount of Mercury (LIX, 3A) is a good omen. It reveals preservation from financial or business losses which could ruin its owner. Indirectly it denotes a person who is inclined to be involved in quite substantial financial risks.

Grille
A grille on the Mount of Mercury (LIX, 2A) is an ill omen. Its owner is apt to engage in hazardous, swindling enterprises, and is liable to run the risk of grave fatality. He is inclined to live the life of a scoundrel and would stop at nothing to gain his ends.

The Upper Mount of Mars

Ascending Line
An ascending, clear and definite line on this mount (LIX, 5A), is indicative of courage, and its owner is capable of showing a great deal of resistance. He can give battle with a genuine will to win.

Multiplicity of Ascending Lines
A multiplicity of lines on the mount is hardly a good indication (LIX, 8B). These betray violent temper and lasciviousness on the part of the owner. He can be rather brutal in matters appertaining to love and usually seems to be a poor partner in marriage. These lines are also a sign of a tendency toward bronchitis.

Cross
A cross on the Upper Mount of Mars (LIX, 5B) shows a quarrelsome disposition. Its owner tends to be obstinate and unbending and his evil instincts can invite bodily harm.

Star
A star on the mount (LIX, 6A) is usually considered to be a sign of a serious wound caused by firearms or something similar. Its owner can be given to jealousy, anger and instincts which can lead to his causing bodily harm to others.

Triangle
A triangle on this mount (LIX, 6B) is an excellent mark and denotes aptitude for the art of war and military tactics. Its owner can be a great warrior and can excel in the technique of disciplined combat.

Square
When there is a well-formed square on this mount, it is a sign of protection against bodily harm (LIX, 8C). It also shows that any tendency of the owner towards violent temper can be held in check: reason will prevail.

Grille
A grille in this area is a very evil sign (LIX, 7A). It betrays the likelihood of a violent end. It is also indicative of a tendency toward haemorrhage.

The Mount of the Moon

Ascending Line
An ascending undisturbed line on the Moon (LIX, 6C) is a sign of the potential to be presentient — of, however, the evil alone. Its owner is usually able to foresee evil happenings or occurrences of an unsavoury nature.

Cross
A cross on the Mount of the Moon (LIX, 5C) is not a good sign to have. It is supposed to indicate a tendency to exaggerate in words or ideas. In point of fact its owner is liable to be untruthful or unable to discern the fine line between exaggeration and dishonesty.

It is also considered to be an evil indication of danger from water, and may show a fear of going into or travelling over water.

Star
A star, when clear and well-defined, is said to be a mark of danger of death by drowning (LIX, 7B). However, other indications on the hand must confirm such prognosis.

Triangle
A triangle on the Mount of the Moon (LIX, 5D) denotes intuition, knowledge of mystical techniques and, of course, wise use of imaginative faculties which are rather highly developed. It is also an indication, in specific cases, of deep interest in maritime science.

Square
A square (LIX, 6D) is a good sign to have here. It denotes protection against any evil tendency associated with the mount. Its owner shows sagacity and wisdom, and is usually able to ward off danger in time.

Grille
A grille is an unhealthy and unfortunate mark (LIX, 8D). It shows sadness, melancholia and nervous trouble. Its owner tends to be continually discontented, given to gloom, nervous spasms and excitability. He is usually under the evil force of an ungovernable and immodest imagination. Such a person is inclined to cause a great deal of depression among those around him and usually gets involved in situations of an unhealthy kind due to his own unfortunate propensities.

The Mount of Venus

Ascending Line
A clear and well-defined ascending line (LIX, 8A) shows warmth, affection and loyalty in love. It accentuates the constructive qualities of Venus and helps harmony and happiness.

Cross
A clear and somewhat large cross on the Mount of Venus is not a very good indication (LIX, 8C). It shows an only love: however, the course of such love is unfortunately neither smooth nor happy. Its owner usually succumbs, for this cross is a sign of fatality in matters appertaining to love. However, if protecting signs are to be found elsewhere in the hand, he could be fortunate and happy in his only love.

Star
A star around the apex of the Mount of Venus is likely to indicate a person who is fortunate in love (LIX, 6E). When misplaced, especially toward the Life Line, it is a mark of sorrow due to the death of a loved one or a close relative (LIX, 6F).

Triangle
A triangle on the Mount of Venus (LIX, 6G) shows calculation in love. In fact all women who follow love as a profession seem to own this mark. Whether in a male or female hand it certainly reveals a strong tendency towards material advantage in regard to love and marital union.

Square
A square in the Mount of Venus is not altoghether a good sign to have. When in the middle of the mount (LIX 7C) it denotes a confined life. If it is near the Life Line (LIX, 7D) it is said to denote imprisonment, not necessarily due to evil acts or crime.

Grille
A grille on this mount (LIX, 5E) is an unwholesome indication, for it betrays a tendency towards lasciviousness and a curiosity which is far from being healthy. Its owner, is apt to go for obscene pleasures and tends to indulge in all that is denegerate in regard to sex.

The Lower Mount of Mars

Ascending Line
An ascending line (LIX, 5F) shows a great deal of courage, and its owner tends to be a fighter with a will to win. His fortitude and audacious approach to things, particularly in matters concerning combat or war, could hardly be ordinary.

Cross
A cross on the Lower Mount of Mars is an accurate sign of an uncontrollable temper and a very quarrelsome disposition (LIX, 7E). Its owner is too apt to be aggressive and usually itches for a fight. He is hardly a desirable person to be around.

Star
A star on this mount (LIX, 8E) is extremely rare, and is usually a mark of the dangerous possibility of injury either in war or by weapons of combat. Its owner, however, seems to be drawn towards such activities or situations which spell danger: he is not really able to control his temper or have a very great deal of

will to avoid being involved in hazardous situations.

Triangle
A triangle certainly is one of the most excellent indications in this area (LIX, 5G). It reveals innate aptitude for the art of warfare and military science. Its owner is usually able to show a mastery of the technique of combat.

Square
A square on this mount (LIX, 7F) betrays a tendency towards violent temper. However, its owner, by some unconscious protective instinct, is able to avoid bodily harm. It helps him to either get out of the danger zone, or, when involved, gives him the sagacity to find a way out unharmed.

Grille
A grille (LIX, 6H) is an ill omen. When marked here, it points to the danger of a violent end, though other signs have to confirm this interpretation. Usually its owner tends to be rather violently inclined and is to apt to look for trouble which usually leads to dangerous consequences. He has neither wisdom nor the essential control of his passions. Obviously he seems to be at the mercy of his own none too healthy inflammable dispositiion.

SCRAPBOOK

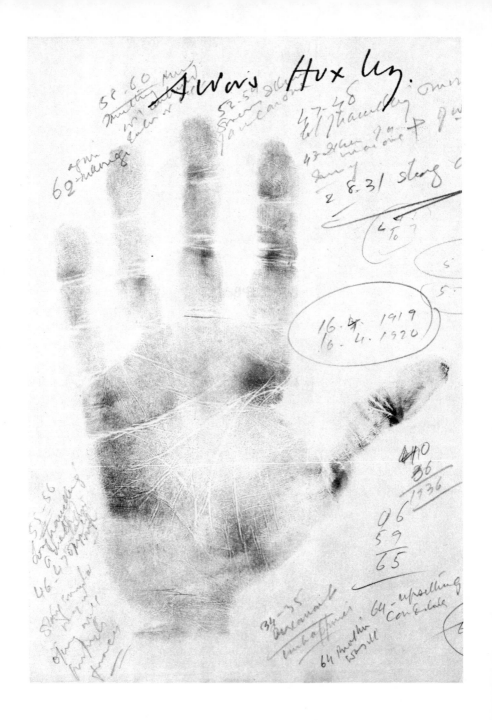

Palmprint of Aldous Huxley with Mir Bashir's original notes

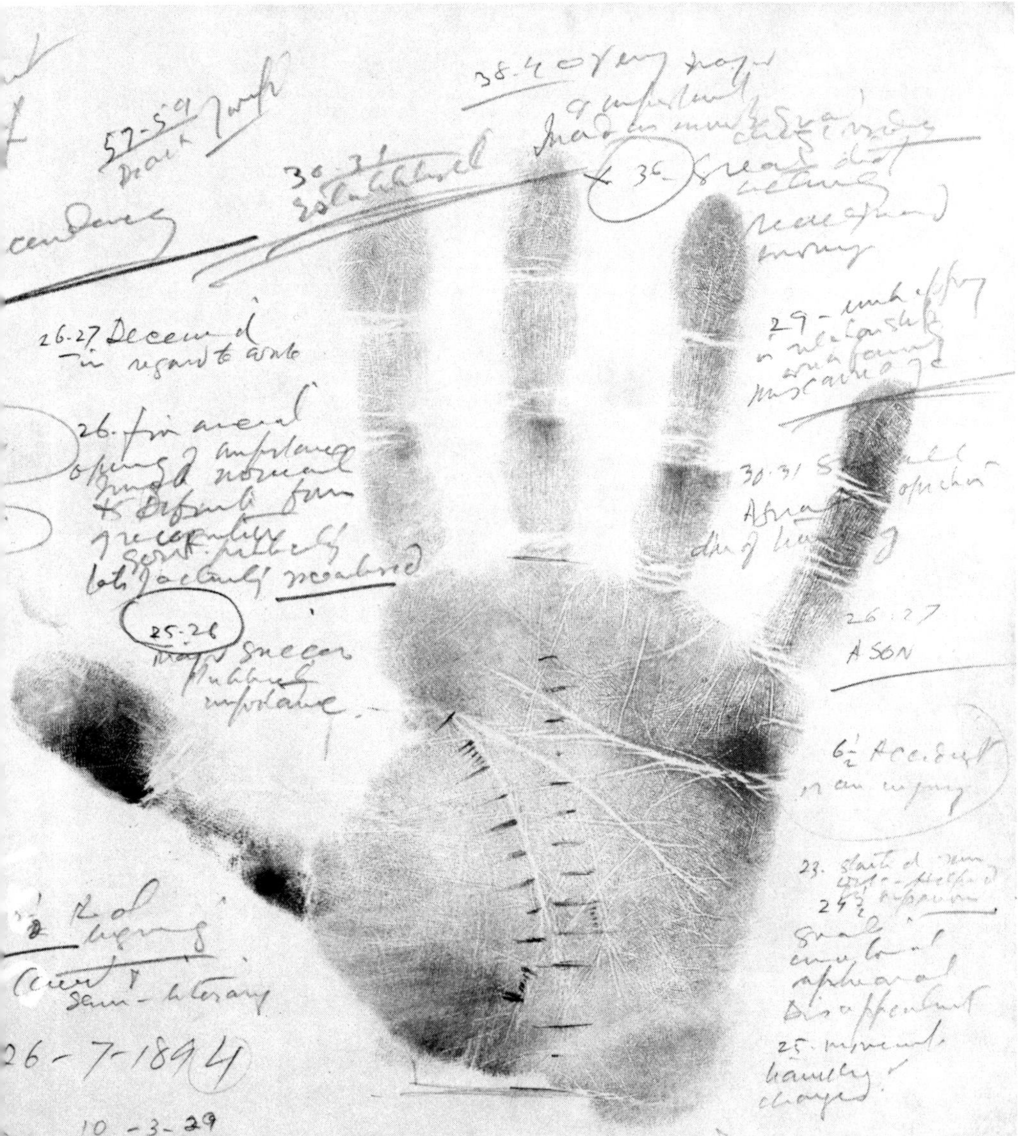
26-7-1894
10 -3-29
A SON

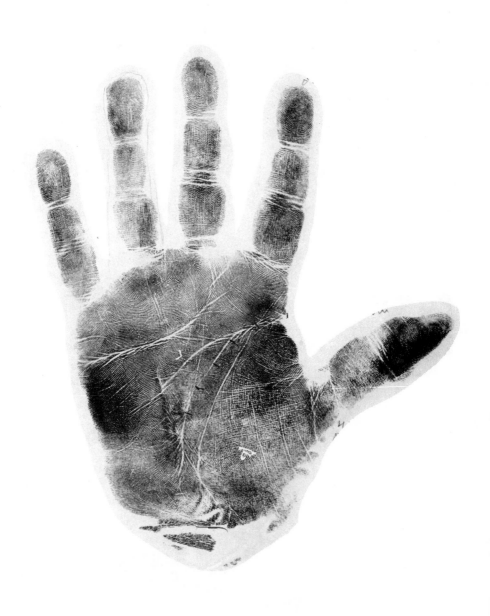

Palmprint of Robert Helpmann

242

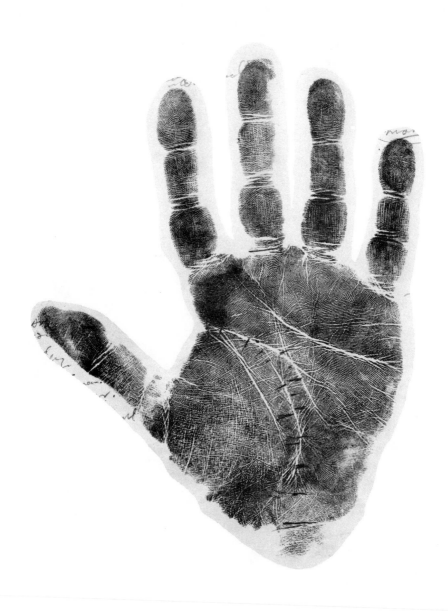

243

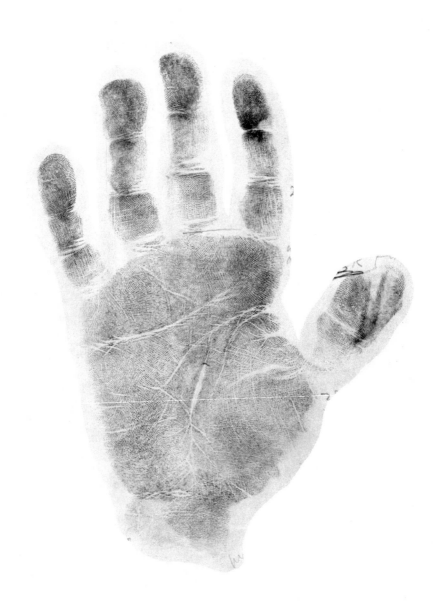

Palmprint of Herbert Lom

244

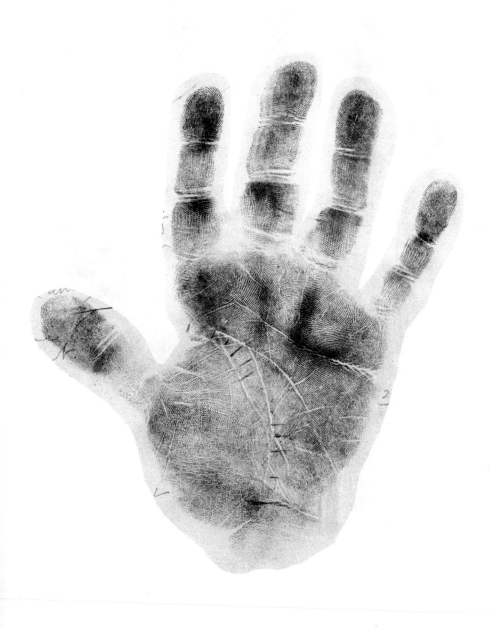

245

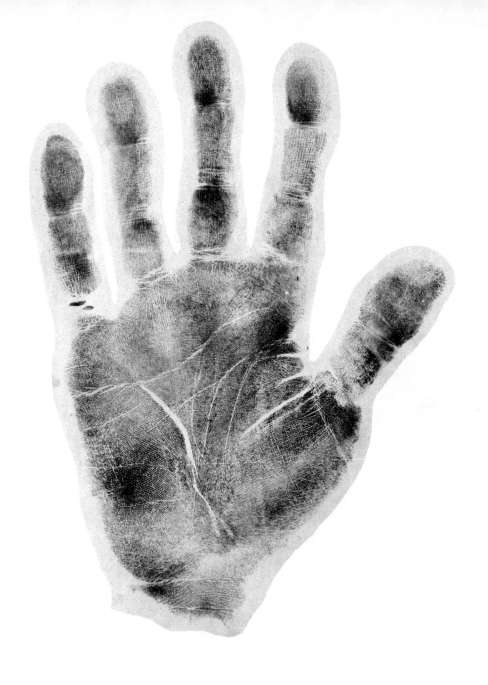

Palmprint of Walter Pidgeon

246

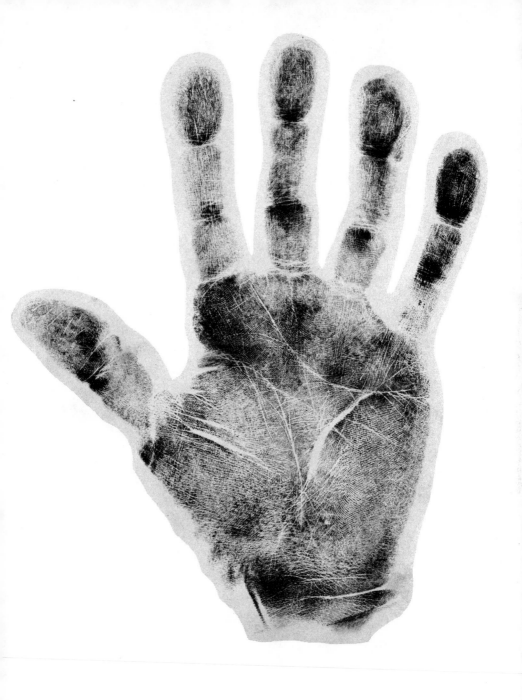

247

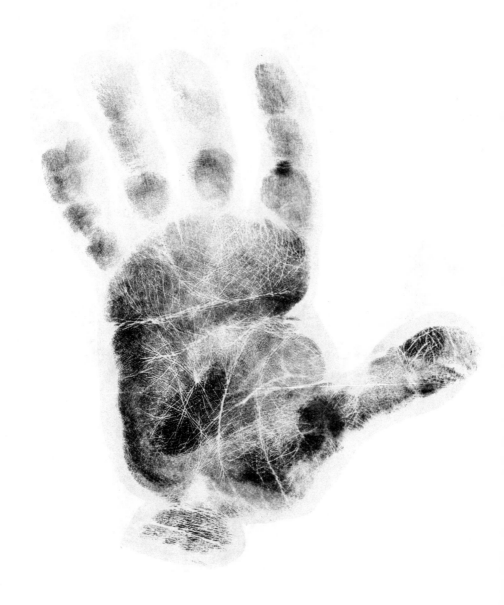

Palmprint of Vicki Baum

248

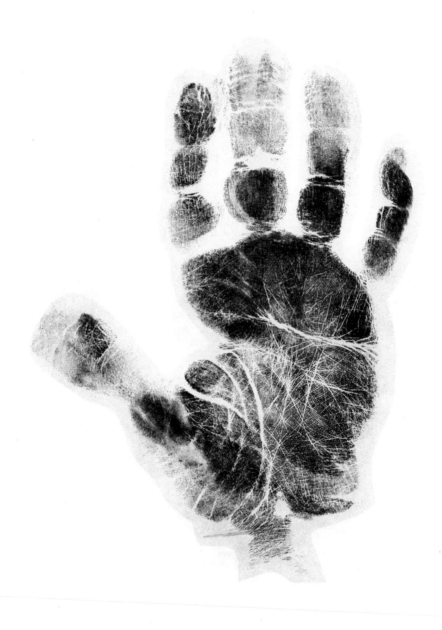

249

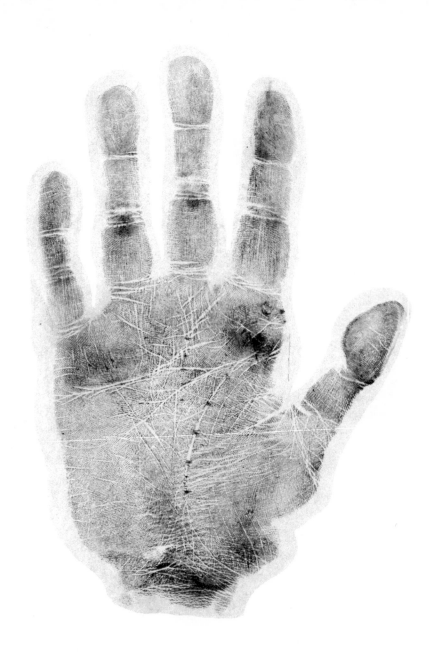

Palmprint of Jawaharlal Nehru

250

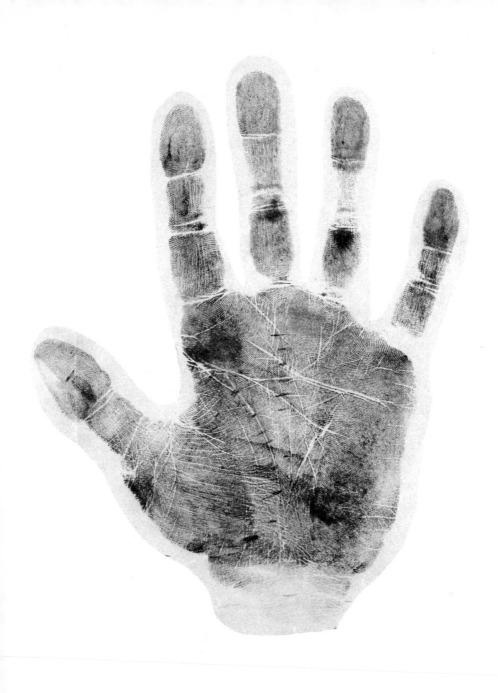

251

INDEX

Because of the specialized nature of this work the Index has been confined to mainly technical references.

Apex, 7
Apollo, Mount of, *see* Sun
Art, Finger of, *see* Third Finger

Balzac, 22
Bracelets, the Three, 9, 85; *see also* Rascette *and* Wrist Lines

Chaldeans, 1
Cheiromancy, 1
Chinese, 1
Chirology, 1, 2
Circles, 9, 189
Conic fingers, 18, 19; *see also* Fingers
Cross, Mystic, 9
Crosses, 190

D'Arpentigny, Captain, 2
Dating system, 9
Dermoglyphics, 7
Desbarrolles, 2
Destiny, Finger of, *see* Middle Finger
Dots (skin indentations), 9, 189

Eastern system, 10
Eloquence, Finger of, *see* Little Finger

Fate, Line of, 8, 9, 83, 130, 148, 154, 166, 177, 185, 187, 189
origins: an island, 141; first bracelet, 134; close to wrist, 135; from Life Line, 135; from Mount of Venus, 135; from Plain of Mars, 135; from Mount of Moon, 136; from Mount of Venus and Mount of Moon, 136; from Head Line, 136
termination: on Mount of Saturn, 134, 136, 137, 138; on Middle Finger, 134, 136, 139; natural point of, 137; at Head Line, 138; at Heart Line, 138; on Mount of Sun, 139; at Mount of Jupiter, 139
nature of: with obstacles, 138; wiry and thin, 139; wavy and irregular, 140; dominant, 141
marks on: cross, 141; formidable obstacles, 141; cross by line, 142; star at origin, 142; triangle, 142; squares, 142; breaks, 142, 143
branches: upwards, 143; merging from Mount of Moon, 143, 144; intersecting, 144; weak intersection, 144; from Heart Line, 144, 145
time scale: 145
Fingers: inclinations of, 29; inward bent, 29; outward bent, 29; towards each other, 31; unbent, 32; spaced, 32
length: longer than palm, 63; shorter than palm, 64
nature: smooth and straight, 15; knotted, 15; knotted top joints, 16; knotted second joints, 16; uneven third joints, 17; even third joints, 17; square, 18, 19
Fingerprints, 56
Fingertips, combinations, 18, 21; conic, 18, 19; square, 18, 19, 20; spatulate, 18, 20, 21

see also 'nails' and under
individual fingers, eg Index
Finger, etc

Grilles, 9, 192

Hands, profusely hairy, 11; hairy,
12; thick hair, 12; thin hair, 12
Handprints, 5
Hasthrikha, 2
Head, Line of, 7, 8, 80, 83, 95, 97,
107, 130, 136, 138, 148, 149,
152, 157, 166, 168, 169, 170,
172, 173, 185, 186, 189
origins: junction with Life Line,
116; within Life Line, 117;
separation from Life Line,
117; origin with Mount of
Jupiter, 117
length: 118, 119, 120
nature: straight, 118; sloping,
119, 121; drooping, 119;
deep and clear, 119; shallow,
120; defective, 120; double,
122; arched, 122; twisted,
123; fragmented, 123;
broken, 123; overlapping
breaks, 123; islanded, 124;
interspaced with Heart Line,
125
branches: 120, 123
termination, 122
Health, Line of, 8, 168, 185, 186
origin: from Life Line and
Rascette, 155, 157; from
Mount of Venus, 155;
absence of, 155
nature: twisting, 155; broken,
158; thin and wiry, 157;
colour, 158; islanded, 158;
with crosses, 157; with
triangles, 158
length, 155
branches: to Head Line, 157; to
Mount of Mercury, 158
Heart, Line of, 7, 8, 80, 98, 115,
125, 138, 144, 148, 149, 150,
159, 161, 172, 173, 185, 186,
189

origins: from Mount of Jupiter,
126; from between Index and
Middle fingers, 126; from
below Middle Finger, 126,
127; from third phalange,
129; from below Third
Finger, 127; from edge to
percussion, 127, 128
length: 128
nature: colour, 128; flawless,
128; twisted, 129; wavy, 129;
double, 129; low at start,
130; forked, 130; merging
with Head Line, 130; merging
with Fate Line, 132; cutting
Fate Line, 130; broken, 132;
islanded, 132; with circles,
132; with squares, 132; with
crosses, 132
branches: giving rise to Sun
Line, 133; upwards, 131;
downwards, 130; to Mount of
Jupiter, 131; to Mount of
Mercury, 131, 132

Index Finger, 8, 17, 46, 68, 126
inter-space 32
phalanges: top, long 35; short,
36; thin, 36; stout, 36
second, long 36; short, 36;
thin, 36; stout, 36 third, long
37; short, 37; thin, 37; stout,
37
marks: First phalange: vertical
line, 192; cross, 192; star,
192, 194; clear triangle, 194;
square, 194; circle, 194;
islands, 195; grille, 195
Second phalange:
associations, 195; vertical
line, 195; horizontal lines,
196; wavy lines, 196; slanting
fork, 196; cross, 196; cross at
joint, 196, 197; star, 197;
triangle, 197; square, 197;
circle, 197; grille, 197, 198;
line from Mount of Jupiter to
second phalange, 198

Third phalange: vertical line, 198; wavy lines, 198; multiplicity of vertical lines, 198, 199; cross lines, 199; forked line, 199, 200; circle, 200; grille, 200, 201
length: 38, 39
tip: conic, 37; pointed, 38; square, 38; spatulate, 38
Indians, 1
Intuition, Line of, 9, 186
origins and end, 163, 165, 166, in an island, 167
main associations, 163-165
nature: wavy, 166; flawless, 166; islanded, 167; broken, 167; cut, 167
Islands, 9, 189, 192

Jung, Dr Carl, 2
Jupiter, Finger of, *see* Index Finger
Jupiter, Mount of, 6, 7, 80, 96, 101, 108, 126, 131, 172, 183, 187, 190, 191, 198
pure Jupitarian, 68; physical features, 68, 70; psychological features, 70, 71; health and ailments, 71;
nature: well developed, 90; excessive development, 90; absence, 90; displacement towards thumb, 97; towards Head Line, 97; towards Saturn, 97

Knots, *see* fingers
Knuckles, *see* fingers

Life, Line of, 8, 9, 80, 85, 96, 100, 116, 135, 142, 146, 147, 155, 161, 168, 169, 171, 185, 187, 189, 190
origins: 102, 104; with Jupiter, 108; marks at origin, 106
termination: inwards, 109; towards Mount of Moon, 109; in a fork, 110; with tassles, 111; demarcation, 104, 105

branches: 110; rising offshoots, 114, 115
dating system, 105, 106
nature: sweeping, 108, 109; straight, 109; separated from Head Line, 107, 108; joined to Head Line, 107; broken, 111; with squares, 111; with crosses, 113; islanded, 113; with cuts, 113; with circles, 114; very thick, 113, 114; thin, 113; travel lines, 110
Little Finger, 6, 8, 17, 34, 38, 46, 77, 92, 143
inter-space, 33, 34
inclination, 34
phalanges: top, long 50; short, 51; stout, 51; thin, 51 second, long 50; short, 51; stout, 51; thin, 52 third, long 52; short, 52; stout, 53; thin, 53; only two phalanges, 53
marks: First phalange, associations, 218; vertical line, 218; cross lines, 218; cross, 218; star, 218; triangle, 218; square, 218; circle, 218, 220; grille, 220
Second phalange, vertical line, 220; crosslines, 220; cross, 220; star, 220, 221; triangle, 221; square, 221; circle, 221; grille, 221
Third phalange, vertical line, 221; wavy lines, 222; crosslines, 222; cross, 222; star, 222; triangle, 222; square, 223; circle, 223; grille, 223
tip: conic, 54; pointed, 54; square, 54; spatulate, 54, 55

Maharishi, Valmik, 1
Major Lines, 7
Marriage, Lines of, 9, 154, 179
origins, 159; numbers, 159; length, 159

nature: curved, 159, 161;
touching Heart Line, 161;
cutting Life Line, 161;
forked, 161; cutting Sun
Line, 162; broken, 162; cut,
162; islanded, 162; offspring,
162
Mars, Line of, 9
Mars, Mount of, pure Martian, 80;
physical features, 80, 81;
psychological features, 82;
health and ailments, 83;
Negative Mount: 7, 172
nature: well developed, 93;
excessive development, 93;
absence, 93, 94; displaced
towards Mercury, 99; towards
Moon, 99; palm proper, 99
Positive Mount:
nature: well developed, 96;
excessive development, 96;
absence, 96; displaced
towards Venus, 101; towards
thumb, 101; towards Palm
centre, 101
Mars, Plain of, 135, 148
Mentality, Line of, 108, 110
Mercury, Mount of, 6, 8, 80, 98,
99, 131, 132, 155, 157, 159,
163, 175, 179, 183, 190
pure Mercurians, 77; physical
features, 77, 78;
psychological
features, 79; health and
ailments, 80
nature: well developed, 92;
excessive development, 92;
absence, 93; displaced
towards Sun, 98; towards the
Percussion, 98; towards the
Heart Line, 99
Middle Finger, 6, 8, 39, 46, 71,
126, 134, 186
inter-space 32, 33
phalanges: top, long 40; short,
40; stout, 40; thin, 40
second, long 42; short, 42;
stout, 42; thin, 43 third, long

43; short, 43; stout, 43; thin,
43
marks: First phalange,
associations, 202; vertical
line, 203; numerous lines,
203; wavy lines, 203; cross,
203, 204; star, 204; triangle,
204; square, 204; circle, 204,
205; grille, 205
Second phalange, vertical
line, 205, 206; crosslines,
206; cross, 206; star, 206;
square, 206; triangle, 207;
circle, 207; grille, 207
Third phalange, vertical line,
207; oblique line, 207, 209;
multiplicity of lines, 209;
crosslines, 209; slanting fork,
209; cross, 209; star, 210;
triangle, 210; square, 210;
circle, 210; grille, 210
tip: conic, 43; pointed, 44;
square, 44; spatulate, 44
Minor Marks, 7, 9
Moon, Mount of, 7, 99, 101, 109,
110, 136, 142, 143, 147, 152,
170, 182, 189
Pure Lunar type, 83; physical
features, 83, 84;
psychological features, 84;
health and ailments, 85
nature: well developed, 94;
excessive development, 94;
absence, 95; displaced
towards Negative Mount of
Mars, 99; towards the palm,
100; towards the Percussion,
99, 100; towards the wrist,
100; towards Venus, 100
Mystic Cross, 185, 186

Nadis, 2
Nails size: long, 22; short, 22, 23,
24; narrow, 22, 24; broad, 22,
24; oblong, 22
moons: 24; large, 25; half-, 25;
absence of, 25
see also under 'Fingers' and
individual fingers

Palm, dimensions: how to measure, 63; narrow, 65; wide, 65, 66; thin, 66
    consistency: flabby, 66; firm, 66; hard, 67; silky, 67
    percussion of: 7, 98, 127
Persians, 1
Phalanges, 15; First, 28; Second, 27; Third, 26 *see also* under 'Fingers' and individual fingers
Physiological aspects, 6
Power, Finger of, *see* Index finger
Psychic Hand, 18 *see also* Fingers

Quadrangle, The location of, 172
    nature: regular, 172; absent, 173; wide, 173; widening, 173; width under Mounts of Saturn and Sun, 173; narrow, 173, 174
    marks: none, 174; criss-cross lines, 174; clear cross, 174; badly formed cross, 174; stars, 174, 175; star below Mount of Mercury, 175; square, 175; circle, 175

Rascette, 9, 85, 155, 181, 182
    First wrist line, 102, 110, 182; islanded, 182; disfigured, 182; upward turned, 182
    branches: to Mount of Moon, 182, 183; to Mount of Jupiter, 183; to Mount of Saturn, 183; to Mount of Sun, 183; to Mount of Mercury, 183
    marks: breaks, 184; angles, 184; triangles, 184; travel lines, 184; crosses, 184

Saturn, Finger, of, *see* Middle Finger
Saturn, Mount of, 6, 97, 124, 130, 134, 138, 173, 176, 183, 186, 187, 190
    pure Saturnian, 71; physical features, 72, 73; psychological features, 73; health and ailments, 73
    nature: well developed, 91; excessive development, 91; absence, 91; disposition of, 73; displaced towards Jupiter, 97; towards the Sun, 97; towards the Heart Line, 98
Saturn, Ring of, 9, 185, 187
Signature of the Thumb, 56; *see also* Thumb
Skin texture, fine, 13; firm, 13; leathery, 13; ridge lines, 7, 68
Solomon, Ring of, 9, 185, 186, 187
Spatulate fingers, 18, 20; *see also* Fingers
Spier, Julius, 3
Square, 9, 190
Stars, 9, 191
Stigmata, The Medical, 9, 185, 187
Sun, Line of, 8, 132, 145, 162, 185, 189, 190
    origin: from wrist, 146; within Life Line, 146; on Life Line, 147; from Mount of Moon, 147; from palm centre, 148; from Fate Line, 148; between Lines of Head and Heart, 148; from Head Line, 148, 149
    termination: 146; at Head Line, 149; at Heart Line, 150
    nature: length, 149; thin, 150; thick, 150; fading, 150; wavy, 152; islanded, 150; with bars, 150
    branches: 152; from Mount of Venus, 153; from Fate Line, 154; from Line of Marriage, 154
Sun, Mount of, 6, 97, 98, 139, 152, 161, 173, 176, 183, 190, 191
    pure Sun types, 75; physical features, 75; psychological features, 75, 76, 77; health and ailments, 77

nature: well developed, 91;
excessive development, 92;
absence, 92; displaced
towards Saturn, 98; towards
Mercury, 98; towards the
Heart Line, 98

Tamil language, 1
Third Finger, 6, 8, 38, 44, 45, 74,
127
inter-space, 32, 33
phalanges: top, long 46, 47;
short, 47; stout, 47; thin, 47
second, long 47; short, 47, 48;
stout, 48; thin, 48
third, long 48; short, 48;
stout, 48; thin, 49
marks: associations, 211
First phalange, vertical lines,
211; numerous lines, 211;
crosslines, 211; cross, 211,
213; star, 213; square, 213;
triangle, 213; circle, 213;
grille, 214
Second phalange, vertical
line, 214; slanting fork, 214;
crosslines, 214; cross, 214;
star, 215; triangle, 215;
square, 215; circle, 215;
grille, 215
Third phalange, vertical lines,
216; crosslines, 216; cross,
216; star, 216; triangle, 216;
square, 216; circle, 216-17;
grille, 217
length, 33, 34
tip: conic, 49; pointed, 49;
square, 49; spatulate, 49
Thumb, 97, 100
angle: normal, 56; narrow, 58;
wide, 58
flexibility, 58, 59
marks: associations, 224, 226
First phalange, vertical line,
224; numerous lines, 224,
225; crosslines, 225; cross,
225; star, 225; triangle, 225;
square, 225; circle, 225, 226;
grille, 226, 227

Second phalange, vertical
line, 226; numerous lines,
226; crosslines, 226; cross,
226; star, 226, 227; triangle,
227; square, 227; circle, 227;
grille, 227
length: 59, 60
inclination, out-turned, 62;
inturned, 62
tip: conic, 61; pointed, 61;
square, 61; bulbous, 62
Travel, Line of, *see* Rascette
Triangles, 9, 190
Triangle, The Great, 168
nature: large and spacious, 168,
169; ill-shaped, 169; narrow,
169
angles: First angle, location 169;
blunt, 169; wide, 170
Second angle, location 170;
sharp, 170; obtuse, 170
Third angle, location 170;
obtuse, 171
Triangle, The Small, 185, 186

Venus, Girdle of, 176, 178
nature: flawless, 177; deeply
ingrained, 177; wiry, 177;
multiple girdle, 177, 178
marks: cutting Marriage Lines,
179; fragmentary lines, 179;
islanded, 179, 180; stars, 180;
crossed by vertical lines, 180;
bars, 180
Venus Line *see* Life Line
Venus, Mount of, 7, 8, 96, 101,
104, 108, 135, 136, 153, 155,
190
pure Venusian, 85; physical
features, 85, 86, 87;
psychological features, 87,
88; health and ailments, 88